On Political Virtue

Carlo Sini

On Political Virtue

Plato's *Republic* and the Politics of Desire

Edited and with an introduction by

Alessandro Carrera

Translated by

Giorgio Mobili and Santo Pettinato

Published by State University of New York Press, Albany

EU GPSR Authorised Representative:
Logos Europe, 9 rue Nicolas Poussin, 17000, La Rochelle, France
contact@logoseurope.eu

For information, contact State University of New York Press, Albany, NY
www.sunypress.edu

Library of Congress Cataloging-in-Publication Data

Names: Sini, Carlo, author. | Mobili, Giorgio, translator. | Pettionato, Santo,
    translator. | edited and with an introduction by Alessandro Carrera.
Title: On political virtue : Plato's *Republic* and the politics of desire / Carlo Sini.
Description: Albany : State University of New York Press, [2026]. | Series:
    SUNY series, Intersections: Philosophy and Critical Theory | Includes
    bibliographical references and index.
Identifiers: ISBN 9798855805178 (hardcover : alk. paper) | ISBN 9798855805192
    (epub) | ISBN 9798855806892 (PDF) | ISBN 9798855805185 (pbk. : alk.
    paper)
Further information is available at the Library of Congress.

Contents

Act Two

Act Three

Introduction

The Politics of Desire: Carlo Sini Reads Plato's *Republic*

Alessandro Carrera

Prologue and Act One

Carlo Sini is one of the few practitioners of philosophy in Italy that truly deserve to be called a theoretical philosopher. He is not, except occasionally, an essayist. He rarely intervenes on the issues of the day unless what he has to say has a direct bearing on his research. As a student of Enzo Paci (1911–1976), he is a phenomenologist by training, but his approach has always been open to other schools of thought. He has incorporated American pragmatism, philosophical semiotics (in divergence from Umberto Eco's brand), hermeneutics, Heidegger, Nietzsche, Spinoza, and post-structuralist trends (Blanchot, Derrida, Foucault), but always from a distance and with a critical eye. In his perspective, Bruno and Vico may in fact play a bigger role than any contemporary deconstructionist school. He looks at the tradition of Western philosophy not as a self-sufficient entity but rather as the product of specific "practices," which originated with the introduction of alphabetic writing in the Greek culture. His strong point is that metaphysical concepts such as Being, Nothingness, Truth, Substance, Subject, Object, the Particular, the Universal, among others, are the result of the power of abstraction that Western alphabetic writing allows. That doesn't mean that those notions don't have real effects, but the belief that all basic concepts of Western philosophy are self-sustaining and permanent entities, independent from the writing and

"

discursive formations that have made them possible (either systems of signs or *dispositifs*, as Foucault would say) is a superstition that affects philosophy as well as science.

It took Sini twenty years, from *Semiotica e filosofia* (1978) to *Teoria e pratica del foglio-mondo* (1997), to establish the coordinates of his "philosophy of practices" (not just of *praxis*, because *praxis* in the singular is still a metaphysical abstraction). In the early 2000s, he systematized his philosophy in a six-volume series called *Transito verità. Figure dell'enciclopedia filosofica*. The six parts were first published separately in 2004–2005 and then collected in one volume in 2012. This present volume, whose Italian title is *La virtù politica. Filosofia e antropologia*, came fourth in the series. Before we delve into the complex rereading of Plato's *Republic* that takes up a great part of *On Political Virtue*, we must understand the meaning of the title that Sini gave to the whole series.[1]

---

1. Few of Sini's writings are available in English so far. See Carlo Sini, *Images of Truth: From Sign to Symbol*, translated and with an introduction by Massimo Verdicchio (Humanities Press, 1993), and *Ethics of Writing*, translated by Silvia Benso with Brian Schroeder (State University of New York Press, 2009). See also Carlo Sini, "The Beyond of Language," translated by Thomas Behr, in *Annali d'Italianistica*, special issue, "Italian Critical Theory," edited by Alessandro Carrera, 29 (2011): 123–129, and "The Desire for Eternal Life: The Platonic Roots of Western Political Science and Its Ethical and Theological Consequences," in *Contemporary Italian Philosophy: Crossing the Border of Ethics, Politics, and Religion*, edited by Silvia Benso and Brain Schroeder, translated by Silvia Benso (Albany: State University of New York Press, 2007), 21–31 (a book chapter that can be read as an anticipation of this volume). On Carlo Sini in English, see Alessandro Carrera, "Consequences of Unlimited Semiosis: Carlo Sini's Metaphysics of the Sign and Semiotical Hermeneutics," in *Cultural Semiosis: Tracing the Signifier (Continental Philosophy VI)*, edited and with an introduction by Hugh J. Silverman (Routledge, 1998), 48–62, and Enrico Redaelli, "A Political Gesture: The Performance of Carlo Sini and Michel Foucault," in *Open Borders: Encounters between Italian Philosophy and Continental Thought*, edited by Silvia Benso and Antonio Calcagno (State University of New York Press, 2021), 117–134. I have subsequently updated and revised my 1998 book chapter in Alessandro Carrera, "Nostalgia di sapienza. Gli anni Ottanta di Carlo Sini, dalla fenomenologia all'etica della scrittura," *Il Pensiero. Rivista di filosofia* 62, no. 2 (2023): 37–54. My 2023 article analyzes Sini's opus from the early works to *Ethics of Writing*. The book that bridges the gap between *Ethics of Writing* (1992 in the Italian edition) and *On Political Virtue* (2004) is *Teoria e pratica del foglio-mondo. La scrittura filosofica* (Laterza, 1997) (*Theory and Practice of the World-Sheet: On Philosophical Writing*), whose first part (on Socrates and Plato) anticipates *On Political Virtue*.

In the conversation with Florinda Cambria that opens the complete edition of his philosophical encyclopedia, Sini points out that *Transito verità* should be understood as a geographical expression, like "Hope Hill" or "Paradise Mountain." It is a precious indication for a correct translation. Perhaps *Truth's Crossing* would convey the idea of a passage, a ford, a bridge, a path that crosses a place called Truth. As the title, *Truth's Crossing: Figures of the Philosophical Encyclopedia* also provides a key to the present volume, which is a commentary on Plato's *Republic* but also outlines an anthropology of language.

Sini bypasses Plato's *Republic* as a "book"—a fictive identity that the ancient texts have assumed over time and have shaped the way we moderns approach them. Sini's reading of Plato is closer to traversing a text (or rather a text-as-event) than to a book commentary. And our introduction is a crossing, too. We will often enter and exit the text, sometimes alerting the readers to where we are with the use of parentheses while at other times the transition will be more nuanced, and readers will have to figure out whether we are channeling Sini or commenting on his comment. Given the nature of *On Political Virtue*, it would be arduous to proceed otherwise.

The artifact known as "book" as we know it dates to around 1300 CE. The history of Plato's *Republic* as a book began with the 1402 Latin translation by Pier Carlo Decembrio, Uberto Decembrio, and Emanuele Crisolora, followed by Marsilio Ficino's translation, published in 1484. That the *Republic* was not a "book" when it was written (possibly around 375 BC) is not just a historical fact. To truly traverse the *Republic*, we must consider its overall history, first as a literary elaboration of a conversation that perhaps, or at least in part, was real, then as a manuscript, first handwritten by Plato himself (who had it close to him on his deathbed and was still correcting it), then copied and ultimately printed and digitized. Sometimes Sini refers to other comments, thus adding a further link to the chain of scholarship, but the object of his research is to reach the crossroads that the *Republic* is, a place where events occur that have then been interpreted as "facts" at the risk of lessening their event-like impact.

At the *Republic*'s crossroads, four directions converge bearing the names of Justice, Virtue, Politics, and Education. At the center of the cross is the city, the *polis*, which in Plato is always a double entity. Everything that happens in the city is duplicated in the soul of the individual, while the soul of the individual is reflected in the soul of the city. At the center of the cross is therefore the *psyche*, as the soul of both the individual and the city.

Like all six volumes of Sini's philosophical encyclopedia, *On Political Virtue* is divided into nine "figures," each theatrically placed into three "acts" and several "scenes." The three-act structure mirrors Sini's interpretation of the *Republic* as an example of Plato's theater, where the dialectical drama replaces the tragic drama. In fact, the *Republic* is a combination of theater and storytelling. Regardless of its many characters, Socrates is the only narrator. It is Socrates who recounts, in a dialogized monologue, the entire discussion around *politeia* as something that recently happened to him. It is Socrates who holds the threads of the discussion, even when the other interlocutors put him in a corner. If the city is duplicated in the soul and the soul has its double in the city, and the text of the *Republic* (both a conversation and Socrates' narrative) is a double of the double, then *On Political Virtue*, which is structured as a narrative (the author's voice is always present, guiding the reader) and as a theatrical work, is a double of the double of the double.

If Plato writes a theater of ideas to supplant tragic theater, Sini writes a theater of comments to shed a critical light on the *dispositif* of the typical academic commentary. But what meaning should we give to the intersection of the three acts and their forty-nine scenes with the nine "figures" that seem to move with a great degree of independence from the theatrical framework?

By analogy, we can think of Erich Auerbach's notion of *figura*.

Tertullian, as Auerbach recalls, introduces the expression *figura futurorum* (figure of things to come, prefiguration) to underline the first time that the name "Joshua" appears in the Bible: "Moses gave Hoshea son of Nun the name Joshua" (Numbers 13, 16, NIV). Tertullian comments: "For the first time he is called Jesus. . . . This, then, we first observe, is a figure of things to come" (*Adversus Marcionem* 3, 16).[2] Such a prefiguration of the future is neither an allegory nor a metaphor nor a symbol. It's a sign, an index pointing toward a time vector. It is also a prophecy, but retroactive, for Moses does not know that by changing Hoshea's name to Joshua he is prefiguring the coming of Jesus. If we understand *figura futurorum* as anagogy, in the sense used by Dante in his

---

2. Erich Auerbach, *Scenes from the Drama of European Literature*, foreword by Paolo Valesio (University of Minnesota Press, 1984), 28.

letter to Cangrande della Scala, a *figura* is a transposition, a transition, a movement from a longing not yet aware of being such to a future resolution. Sini's *figurae* are certainly not biblical, but each is a sign of a new soul to come, because the soul, in Sini's interpretation, is the greatest stratagem invented by Plato.

In addition to the three acts, scenes, and figures, Sini adds further theatrical devices consisting of Prologue, Interlude, and Epilogue. In the Prologue and Epilogue, however, the protagonist is not Plato but rather a *figura Aristotelis* who introduces the fundamental political notion, according to which "man is a political animal . . . endowed with the gift of speech" (*Politics* I, 1, 1253a). To frame Plato, Sini stages the Aristotelian definition of man, which holds nearly the same power over us today as it did 2,400 years ago. The staging of Aristotle reminds us that the modern reading of the *Republic* is contextualized by Aristotelian politics and ethics. After Aristotle, we no longer read Plato as Plato; we read it as Aristotle's posterity. The modern notions of society and justice are not those of Plato, which in fact are not yet definitions but lines in a dialogue, open to all the variations and refutations that a dialogue can generate. They point toward a theory, but they are not yet *the* theory. Plato suggests a way of thinking, sometimes very decisively, as only his Socrates can do, but it is Aristotle who explicitly tells us *what* to think and *how* to think, and he has never stopped doing so.

Once the theatrical structure has been set, Sini divides his analysis into the four "descents" that punctuate Plato's text. The first is Socrates' descent to the port of Piraeus to participate in the feast of the goddess Bendis; the second is Gyges' descent into the bowels of the earth, where he finds the ring that makes him invisible and gives him the power to give vent to his desires; the third is the philosopher's descent into the Cave in an attempt to free the prisoners who are chained there; the fourth and last is the journey of Er, son of Arminius, originally from Pamphylia, also into the bowels of the earth and back up to the surface to testify to the fate of souls in the afterlife and instill the proper fear in those who are not convinced that all the acts performed in one's life will be judged between one incarnation and another.[3]

---

3. Sini adopts the "four descents" frame of interpretation from Mario Vegetti, "*Katabasis*," in Platone, *La Repubblica, Vol. I, Libro I*, translated, edited, and commented by Mario Vegetti (Bibliopolis, 1998), 93–104. Vegetti's monumental commentary in seven volumes, with many contributors, and published between 1998 and 2005, has been Sini's main source.

In Sini's text, however, the first dissection of this double movement of descent and ascent leads to the first of many detours that readers will encounter. Socrates is down at the Piraeus, the port of Athens, the greatest melting pot of ancient Greece, to participate in the celebration of a divinity tenuously related to the Greek Pantheon. The goddess Bendis comes from Thrace, but she may be related to the Greek Hecate, who guides souls to the kingdom of the dead and also stands for the new and invisible moon. Sini's text is a play or, if you will, a script. Each figure is a sign of the future figures that the reader will find later. In the Bendis-Hecate figure two themes are announced, namely, the fate of the dead, which will reappear in the myth of Er; and invisibility, which will acquire great importance throughout the entire book.

Sini uses Bendis-Hecate to evoke three other goddesses of the Greek Pantheon: Artemis, Aphrodite, and Hera, symbolizing the three phases of the visible moon, while Bendis-Hecate, as we have said, stands for the invisible moon. Among those goddesses, Aphrodite and Hera are linked to the possession or lack of Aphrodite's Girdle. This small object of desire, often painted as a belt or a breast band, makes any woman who wears it desirable (by making her more visible—the opposite of Gyges' ring, which makes one invisible). The Girdle passes from Aphrodite to Hera and back as a signifier (or as E. A. Poe's stolen letter, which was invisible and at the same time clearly visible).

Paris, who has been enchanted by Aphrodite's Girdle, has lost his freedom, if he ever had it. He is in debt, even if he doesn't know it, because the reward that he receives from Aphrodite, after he has chosen her as the most beautiful of the goddesses, is the injunction to chase another object of desire, namely, Helen. The Girdle is the female equivalent of the phallus. It works by diverting the view from the genital organ and making it more desirable by taking its place. Because the Girdle functions as a master signifier, his transpositions, always oscillating between visibility and invisibility, make every other signifier "visible" for our interpretation. Especially, Sini says, those mobile, exchangeable, invisible signifiers that we call economic exchange, speech, and money, up to the "invisible" democratic vote, dangerously close to an exchange vote, because it is always an exchange vote. (We vote for someone to receive something in return, either real or symbolic.) The sudden transition from the invisible Bendis-Hecate to the very visible Girdle and then to the invisibility of speech, money, and the democratic vote is just the first of many leaps that the readers of this book will have to take.

This is how Sini summons and at the same time "deactivates" Aristotle, by introducing figures of desire that long precede Aristotle's supposedly objective gaze. Only after such digression does Sini introduce the reader to the heart of the *Republic*, Book I, the initial scene at Cephalus' house, which leads to the subsequent *agon* with Polemarchus, Thrasymachus, Glaucon, and Adeimantus.

It is no coincidence that Socrates and Cephalus, an elderly man who is beginning to fear death, first discuss the lack of desire in old age and the possibility that a certain financial security, which Cephalus achieved as an entrepreneur, can free old age from livelihood precarity. If then, immediately after that brief conversation, Cephalus disappears from the scene never to return, it is because he admitted that he no longer feels desires for food and sex. Cephalus is dismissed because, once deprived of desire, he can no longer be a political subject. He cannot, in other words, desire the city. If politics is a question of pedagogy (*paideia*), it will have to be aimed at young people, whose desires are intense, because in the education of the politician it is crucial that the desire be strong and even dangerous (think of Alcibiades), so much so that Socrates will later warn that young people will have to reach a certain age before they can access political offices (and philosophy will be the cure for their excessive desire).

If the first figure is an introduction to desire, the second figure is dedicated to strength and/or force. As soon as the conversation begins, it is not difficult to find in Polemarchus (according to whom justice consists in doing good to friends and evil to enemies) a *figura* of Carl Schmitt, indeed a prefiguration of Schmitt's thesis that politics begins with the distinction between friend and foe. In the same way, it is not difficult to identify in Thrasymachus the *figura* of a trivialized Nietzsche, read badly (or perhaps well, with Nietzsche you never know) by any tyrant in the history of the twentieth century and beyond. Yet Thrasymachus is an extraordinary character, the strongest in the *Republic*, whose figure radiates through historical time like the spokes of a wheel. Hobbes and Lenin were captured by it, and perhaps Kissinger and Foucault, too (the juxtaposition of extreme thinkers and equally extreme realpolitiker is ours and not Sini's).

Socrates' criticisms of Polemarchus—no more than a sparring partner compared to the much more aggressive Thrasymachus—modify what was, at the time, the common concept of virtue. *Areté*, like *virtus* in Latin, means force, strength, powerfulness, ability, skill, manliness (the notion is unsurprisingly masculine). According to Socrates, however, for virtue to be political and therefore serve the common good, it can no longer be the *areté* that the Greeks learned from Homer. It can't be the spectacular yet senseless brazenness of Achilles, who does not fight for any political ideal but only to satisfy his desire for glory. Force, as Simone Weil names it in her essay on the *Iliad* as "the poem of force," is the virtue that precedes politics, and which must be contained so that it does not annihilate the possibility of politics.[4] Yet no politics can do without force. Once political virtue becomes established power—it becomes law—it must keep force at its side. Not even a metaphysical justice could do without it, just as it is not possible to imagine a law that renounces the threat of violence.

Indeed, as Socrates tries to find a substitute for force, he can only come up with the "noble lie" of the myth of autochthony, which should convince the guardians of the city to give up all their possessions and desires in the name of the "soil" (the soil of Athens) from which they were born (and not from a woman; we will see the implications later). It is an admission on Socrates' part that justice cannot be founded rationally. Implicitly, Socrates says even more: that every myth, no matter how necessary it is to a community, is a lie. It is one of the statements that will cost him the accusation of blasphemy, and ultimately the death sentence. Yet Socrates fears that without the myth of autochthony the guardians will never feel connected to their "soil" enough to sacrifice their life. In a society without myths, and founded exclusively on the desires of individual citizens, no one can ask anyone else to sacrifice themselves for the common good, no one can be told that "it is sweet and proper to die for the fatherland," as Horace later will say (*Odes* III, 2, 13).[5]

In the next discussion between Socrates and Thrasymachus the topic shifts to the distinction between right and wrong. Hesiod gives Justice,

---

4. Simone Weil, "The Iliad, or the Poem of Force," in Simone Weil and Rachel Bespaloff, *War and the Iliad*, translated by Mary McCarthy, introduction by Christopher Benfey, with an essay by Hermann Broch (New York Review Books, 2005), 1–37.

5. For this interpretation, see also Allan Bloom, *The Republic of Plato*, translated, with notes, an interpretive essay, and a new introduction by Allan Bloom, 2nd ed. (Basic Books, 1991), 367–368.

if not exactly the status of a goddess, certainly a semi-divine quality as daughter of Zeus and Themis (*Theogony* 901–902). But the Gods to whom Socrates pays homage are not exactly the Gods of the major Greek Pantheon, even when the names are the same. Besides, Hesiod's *Dike* is not the Law. For that, we have *Eunomia* (lawfulness), another daughter of Zeus and Themis. It may surprise us that Plato does not elaborate a transition from justice to law, which would be in fact a rationalization of what Hesiod suggests, given that they are sisters. But the transition would be premature, for Socrates does not yet know where to place "his" justice, which is political and not divine. Three of the cardinal, or rather heroic, virtues are necessary for the citizen: wisdom, courage, and moderation. The fourth virtue, justice, seems to be nothing but the harmony of the other three virtues, which comes down to every member of the community doing what he or she is supposed to do. Justice is not for the individual; it only belongs to the community.[6]

This is where Sini introduces his first deconstruction of the Platonic theater—the first of many to follow. Each scene is duplicated backstage, where the Platonic dialogue is weighed according to the anagogical direction of its figures, in their being part of a movement. In theory, as we have said, before politics there should be Law, and before the law there should be Justice, beyond which we cannot venture without encountering the terrifying figure of brute force. In Sini's reading, however, there is something that precedes force, and that is desire.

Which is, ultimately, the desire to be desirable. Everyone wants to be "recognized" as desirable. The wound of not being recognized as desirable may in fact turn instantly into a desire for predominance (*pleonexia*). Why is power desirable? Can we say that power is desirable, and predominance or prevarication is a legitimate way to acquire power, for it compensates for the lack of recognition? Yet we see that even in the presence of recognition, power continues to be desirable, and so does predominance.

One could say that power is desirable because it guarantees survival, but as Socrates explains, power doesn't shield anyone from aggression. The tyrant is never safe. If man only had to worry about survival, he might as well live in a peaceful, egalitarian, and law-abiding society. Even if pure politics based on force—or rather the realpolitik that Thrasymachus embraces—may seem like a *figura* of Nietzsche, is not at all the "great

---

6. Eva T. H. Brann, Introduction, in *Plato: The Republic*, edited and translated by Raymond Larson (Harlan Davidson, 1979), xlv.

politics" that Nietzsche hoped for. In a way, the death of Socrates will prove Thrasymachus right. Socrates is condemned by a force that has worn the mask of the law, yet he could never yield to the equivalence between the law and force. Force destroys the city, while laws create it. Socrates dies as an anti-Antigone, who on the contrary died because she recognized only the unwritten laws of the Gods and not the laws of the city. Yet in the eyes of Thrasymachus, who is not convinced, Socrates' reliance on the laws is his weakness.

It is inexplicable that Socrates seems to be unable to respond to Thrasymachus. In fact, Socrates cannot convince anyone (not in Book I, at least) of the reasons why the just man should be happier than the unjust man. That the answer to this crucial question should be so tortuous is the real "scandal" of the *Republic*—a scandal that still torments us today. Sini's thesis is that from the end of Book I onward, in order to limit the scope of that scandal (i.e., the impossibility to respond in terms that Thrasymachus would understand), Plato intends to expound a philosophy of anti-desire, for only by eliminating the anarchy of desire is it possible to give the city political virtue.

(Here too we come close to a figure of our times. No desire is the same as another desire. Desire is neither equal nor fair and cannot guarantee an egalitarian society. What is identity politics today if not an awkward Platonic experiment, a schizophrenic politics, founded on the exaltation of differences and at the same time on pure equity—which to be such must remove the differences themselves, and therefore, desire?)

One of the few arguments that Socrates can put forward against Thrasymachus is of a deductive nature: if right and wrong are a product of power, it makes no sense to say that injustice, having more power, holds power. If it is power that determines what is right and wrong, then power is always just. On the other hand, Socrates points out, ironically, that not even a society of thieves could be based on injustice. Even thieves must agree on the fair division of the loot.

(It might be said that the criminal must be honest with other criminals insofar as he is outside the protection of the law. In the law of democratic societies—and this is an embarrassing yet inevitable fact—the law serves above all to protect the guilty. But if someone establishes a society that cannot hide from the law, then that society will have to be internally honest, thus arriving at the paradox whereby organized crime might even be less corrupt than the society of which it is a parasite. Here a clever line from Don Siegel's *The Lineup*, a 1958 crime film, comes in handy. A seasoned criminal instructs an apprentice not to forgive any transgressions by the gang members: "To live outside the law, you must eliminate dishonesty." Of course, the society of crime is anything but peaceful and is based on betrayal and violence, but this also applies to societies that portray themselves as just. So where is the difference?)

Glaucon's solution is to consider predominance as a state of nature that precedes the social pact. Glaucon supports his thesis by recounting Gyges' story, which introduces the crucial theme of the visible and the invisible, of desire and the signifier—not to mention money, albeit implicitly, since King Gyges of Lydia, according to the legend, invented money (the invention might have happened shortly after his death, but myths don't pay attention to these details). In Sini's interpretation, the myth of Gyges is of exceptional importance, even more so than the myth of the cave. It is at this juncture that Sini activates his "genealogical retroflection," an ethics of research which consists in acknowledging the limits of research itself. Starting with the result of a thought process, we can never go back to its origin, for it is the result that creates the origin. Contrary to what Glaucon states, the state of nature is not what precedes the law but rather what the law presupposes as "other than itself" to legitimize itself. Without this genealogical retroflection (we could call it the rearview mirror critique), we would end up with another paradox: the man of predominance would behave like a "natural man" and therefore enjoy a higher legitimacy than the man of the law.

The clash between the man of predominance and the man of the law occurs without mediation (this crucial passage is in Sini's par. 70) because when men sign the social pact, they also implicitly sign the rules of transgression. We may think of St. Paul's apparently paradoxical statement about the law creating its own transgression (Corinthians I, 15, 56; Romans 7, 7–9). But perhaps for Paul it was not really a paradox. Because of his upbringing as a Pharisee, the sovereignty of the Law was indisputable to him. Law and transgression are linked for no one ever escapes from the Law (as Kafka knew quite well). To this it must be added that the Law, even if divine, circulates among men as a written tablet, and everything that is written, Sini would say, is a signified that makes its signifier (the event of its being written) invisible (as Jahve is invisible to Moses and cannot be represented). Writing does not erase what was not written before; rather, it erases the "before" itself. What was not written is now within the written. It is not entirely true that there is nothing outside the text ("il n'y a pas de hors-texte"), as Derrida has stated.[7] The outside exists, but it, too, is in the text. There's no other place where it can be found.

Socrates' response to Glaucon shifts the place of justice from the individual to the city, which is or should be founded on the need for community and not on the desire of the individual. But that doesn't refute Glaucon's statement, which instead concerned the individual: anyone, if they could give vent to their desires without fearing consequences, would do so. Faced with this wall, which he cannot climb, Socrates removes desire from politics altogether.

(Here, too, we find another *figura futurorum*. The removal of desire was the project of Soviet Communism, not only in the collectivism imposed on the workers, which were the defenders of the state as well, but also in the equalization of the individual desires to eliminate any remnant of the supposed state of nature. It was a die-hard myth that we even find in late and more liberal Marxism, for instance in Ágnes Heller, who is Platonically certain that the working class has no interests, only needs.[8])

In Sini's interpretation, however, need is inscribed in desire to the extent that desire appears in language (here we perceive a concordance with Lacan). But together with language we have exchange, and economy begins. The human impulse to exchange, as Adam Smith called it (Sini quotes Smith in par. 89), where desire and need are united, is what gives rise to "value" (how much what I want to exchange is worth compared to what you want to exchange), just as it gives value to the signifiers that "transport" value (from speech to money). It is then a question of understanding what speech wants, and what we really exchange for

---

7. Jacques Derrida, *Of Grammatology*, translated by Gayatri C. Spivak (Johns Hopkins University Press, 1974), 158. Italo Calvino's distinction between the "written world" and the "unwritten world" was based on his concern that the "written world" was devouring the unwritten world. His insight remains valid, but only if we add that the unwritten world is already entirely inside the written world, which after the invention of alphabetic writing can do whatever it wants with the unwritten world. See Italo Calvino, *The Written World and the Unwritten World: Essays*, translated by Ann Goldstein (Mariner Classics, 2022), 95–102 (electronic edition).

8. Ágnes Heller, *The Theory of Need in Marx* (Allison & Busby, 1976; repr. Verso, 2018).

money. If here it seems that Sini has distanced himself from Plato's text, the continuation of his argument will show that this is not the case.

Interlude and Act Two

Thus ends the First Act, followed by the Interlude, whose main theme is that political virtue was not, in its origin, a political problem; rather, an anthropological one. If a "new man" is needed to establish the new science of politics, then an anthropological foundation is necessary. In Sini's theatrical reading of Plato, a backstage retreat is needed to reveal the mechanism of metaphysical questions such as "What is man?," "What is politics?," "What is language?," "What is justice?," or "What is virtue?"

It won't be easy, because we are always-already captured by our implicit, post-Platonic and post-Aristotelian metaphysics. It is therefore impossible to move in the opposite direction, toward the origin. An origin begins to exist only when we define ourselves as derived from it. We cannot distance ourselves completely from Plato's gesture, because we are already captured by it (in its own way, the figure of Aristotle in the Prologue is also captured by the Platonic gesture, although in turn Aristotle has captured us moderns even more than Plato). The institutive gesture of philosophy is Plato's philosophical theater, but as soon as we say so we have already replaced the backstage (the origin) with *our* stage (the meaning). Is there a way out? Or better, do we need a way out?

Sini's approach, as we have seen, combines phenomenology and genealogy. In his thought, Nietzsche, Foucault, and Derrida (not all Foucault and not all Derrida) are in dialogue with Husserl, Heidegger, Whitehead, and American pragmatism (C. S. Peirce, Chauncey Wright, William James). But, as we have already said, the presence of Bruno and Vico is equally strong, and strongest of all is Vico's warning to never forget that all origins are rough, mysterious, much older than we think, and we cannot have a clear and distinct idea of them. Arguably, Sini's *Ethics of Writing*, the key to his "mature" philosophy (see footnote 1), has been Italy's strongest response to Derrida, mainly because Derrida has basically ignored Vico.

As we have said, the *figurae* that Sini brings into play can be read in an anagogical key, but they don't necessarily go upward, or toward an ever-greater clarification. Anagogy can also take place on a horizontal plane of immanence. That's because metaphysics cannot be vertically "overcome." Every attempt to venture "beyond" metaphysics simply adds another chapter (another "scene") to it. For this reason, Sini insists, we must take a step back and disclose the autobiographical nature of philosophy, where "autobiographical" must be divided into "bio" and "autographic." It is the autographic / autobiographical character that differentiates philosophical speech from other speeches. Not because philosophers write autobiographies, even if they sometimes do, but because the subject of philosophy is the very gesture of writing that gives philosophy birth, and that gesture coincides with a *grapheme* and with a *bios*, an individual life that is affected by that gesture. In other words, it is a question of making visible what philosophy, starting from Plato, does its best to make invisible, that is, its own act of writing, which in Plato is masked by Socrates' seductive "voice."

(Here we might add some observations on the enmity between poetry and philosophy. Plato may have been right or wrong in banishing epic-mythological poetry from the city, but he certainly knew that philosophy's attempt to show the invisible *by leaving it invisible*, as a procession of ideas that can only be seen with the mysterious eyes of the mind or soul, was going to encroach on the turf of poetry. In Plato's rejection of poetic mimesis lies the *figura* of what Rilke said about what poets do: "We are the bees of the invisible. *Nous butinons éperdument le miel du visible, pour l'accumuler dans la grande ruche d'or de l'Invisible.*"[9] Philosophy, on the contrary, accumulates the invisible in the hive of the visible, yet leaving it invisible. If Plato chases the poets from the city, it is not just because he considers them pernicious to the education of the ruling class. By leaving the poet and the philosopher side by side, anyone would notice their uncomfortable closeness. Although the purposes are different, what poetry and philosophy have in common is precisely the invisible, because the invisible is in language, it is language itself. To quote the locus classicus of another Platonic poet, "I say: a flower! And . . . there arises musically, as the very idea and delicate, the one absent from every bouquet."[10])

---

9. "We pilfer distractedly the honey of the visible to collect it in the big golden hive of the invisible." Rainer Maria Rilke, Letter to Witold von Hulevicz, November 13, 1925 (Letter 218), in *Letters of Rainer Maria Rilke 1910–1926*, translated by Jane Bannard Greene and M. D. Herter (Norton, 1969), 308 (electronic edition).

10. Stéphane Mallarmé, "Crisis in Poetry" (excerpts), in *Selected Poetry and Prose*, edited by Mary Ann Caws (New Directions, 1982), 65 (electronic edition).

The invisible is what the myth of the cave is about, but Sini avoids lingering too long in that place, which is already very populated. He prefers to reflect on the consequences of coming back *from* the cave, for it is outside the cave that the freed prisoner will have to see the invisible in the visible, *always leaving it invisible*—that is, leaving it in speech, and even more so in writing.

Essentially, there are two reasons why Sini, in the Second Act, dedicates only one page to the myth of the cave. The first is that the discussion on the visible and the invisible replaces yet another recapitulation-interpretation of the myth. (Rousseau and Werner Jaeger for whom the *Republic* is about education and not politics, and then Kant, Hegel, Wilamowitz, Friedländer, Stenzel, Heidegger in *The Essence of Truth*, Gadamer, Jan Patočka in *Plato and Europe*, A. E. Taylor who believed that Plato's Socrates may be closer to the real Socrates than we think, Popper for whom Plato is the archenemy of the open society, Leo Strauss, Allan Bloom, John Niemeyer Findlay and his mysticism of the cave, Julia Annas, Giovanni Reale—who hasn't tried to appropriate Plato even when hoping to get rid of him?[11])

But the second reason is more relevant, and it brings us back to the very beginning. After the entertainment that he enjoyed at the Piraeus, Socrates is about to go back to Athens, but when he meets Cephalus, Polemarchus, Thrasymachus, Glaucon, and Adeimantus, they all want to stop him. No, Socrates, you can't leave, you can't go back up there to Athens where the beautiful Acropolis is, you must stay with us, here at the bottom, and convince us that there are indeed things like Justice, Virtue, Politics, and Education. The real cave into which Socrates descends is Cephalus' house, where the whole conversation takes place. Having entered reluctantly, as happens to every good citizen who is involved in the politics of the city against his will, Socrates does his best to bring his dialectics of the invisible to the chained people down at the bottom. The chained resist, they are not used to seeing the invisible, *by leaving it invisible*. They are used to seeing shadows, and they think that those shadows are real, or at least they are visible, and they want "visible" answers. It is no coincidence, as we have already said, that the entire *Republic* is a story told by Socrates after he left Cephalus'

---

11. On the modern reception of Plato's *Republic*, see Franco Ferrari, *La Repubblica di Platone* (il Mulino, 2022), 183–192 (I have added Allan Bloom, John Niemeyer Findlay, Paul Friedländer, Jan Patočka, and Giovanni Reale to Ferrari's list).

house (Cephalus' cave) and came to report to those outside—to the philosophers, to *us* (we're being generous here)—how difficult it was to make those "prisoners" listen to reason. With Thrasymachus, Socrates didn't really succeed. Maybe he was a bit more successful with Glaucon and Adeimantus, but he didn't give a direct answer to their doubts and objections, or at least not the way they wanted it. Those answers lie between the lines, in the latest books of the *Republic*, but they will never have the chance to read them, for the *Republic* is a conversation among dead people.

The main theme of Sini's Interlude, however, is the return of desire. If desire is essentially "singular" and therefore unequal, political virtue will then have the task of harnessing it. Plato explains it now with greater clarity: political virtue coincides with the repression of desire. As appears in the conclusion of Book II and the beginning of Book III, it was Plato who invented cancel culture. It is Plato, by means of Socrates' voice, who decides which verses of Homer should be taught in schools and which should not—because they are not suitable for the young, because they would give them wrong ideas about the nature of the Gods (who cannot be anthropomorphic and subject to the same weaknesses as ordinary humans), let alone the nature of heroes. Achilles cannot be described as a senseless defender of his property, whose rage throws an entire military operation into crisis. What's the educational value in such a character?

To establish his new and revolutionary discipline, which is political philosophy, Plato must also downsize Aristophanes, who had ridiculed Socrates in *The Assemblywomen* and *The Clouds*. Plato responds therefore to Aristophanes' "comedy" with the "comedy" of the *Republic*.[12] Aristophanes can laugh at Socrates all he wants, but it is Socrates, not Aristophanes, who knows what is good for the city. Yet the desire to harness desire is itself a desire, which therefore requires its own motivation as well as its own genealogy. What, then, does politics want?

Politics longs for peace, harmony, the industriousness of the hive. Plato is a thinker of peace, not a thinker of conflict as Heraclitus was. He wants the peace of desire, peace *from* desire, and the sublimation of desire into virtue, which is no longer the brute force of Achilles' wrath,

---

12. Bloom, *The Republic of Plato*, 376–381.

but rather harmony and obedience. And, to eliminate the danger of desire, the first thing to do is to reorganize sexuality.

Here is where Gyges' story becomes central again. The myth of the cave is intended to be self-explanatory and to give us the perception of being easy to understand. The myth of Gyges does not act in the same way, in part because Plato borrows it from Herodotus (*The Histories*, Book I, 8), though with substantial modifications. Gyges, a bodyguard of Candaules, the king of Lydia, one day sees the queen while she's naked. In Herodotus, it is the king himself who shows the queen to Gyges, out of pride for his wife's beauty and perhaps also out of his infatuation with Gyges, with whom he seems eager to share some sexual excitement. In Herodotus, it is the queen who then proposes the pact to Gyges: you have seen me naked; now you can only die or kill the king and marry me.

In archaic societies based on the violent removal of power, this second option is legitimate. Sini claims, in fact, that this is what Paris should have done once he "conquered" Helen. He should have killed Menelaus. No one would have taken Helen from Paris if he had killed Menelaus in some sort of ritual murder. By leaving Menelaus alive, Paris made a mistake. If he had done otherwise, he would have taken responsibility for his actions and there would have been no Trojan War. Helen would have given Paris the power to make her submissive to him, because in the archaic rule of law, long before there was a law, sovereignty belonged to the man, but only insofar as it was granted to him by the woman, in a ritual transfer of power which is perhaps the remnant of a much older matriarchal order whose memory has been lost.[13]

Such a way to achieve public power sounds primitive if compared to Socratic justice (understood as the division of labor between the classes that make up the city), just as it is not subjected to Aristotelian justice (the just man is he who respects the contracts). In the archaic world, justice, *Dike*, is not yet a positive *Nomos*; it is not yet a law issued by the "good city" (*kallipolis*). On that respect, Thrasymachus and Glaucon, with all their realpolitik and imaginary "state of nature," are just like Socrates. They have no ties to the sacredness of power. Even Thrasymachus, in his own way, is for positive law: power is always right, he says, and it is power that makes the laws. Nothing in Thrasymachus' speech suggests that law and power come from a God. And the state of

---

13. See Francesca Falabi, "Gige," in Platone, *La Repubblica, Vol. II, Libri II e III*, translated, edited, and commented by Mario Vegetti (Bibliopolis, 1998), 173–188.

nature to which Glaucon appeals answers to no sacred order. It is the queen of Lydia who reintroduces the sacred, offering the pact to Gyges.

In Glaucon's retelling of the story, Gyges first penetrates underground, where inside a bronze horse he finds a ring that can make him invisible. Subsequently, he penetrates the queen's body. He then becomes king and, as we know from other sources, invents money, that is, something whose value is invisible like Gyges himself when he wears the ring. What happens to Gyges is the perfect combination of the state of nature and desacralized politics.

But Socrates doesn't care about Gyges' desires. He intends to destroy the politics of desire at its roots, of which he has seen the results: the Peloponnesian War, Alcibiades constantly switching sides, the victory of Sparta, the thirty tyrants, and the democratic regime which will eventually put him to death. If these are the consequences of the politics of desire, it is much better to abolish it, but at what price? By making the city a place of satisfied pigs, as Glaucon sarcastically defines it—a city based on state lies and forced happiness, a true *figura* of George Orwell's *1984*?

What strategy can convince the citizens to live in a hive governed by the invisible? The device is the abolition of sexual difference among the defenders of the city, and therefore of the desire that arises from difference. If that seems inconsequential (What has sexual difference to do with the politics of the invisible?), we may recall that sexual difference is one of the first things that the child "sees" and inquiries about. Such an explanation may sound too Freudian, and it isn't Sini's. The abolition of sexual difference—this is Sini's point—leads to an extraordinary result, no less than the invention of the Platonic soul which has no sex. And from the invention of the soul comes the replacement of sexual desire with philosophy, which is still *eros*, but *eros* directed toward the knowledge of the Good. Philosophy thus becomes the only legitimate desire, the only purpose worthy of *eros*. It is this strategy that grants the philosophers the ability to govern. They are those citizens who are willing to renounce every desire except that for the Good.

Here Plato reveals the anti-genealogical procedure which Sini never ceases to highlight. It consists in overturning the metaphorization carried out by language to make metaphors appear "real" while their phenomenal basis is reduced to a metaphorical status.

The most striking example of this reversal is the analogy between the sun and the Good. The sun that nourishes the earth is the source of the idea of Good. Or at least it would be so in a cosmological, mythical, and sacral frame of mind, as in Vico the lightning and thunder generating in the "feral creatures" (*bestioni*) of the primordial forest the idea of a God who hurls lightning. Apologies to Vico, of course, for we have used his explanation in a reductively "rational" way. However, Plato does just the opposite.

Instead of placing the light and heat of the sun as the origin of the metaphor of the Good, Plato puts the Good as the origin of the sun. Instead of placing the heroic virtues—wisdom, courage, and moderation—as the foundation of political virtue, he puts political virtue as derived directly from the state and as the thread that binds the other virtues together. The same inversion also affects justice, understood as the harmony between the classes that make up the state. Except this isn't justice in any legal or moral sense; it does not show what is right but rather what is preordained to function together with the other parts that make up the whole. It is a division of labor, the true figure of a caste system, and has nothing to do with "what is right" or even respect for contracts. Harmony, which should be the outcome of justice, becomes its foundation instead. Yet the inversion succeeds; indeed, it is the foundation of the entire edifice of metaphysics.[14]

In this regard, Sini points out that trying to resolve political problems exclusively through public conversation, in the sense desired by Apel, Habermas, Gadamer (and by Kant, with his dream of perpetual peace), merely repeats the original inversion from which the Platonic state was born. In the name of civility, it repeats the Platonic rejection of desire and its replacement with speech, ignoring therefore that the desires expressed by the community must be faced for what they are and not at the level of abstraction allowed by speech—not to mention that speech is always associated with money (they are both invisible), which means economic exchange, and therefore commodity, and therefore speech fetishism and commodity fetishism.[15]

Two observations must be added here: first, the equivalence between the soul of the state and the individual soul involves the reduction of the "outside," or cosmological thought, which will be now confined within

---

14. On the Platonic strategy of overturning metaphors and phenomena, see Alessandro Carrera, *La consistenza della luce. Il pensiero della natura da Goethe a Calvino* (Feltrinelli, 2010), 40–47.

15. Sini makes the same point in *Teoria e pratica del foglio-mondo. La scrittura filosofica* (Laterza, 1997), 32.

the "inner life" of *psyche*. Such reduction of the cosmological soul (*anima mundi*) to the individual soul (which Plato himself will try to correct in part in the *Timaeus*) will then extend to every other discipline and is in fact the project of modernity.[16] The second is that, according to Sini, Plato did not "liberate women" at all by admitting them into the caste of defenders of the city or even into that of philosopher-kings. Socrates says that women can do everything men do, apart from the limitations imposed by different physical strength, and that statement looked revolutionary to many (it certainly was in Plato's time). But saying that women and men are equal means that sexual difference must be erased while *logos* will remain entirely male.

The "phallogocentrism" that Derrida used to denounce as male privilege is here further confirmed. In the Socratic-Platonic city, the woman-guardian who is equal to man is the woman who desires exactly like a man and for this very reason can sleep with all the men of her caste and have children with each of them without even having to acknowledge them, thus repeating an all-male model. Physical strength aside, the woman is "elevated" to the level of the man, but she is not "recognized" in her difference (she is not even "asked" whether she wants to keep her difference or not).

Sini's point is that political virtue (which now can be called political science, as it guarantees the rational exchange of speech and goods) is a new promise of eternal life. It is not the eternal life of the animal, which is based on the absence of speech and on openness to the world. No, the politics of eternal life is that of the eternity of the "city of man" (and woman-as-man). It is the promise, often sincere, that "the honest and just / civic conversation" hoped for by Leopardi in *La ginestra* (*The Broom*), but also by Habermas and others, will be able to smooth out the edges and pass off the "justness" of the city as realized justice.

The conclusion of the fourth figure, dedicated to sexual difference, is supported by a recent occurrence, namely, the March 23, 2022, congressional hearing in which Judge Ketanji Brown Jackson, the first African

---

16. See Carlo Sini, *Passare il segno. Semiotica, cosmologia, tecnica* (Il Saggiatore, 1981). The mythical, cosmological, sacral awareness of the world has flown entirely into the psyche, so much so that it is not difficult to find in the Platonic tripartite soul (appetitive, irascible, and rational) the blueprint of the dynamic model of the Freudian psyche (id, ego, and superego).

American woman appointed to the Supreme Court, was questioned by senators to ascertain her competence and political inclinations. Republican Senator Marsha Blackburn asked her, rather surprisingly: "Can you provide a definition for the word 'woman'?" Judge Jackson responded: "No, I can't. I'm not a biologist."

If Judge Jackson had given an inclusive response, related to gender and not to sex, she would have exposed herself to criticism from the conservative component of the commission. But if she had given a merely biological answer, she would have exposed herself to just as much criticism from the progressive side.

Judge Jackson's choice was to both deny and affirm her difference. By saying, "I'm not a biologist," she affirmed her belief in science as a neutral yet authoritative terrain that she, not being a scientist, was not allowed to cross. Senator Blackburn retorted: "Is the meaning of the word 'woman' so unclear and controversial that you can't give me a definition?"

Senator Blackburn could have done better. For example, she might have asked, "Since neither you nor President Biden are biologists, how does the President know that he has nominated the first African American *woman* to the Supreme Court? And how do *you* know that you are the first African American *woman* nominated to the Supreme Court?" And Judge Jackson could have answered, "But I know that I am a woman. I just don't know what's the *definition* of woman." And the answer would have been *scientifically* correct.

But imagine for a moment that the senator had asked a male judge, "Can you provide a definition for the word 'man'?" The answer would have been very easy, we have carried it with us for 2,400 years. It is in the Prologue, when Aristotle comes forward and says: "Man is a political animal . . . endowed with the gift of speech" (again *Politics* I, 1, 1253a). Aristotle says *zoon*, animal, and not *aner*, male, but it is clear what he means. The state is made up of families who gather in villages, and the head of the family is a man. Man has *logos* and is *logos*. Can woman possess *logos*? Aristotle doesn't deny that, but it isn't a political *logos*, otherwise woman's social status would not be halfway between man and slave. And according to Socrates-Plato? Yes, women can participate in the political *logos*, but only if they renounce their difference.

(A little aside. Just think of the innumerable comics, movies, and television series about superheroes or secret agents. All those intrepid defenders of the homeland must be ready at any moment to give up all their emotional ties. They can have sex as much as they want, but they cannot marry or have children because sooner or later their spouse will be killed, and their children kidnapped. They are the "guardians of the city" imagined by Plato. They can have no other desire than to save the "common good," and as such they continue to live among us, if only as cheap entertainment.)

As we have mentioned, Sini quickly shifts from the myth of the cave to the visible / invisible issue. The point is to understand who the philosopher is, this unique being, who can convince the prisoners to come out of the cave to contemplate the Good in the shape of the sun (which cannot be looked at) and the truth in the shape of what they cannot see. What does it mean, therefore, to see the truth? Is it perhaps the equivalent of Gyges seeing the naked queen? Would the truth be the equivalent of a primary scene?

If that is the case, truth becomes the only object worthy of *eros*. As bearer of the soul, the philosopher can now testify that access to the realm of truth requires setting aside the desirability of the body. "Nor is there male and female," as St. Paul would later say (Galatians 3, 28). What in St. Paul is eschatological universalism, in Plato has an immediate political function. Citizens must feed and reproduce, but the city must not limit itself to taking care of their bodily functions. The politician cannot be a political "animal." He or she will be a de-eroticized soul, whose eros is entirely taken up by Good and Truth. This is why true power, which is power over souls, can only be obtained if one does not desire it. Or, better said, if one's desire is not to desire it.

To have and keep power, the politician must look at reality with practical and ethical disinterest. As we know, disinterest in the service of the common good culminates in Kant's ethics, which Nietzsche then mocked mercilessly. But disinterest does not mean neutrality, because politics is not neutral, it takes a position, it entails parts and parties. To serve the common good one must take a position and therefore renounce, temporarily or strategically, the very common good one would like to serve. The separation of the parties is inevitable, just as it is inevitable that separation generates passion. Socrates may say as much as he wants that philosophers can rise to a divine status despite their limitations as human beings. The fact is that passion can always corrupt them as it corrupted Alcibiades, the most brilliant of his students.

In these terms, the question is unsolvable, and besides, we must drop it here because Sini wants to go back to the topic of writing.

The philosopher, as we know, must show the sun to those who have come out of the cave, but the philosopher does not see the sun; he sees the Highest Good, even if he needs the help of light, which is the support of his vision. But the vision of the "oral" philosopher who does not write cannot be communicated beyond a limited circle. To achieve a larger audience and be politically more effective, the philosopher's vision must transition from the support of light to the support of papyrus. Plato does not write *about* Socrates; he *writes Socrates* so that Socrates can be *read* on papyrus and in the light. Thus, over all the senses stands the privilege of sight, which erases the ancient acoustic primacy of the world that takes shape in the dark, where creation is not seen but heard.[17]

The myth of the cave lowers the creative function of darkness (conception occurs in the dark), staging shadows that have no sound, just as those who move puppets and signs behind the prisoners make no sound. The archaic, acoustic cosmos is erased; sound will only reappear later, but it will be inaudible, just like the vision of the Highest Good is invisible. That new sound which is not a sound is the "voice of conscience" or, rather, the voice of truth that philosophy transcribes. But philosophy doesn't really "transcribe" anything; rather, philosophy *writes* it, it does nothing but write it.

Sini's analysis of the imperialism of writing is his similarity and at the same time his point of contention with Derrida (because, as we have seen, of Derrida's insufficient genealogical gaze). Both, however, make very clear that the voice of conscience, or the voice of truth (the voice of Socrates, that is) is not a voice at all. It is an extrapolation of writing, and only because of writing do we readers perceive it as "the" voice.[18]

As we have seen, Socrates does not really define what justice is, except as harmony of the parts of the city. But the same happens with the Good. Socrates cannot give a definition because the Good is beyond essence (*epekeina tes ousias*), and philosophy cannot but stop at essence. Beyond the *Republic*, and almost beyond philosophy itself, the answer will have to be once again cosmological rather than rationally metaphysical. It's no coincidence that Plato returns to religious cosmology in

---

17. On the acoustic creation of the world, from which the myth of the "music of the spheres" derives, see Alessandro Carrera, *Polvere di stelle. Dalla musica delle sfere ai concerti negli stadi* (Mimesis, 2023), 11–127.

18. On this theme, see Alessandro Carrera, *L'esperienza dell'istante. Metafisica, tempo, scrittura* (Lanfranchi, 1995), 11–62.

Timaeus, which is explicitly the sequel of the *Republic*, thus showing that the secret of philosophy (to use Hegel's expression) is theology. On this point, which Sini highlights, we need to spend some time, but starting from afar; namely, from the genealogy of alphabetic writing.

Philosophy gives a *sign* of the Good, but the Good cannot be written. The Good is therefore that which is supremely visible to the philosopher and can be reduced to a word, just as everything can be reduced to a word, though the word that indicates the Good is far removed from the Good itself. Yet the signifier "Good" carries the genealogy of what we cannot define. The words we use come from ancient images, combination of pictograms that were supposed to be "seen" and not just "read." The paradox is that writing claims to be the transcription of an "orality" of which it is in fact the origin. Only from the point of view of writing is it possible to conceive a primordial orality. In cultures with no writing (although it would be very difficult to find a society without any form of writing, even if it is just a notch on wood), people do not say, "We belong to orality." Our idea that there is such a thing as orality that precedes writing is another example of the perceived "after" retroactively creating its "before."[19]

Unlike iconic scripts, be they Egyptian hieroglyphs or ancient Chinese ideograms, alphabetic writing doesn't say much. In terms of information theory, it has very little redundancy, but neither does it have a high level of information, certainly less than pictorial or ideogrammatic writing. When Leonardo da Vinci said that he was no intellectual (*omo sanza lettere*) and that he would think in images, he was placing himself outside alphabetic writing, but he was also pointing out that a painting provides much more information than the page that describes it. One needs to know a remarkable degree of context to derive meaning from alphabetic writing. It is, after all, a set of instructions. Sini (who has a diploma in piano) even suggests that it is close to a musical score. And

---

19. Sini often mentions Alfred Kallir, *Sign and Design: The Psychogenetic Source of the Alphabet* (James Clarke, 1961) as an inspiration. Kallir (1899–1983), a Jewish Austrian who fled to England in 1941, was motivated by Winston Churchill's two-fingered victory sign to begin his independent research on the Greek and Latin alphabets, focusing on the visual genealogy of letterforms. On the transition from orality to literacy, Sini refers mostly to the work of Eric A. Havelock (1903–1988).

written music, which is only a small part of all music, requires plenty of context and many gestural and mnemonic practices to be performed. The score is not enough.

In Sini's view, structuralism (Piaget, Lévi-Strauss, Barthes), the theory of enunciations and enunciates (Foucault), and the difference between trace and writing (Derrida) do not touch the heart of the matter, which is the real genealogy of the Western mind. The true field of investigation is the practice of alphabetic writing. No other research will show to what extent those abstractions known as signifier, signified, speech, and language are "partial objects," namely, objects whose reality does not extend beyond the frame of alphabetic writing and the civilization that alphabetic writing has created. This is the basis of the genealogy of writing which Sini has outlined since the 1980s and which finds an important chapter in his analysis of the *Republic*.

Sini's thesis is radical, because it dismantles the universalistic assumptions of Western metaphysics with the very tools of Western metaphysics. No doubt, it can originate aporias; it can be discussed and corrected. But it helps explain why cultures that have developed different systems of writing also have different practices of knowledge. Non-Western philosophies who are not fixated on the Western notions of Being, Nothingness, Identity, and Difference are perfectly understandable and fully functional for those who inhabit them, while the Western mind struggles to bring them within the metaphysical parameters, based on determinations, clear and distinct definitions, and on the principle of noncontradiction. Non-Western concepts that originated in nonalphabetic writing provide "too much" information, which to the Western mind sounds like "contradiction."

Sini doesn't want to create a "philosophy" of writing. He would rather call it an "ethics." The task of the ethical philosophers is to show the genealogy of their writing gesture in the same act of writing down their "theories," and the gesture of showing the gesture of writing in action is more important than any new "theory." Yet, the honesty of putting on display one's practice in the act of practicing it does not elude the general problem of phenomenology, which is the habit of thought from which Sini never broke away. While looking for yet another backstage, or the backstage of the backstage, don't we run the (also very Western) risk of infinite regression? As in the most archaic mythologies, where a god is always preceded by another forgotten deity, hidden in the depths of the earth or the sky, behind any genealogical research there hides another genealogy, a pre-genealogy that probably won't ever lead us to the *ur*-genealogy. As Nietzsche argued, "We cannot reject the possibility that it [the world] may include infinite interpretations" (*The Gay Science*, 374), but genealogies are also interpretations, and when we extend them to the infinite, they may block research instead of carrying it out.

The secret of alphabetic writing, thus, becomes a semiotic equivalent of the Highest Good, which we can point to, we can hint at, but when we try to "say it" we must do so with the tools of alphabetic writing. Yet admitting this limitation, and at the same time never ceasing to put it to the test, is precisely the ethical habit of the philosopher that Sini wants to be. The less information the alphabet provides compared to iconic writing, the more its power of abstraction increases. And nothing can be more abstract and at the same time more pressing than the Good. But that the Good cannot be defined does not make it a mystical super-essence (Plato's theology in the *Republic* is secular, not negative); it makes Good a "name" which cannot escape from itself and which circulates in the entire system combining speech and writing (the name, Sini clarifies here and there—echoing Plato's *Sophist*, 218c—is not yet a definition; is not yet part of *logos*).

But if Writing and Good are indefinable names, or if calling them Good and Writing does not do them justice, well, this is also a fact. Not a fact of the world, but the fact that "made" the world, or rather, the fact of Socrates and Plato (two eccentric Greeks, as Husserl called them) who one day decided to "make the world," that world in which the West still lives. It was the Socrates-Plato event, that indefinable signifier, that made the West what it is. The Good which we cannot define except as self-generating (*effusivum sui*, as Thomas Aquinas said) and the alphabetic writing that tries to unite the greatest abstraction with the greatest effectiveness are the aftermath of that event.

Act Three and Epilogue

Plato's political philosophy was a response to the destructive power that the Greek civilization experienced with the Peloponnesian War. By resisting the Persian invasion, the Greeks had discovered themselves as a people, as One. With the Peloponnesian War, they became Many again. Plato intends to remedy the chaotic awakening of the Many after the interrupted dream of the One. He must therefore conclude the *Republic* with the final descent of Er, son of Arminius, into the world of the dead, to learn about the fate of souls. The Spindle that regulates the double anagogical movement (some souls ascend, other souls descend, and Er must ultimately ascend as well) is the cosmic point where all destinies become one. And only here, in the face of death, the leitmotif of Justice can be played out in its entirety. Announced since Book I, unresolved, subsequently identified with the harmony of trades in the city and the tripartite soul in the individual, Justice finds its place only in Book X. While Thrasymachus wished to believe that everything the sovereign decided was just, Socrates' account of the myth of Er wants to believe that all mortals will have to be subject to the calculation of good and evil deeds that they accomplished in life, so much so that the tyrant (the very one for whom, according to Thrasymachus, his will was always right) is the one who suffers more in Hades.

The myth of Er is Socrates' response to the war of all against all, to the state of nature and desire unchained. Sini, however, points out how problematic this response is. First, because it diverts the problems of politics from project to myth; second, because one must accept the postulate of the immortality of the soul to instill fear in men, pushing them to be just to avoid punishment in the afterlife. Which is what Socrates apparently didn't want at first. Man had to be just because the harmony of the city had a value, not out of fear or the expectation of a reward. Where did virtuous disinterest and public-spiritedness go? It seems that Cephalus was not entirely wrong to worry about the future of his soul. He didn't make a mistake when he abandoned the discussion to offer sacrifices to the Gods. The myth of Er is the return of his ghost, and with it, of theology.

We can draw two conclusions from Sini's claim that theology is the fulfillment of philosophy (par. 206). First, if philosophy was born to give order to the chaos of pre-politics, then theology is the only device capable of giving order to the chaos of politics. Political theology, a major theme in twentieth-century philosophy, is therefore the measure to evaluate the entire political project of the West. Obviously, political theology has nothing to do with theocracy, which subjugates politics, while political theology acts from within politics. As in Walter Benjamin's well-known aphorism, theology is the little hunchback who knows how to play chess and moves from within the chess-playing automaton of "historical materialism" (the quotation marks are Benjamin's) and maybe the entire philosophical machine.[20] Second, the fulfillment of philosophy is double. It gets redoubled like the particles of light that pass through the Einstein-Podolsky-Rosen experiment. In other words, the fulfillment of philosophy is all in theology, and yet, at the same time, it is all in technology, or rather, techno-science.

Throughout the twentieth century, both political theology and technical theology (as we might call it) have fought for the legacy of philosophy. Plato's theology, which had the world of myth behind it, intended to replace the myth of God with the *episteme* of God, otherwise known as the Good. Techno-science, however, has also asserted its right to inherit philosophy, and with equally valid reasons, which can be summed up in the mathematical language that techno-science has developed in the last four centuries.

Sini has often repeated that Galileo's statement about the universe being written in mathematical symbols must be taken in all its implications.[21] Yet humanistic philosophy has struggled, and still struggles, to give that statement the gravity it deserves. Now, if the language of "natural philosophy" (the term for science in Galileo's time) is mathematics, we might say that philosophy can now celebrate both its funeral and its triumph. The former for having committed suicide to make room for techno-science, and the latter for having generated a progeny more powerful than philosophy was in its most glorious times.

(The Galilean-Leibnizian turn that occurred when mathematical writing took over discursive writing is an epochal rupture as decisive as Plato's invention of the soul. If philosophy concludes its adventure both in techno-science and in political theology, it becomes necessary to retrace this "catastrophe" in all its ramifications. From this point of view, the last will and testament of European philosophy can be read in

---

20. Walter Benjamin, *Theses on the Philosophy of History*, in *Illusions: Essays and Reflections*, edited and with an introduction by Hannah Arendt, preface by Leon Wieseltier (Schocken Books, 1968, 2007), 253.

21. "Philosophy is written in this all-encompassing book that is constantly open before our eyes, that is the universe; but it cannot be understood unless one first learns to understand the language and knows the characters in which it is written. It is written in mathematical language, and its characters are triangles, circles, and other geometrical figures; without these it is humanly impossible to understand a word of it, and one wanders around pointlessly in a dark labyrinth." Galileo Galilei, "The Assayer," 7.1 (1623), in *The Essential Galileo*, edited and translated by Maurice A. Finocchiaro (Hackett, 2008), 175 (electronic edition).

Husserl's *The Crisis of European Sciences* and in Heidegger's *The Question Concerning Technology* plus *Letter on Humanism.* But what comes after the last will? Not deconstruction or genealogy, which are still part of the will. Perhaps the dream, harbored by the philosophy of mind, to be able to survive as a handmaid of science? Or perhaps, and with more legitimacy, Whitehead's "process philosophy," whose closeness to Sini's philosophy of practices is still to be investigated?)

Plato's project was to secure the positive dictatorship of philosophy; a tyranny of thinking, founded on the universalizing claim of alphabetic writing. However, Sini argues that what Plato *really* wanted to eliminate with his dialogical writing wasn't only Homer but, and perhaps even more, the original writing of the theater, of staging, of the speech which is representation even without being turned into a strip of words written on a support. Theater and poetry are older than philosophy and were born with other purposes. Philosophy makes use of both, occasionally, and perhaps in a vampiric way, just as theater and poetry can do toward philosophy. But Aeschylus believed in the gods of tradition; philosophy does not. At most, philosophy believes in "God" who can be the Supreme Good or the Prime Mover. The spirit of tragedy (Euripides excluded) is the recognition of the terror that the gods instill in mortals; the spirit of philosophy is to find ways to overcome that terror.

While theater does not really need philosophy, philosophy cannot help but create its own theater; it just avoids the embarrassment of presenting the philosopher's body on stage. The teacher may be physically present in the classroom, but the institution of higher education functions as the "curtain" that separates teachers from students. Sini would say that it is almost the same curtain behind which, it is said, Pythagoras imparted his teachings.[22] Socrates was the first to raise that curtain (the curtain of initiation), but then he replaced it with the curtain of his questioning, which is more insidious insofar as it's invisible. Yet Sini points out that philosophy, in its attempt to replace the scene of tragedy with the scene of dialectics, has got the wrong objective. The real place

---

22. The entire first section of *Teoria e pratica del foglio-mondo*, 5–60, is dedicated to the question of the initiatory "curtain," which Socrates replaces with "his" invisible curtain, replacing initiation with education, wisdom with the search for knowledge, and religion with politics.

of the theater is not the scene but the complementarity, which is also complicity, between actor and spectator, accompanied by an inevitable dose of mutual erotic attraction (par. 212–213).

It is true that this complementarity-complicity is also present in the philosophical articulation of teacher and student, subject and object, which are the actor and spectator of philosophical theater. But in doing so, philosophy must give up on its uniqueness. There is no world without the image of the world, just as there is no theater without that ambiguous threshold between representation and represented. Following Artaud (who is very much present in Sini's late work), that threshold is the double of the theater itself, and philosophy cannot call itself out of it.[23]

Can a combination of phenomenology and genealogy reveal the internal engineering of this endless duplication of the world? Or isn't genealogy itself the opening of an abyss into which the postmetaphysical philosopher sinks, trying in vain to speak a nonmetaphysical language? Yet the duplication of the world, Sini argues, is there even in the simplest communication, even in saying "Pass me the salt," because the "salt" that I "say" will never be the salt that is passed to me but rather a bastardization of the Platonic concept of salt.

Theater stands for the persistence of what Plato's philosophy would regard as obsolete, that is, imitation, identification, and even catharsis, as Aristotle would later call it. Yet these theatrical gimmicks are at work in philosophical discourse as well. If theology and techno-science are the fulfillment of philosophy, theater, as well as poetry and myth, are its origin. Plato knows that, but he doesn't want us to be aware of it, or at least not too much.[24] The wisdom of tragedy is foreign to the new philosophical order, which in fact rejects tragic wisdom as the knowledge that one can "possess." Philosophy, on the contrary, is the love of wisdom that is not possessed and cannot be possessed. Tragedy and poetry held the keys to destiny and nature, but that did not give them the political power necessary to manage the world of the Many. Sometimes Plato looks at wisdom, drama, and poetry as one might look

---

23. See Antonin Artaud, "For the Theater and Its Double" (1931–1936), in *Selected Writings*, ed. and with an introduction by Susan Sontag, translated by Helen Weaver (Farrar, Straus and Giroux, 1976), 213–276.

24. See Carlo Sini and Antonio Attisani, *La tenda. Teatro e conoscenza* (Jaca Book, 2021). Sini's interest toward the theater is almost unique in contemporary Italian philosophy.

at a noble failure, or as a pragmatic politician who is asked to fund the liberal arts and dismissively replies, "What's their use?"

Political virtue is the skill to substitute the discordance of poetic sublime and tragic catharsis with a less dazzling but, hopefully, more lasting harmony. The happiness of politics (a theme that Aristotle will make his own and will affect Thomas Aquinas, Dante's *Monarchia*, and the theories of public happiness in eighteenth-century France, all the way down to Hannah Arendt) is founded on the assumption of the universality of reason. To affirm that reason is universal, or that all men are naturally philosophers though they may not know it, imposes Western reason on the rest of the world by passing it off as a gift—a gift that should be feared ("Beware of Greeks bearing gifts," *Aeneid* 2, 49), as is in fact often feared.

(For there are gifts that cannot be refused, and not only because they arrive accompanied by a conquering or liberating army—which is often the same thing—but also because they appear in the format of the alphabetic and mathematical writing that the West has produced. And, as soon as the "universal" paradigm of Western writing and techno-science is adopted, it becomes difficult to criticize the made-in-Europe brand of universality. For instance, postcolonial philosopher Dipesh Chakrabarty has sought to overturn Europe's universal claim by reducing Europe to a province of the world.[25] Which is fine but claiming that Europe is guilty of hypocrisy because it has not maintained the standards of universality it had set out for itself reiterates, in fact, that European values should be even more universal than they are. European thinkers are often much more critical of their tradition than authors from other provinces of the world. Who criticized Enlightenment universalism more ferociously than Adorno and Horkheimer?)

The trouble with the West is consubstantial with its political theology, which perhaps did not even originate solely with Plato, and not necessarily in Greece, but with the Tablets of the Law. Sini insists that the "name" is the real issue, the name that comes before *logos* and is irreducible to *logos*; the name that is given to us, that we are and we have not decided to be; the Name of the Father; and the name, we can

---

25. See Dipesh Chakrabarty, *Provincializing Europe: Postcolonial Thought and Historical Difference* (Princeton University Press, 2000).

add, that we place as guarantee of the law that we want to observe and transgress at the same time. The commandment says: "Thou shalt not kill" (Exodus 20, 13, KJV), but in the name of the commandment, and in the name of the God who commands it, or the city that promulgates it, I can kill anyone who opposes my God and my city. What has long been debated as the mystical apparition of power, law, and violence, from Georges Sorel to Benjamin, from Bataille to Derrida, lies in the legitimation that the name provides.[26]

In the "name" of democracy, a state of exception can be established that abolishes it. In the name of the Good, one can commit Evil. In the name of the liberation of an oppressed people, the same people can be oppressed. The whole *arcanum* of power lies in this terrifying feature of the name, whereby the spell with which I invoke a God who forbids me to do evil is the very same spell that allows me to do it. The essence of political mysticism is framed in this unsolvable interweaving of prohibition and authorization. The law tends to erase its past (*Nomos* wants to be done with *Dike*). Prior to the law—the law states—there must be nothing (there must be no Antigone prior to Creon). But the spell that allows us to break the law is cast together with the law. The pact is broken the moment it is sealed, the seal is broken the moment the pact is signed.

The first edition of *La virtù politica* dates to 2004. The book is certainly affected by the political temper of those years, marked by a hedonistic Italian government—deeply reactionary, but as if it all were just a joke—and the occupation of Afghanistan and the second USA-Iraq war, both begun with the aim to abolish dictatorships whose brutality was beyond question but dragged out to impose Western democracy on peoples that, although oppressed, showed little or no desire to adopt it.

But what Western civilization really exports with alphabetic writing and mathematics, political theology and techno-science is not so much democracy as the specific knowledge of death that the West has acquired in its history. It is Mallarmé's flower again, the one "absent from every bouquet"—the correlation between language and death that Hegel had already grasped in his Jena lectures (1801–1806). The word "flower" is the death of the flower, just as, according to Sini, the four descents that mark the *Republic* are descents into the depth of the relationship

---

26. See Jacques Derrida, *On the Name*, edited by Thomas Dutoit, translated by David Wood, John P. Leavey, and Ian McLeod (Stanford University Press, 1995).

between language and death. The journey ends in the knowledge of death experienced by Er and in a promise of immortality of the soul even more mythical than the myth itself. Because the immortality of the soul is the abolition of "eternal life," of the animal life which does not know death, cannot verbalize it, and therefore is the only life that can be called eternal. Eternal life is what the immortal soul can no longer afford and wants to replace with immortal growth (growth of knowledge and *logos*, growth of production, growth of capital).[27]

Time does not happen in speech; the word "flower" does not contain the past of the flower, nor its future; it does not even contain its present. Yet knowledge is no other than this: knowing that you cannot say time. And the highest knowledge will tell you that if you want immortality, you deny yourself eternal life.

"What, then, is time? If no one asks me, I know: if I wish to explain it to one that asks, I know not." Augustine's discourse on time (*Confessions*, Book XI, 14) is valid for all metaphysical entities, that is, for all the definitions that alphabetic writing can abstract from the flow of "eternal life." If no one asks me what "man" is, I know; if someone asks, I know not. And, as we have already seen, if no one asks what "woman" is, a woman knows; if someone asks, she may not know. Like politics, the Law, or the Good, words can only be overcome "in the name" of the words themselves. Only by speaking in the name of speech do I transcend speech and bring to light the desire that speech signifies without saying it. Pragmatist and Darwinian Chauncey Wright once said, "All the ends of life are, I am persuaded, within the sphere of life."[28] Yet it is equally true, as Sini comments, that "once life has inscribed itself on the threshold of speech, it no longer suffices unto itself" (par. 268). Once we have access to language, Lacan would say, we lose access to *jouissance*. That's why there is no philosophy of *jouissance*, just as there is no philosophy of eternal life.

Yet the desire persists, in philosophy as well as in politics. All political regimes think of themselves as eternal, either out of lust for power or because they presume to know that only the Flood can come after them. Toward the end of the twentieth century, Western capitalism

---

27. On the "economy" of eternal life, see Carlo Sini, *Del viver bene* (Jaca Book, 2015).

28. Chauncey Wright, Letter to Miss Grace Norton, July 29, 1874, in *Letters of Chauncey Wright, with Some Account of His Life*, edited by James Bradley Thayer (Harvard University Press, 1878), 274.

and democracy declared themselves eternal. While no one is seriously threatening capitalism, democracy is always under attack. Not everyone wants the end of democracy, but it is remarkable that democracy is still surprised that someone may want it to end.

Plato would not be surprised at all. In the *Republic*, Book VIII, democracy (which he understands as demagogy) is only part of a cycle of natural (and therefore eternal) generation and degeneration that includes tyranny, timocracy (a regime founded on pride and warrior values), oligarchy, and hopefully, an aristocracy of philosophers. Yet Plato has truly outlined a new anthropology, a new eternal life that overcomes animal life. It is not the eternity of this or that regime, but the eternity of politics itself. This is the threshold that Plato crosses and makes us cross. After reading Plato, Sini points out, it is almost impossible to understand the politics of the ages before politics. What can we say, for instance, of the prephilosophical, yet indisputably political, rituality of Aeschylus' *The Persians*? Does Plato help us understand it? No, we must use other paradigms, which happen to be those of the theater.

As we have already said, one can always kill in the name of "Thou shalt not kill," yet Sini points out that the paradox of the new anthropological politics is precisely the prohibition to kill (par. 301–305). Obviously, Sini refers to ritual and sacral killing, like Gyges who kills the king with the permission of the queen—a killing not made "in the name" of anyone. Having singled out this interdiction on which politics is based (no matter how easily it can be eluded) seems to place Sini in contrast with Giorgio Agamben's theorization of *homo sacer*, where, on the contrary, politics, or rather biopolitics, begins with a procedure of absolute exclusion, the "license to kill" an ostracized citizen without being brought to trial. The mystery of politics always revolves around death, as Foucault understood by examining sovereignty and biopolitics, both being different ways of managing death. Through death, politics desires peace, but because peace is its only desire, it is also a desire that must be absolutely satisfied, and the instrument for achieving peace is war.

The abolition of sexual difference is necessary for peace, not only because it creates a caste of warrior men and women totally devoted to the city, but because the inequality of desires would make it impossible to desire peace. Politics is the politics of desire, even when desire is contained or repressed. But can desire be repressed indefinitely? Here we must tread very carefully, because our answer, which is derived from Sini while not exactly his, walks on a very thin line. The more politics represses desire, the more it defers it. And an indefinite deferment of desire achieves the paradoxical result of making it truly eternal. Thanks to Sini's analysis, which is admittedly difficult to follow in its thousand twists and turns, perhaps now we can answer the question we asked at the beginning: Why is power desirable? Not only that; we may begin to understand what absolute power may consist of, that is, the possibility to extinguish desire not once and for all but through eternal deferment, thus keeping it alive in a suspended state and without end. If the "gentlemen" of Sade's *120 Days of Sodom* despaired because their enjoyment could not last beyond the death of their objects of pleasure, absolute power makes sure that desire will be eternally extinguished, which means ad infinitum, like losing sight of a straight line that proceeds to infinity.

But absolute power is like the Highest Good; it's just not there. Eventually, death of the single or the death of state will put an end to the eternal extinction of desire. Socrates sounds naïve when he says that the only happy man is the just man, that only the man who doesn't want power can be happy, and the sensible man feels no temptation whatsoever to get involved in politics. But what Socrates says is not at all naïve. On the contrary, it is the strongest criticism of any policy based on pure utopia, on the "long-term plan" and the "good of the greatest number of people" in whose name all the bloodthirsty regimes have always found their justification. The *kallipolis* does not exist and will never exist, even if the tyranny of *logos* were established, except in speech, in the invisible and in the idea.[29] The tyrant's perpetual dissatisfaction is there *from the beginning*, because his power is not inscribed in the eternal life of the lower animal or God (for the third time, *Politics*, I, 1, 1253a) but only in the mortal speech that makes him king.

Better said: the just man enters politics out of duty, not for pleasure. He knows that power might allow him to extinguish his "natural" desires for food, sex, and predominance, but such extinction, achieved through good or bad expedients, would be as infinite as desire itself. It would never give him peace, nor would he reach pure *jouissance*, the nonpolitical state of the lower or higher forms of life. Even the worst of tyrants will always be too much of a man to turn into a lower animal, nor will he

---

29. See also Bloom, *The Republic of Plato*, 410.

ever be godly enough to feel like a god.[30] This is the true reason why the unjust man cannot be happy, the reason that Thrasymachus finds it so difficult to understand and that Glaucon and Adeimantus hopefully one day will be able to understand.

Currently, many understand desire as a liberating force. But desire, once politicized (and in the city it can only be politicized), has a totalitarian nature. Plato desires the dictatorship of the rational soul embodied by the philosopher; Marxism desires the dictatorship of the inheritors of bourgeois reason embodied by the working class; in some figures of post-structuralism, we find elements of a dictatorship of desire in its purest state (the desire of the newborn baby who is already satiated but continues to desire the breast). There is very little in this desire that resembles a project of emancipation. Politicized desire is condemned to the Tantalus torture of being eternal and at the same time eternally extinct, extinct and at the same time eternal, and in fact it is no different from the infinite desire that haunts advanced capitalism, the torment of Faust, the inner totalitarianism of modernity, of opulent societies in which no one is satisfied, and of neoliberal capitalism, triumphant, eternal, and at the same time eternally extinct as it has always-already surrendered to the techno-scientific promises of endless desires yet to come.

This is how impossible requests arise, in politics as in morals, or rather that phenomenon that Sini defines as "universal indignation": global moral reaction, triggered by the media as soon as the wishes of the individual, be they biological or technological, are not promptly and absolutely satisfied (par. 334).

The resulting society no longer has an interest in the future; it is only interested in the present time, mistaken for eternal life. The search for universality collapses into the innumerable, particular universals that never reach the stage of the concrete as they seek to embody a non-mediated universality instead of building their universality from their particularity.[31]

It is no surprise that human universality no longer seems an ideal worth pursuing. The theories of the posthuman and transhuman are in fact

---

30. In a certain respect, the king can indeed be an animal, although not a "low" one. On the relationship between animality and sovereignty, see Jacques Derrida, *The Beast and the Sovereign*, 2 vols., edited by Michel Lisse, Marie-Louise Mallet, and Ginette Michaud, translated by Geoffrey Bennington (University of Chicago Press, 2009).

31. See Todd McGowan, *Universality and Identity Politics* (Columbia University Press, 2020).

clumsy attempts to escape the infernal combination of inextinguishable and ever-extinguished desire. Occasionally, what we have is technological Gnosticism: the dream of being able to do without the decaying human body by transferring mind and consciousness (whatever that means) onto another support. Marketing plays a role too. Every experiment in human or transhuman engineering, every political-anthropological project of a "new man," which in fact begins with the *Republic*, is today presented as a new product, a new brand of eternal life.

Man must be overcome, Nietzsche said. Unless we go back to the apocalyptic sects of the second century, never have so many men and women wished to overcome "man" as they wish today, but no one is able to give up the most updated version of eternal life on the market. No one can give up the impossible project of extinguishing their desire while keeping it alive eternally. Desire wants to be recognized, like children who want their mother to recognize them far beyond their satisfied need. But every desire for recognition is always accompanied by the possibility of *not* being recognized, otherwise there would be no desire, or even recognition; there would only be fusional identity. Currently, life is lived as a galaxy of occasions, because "individuals are only worth anything for the occasions they have; that is, for the opportunities they come across to invest a certain amount of money in the market of the endless goods" (Sini, par. 339). And eternal life is one of these endless goods. But that might not be the only destiny in store for us. Life as an occasion might usher in the decision *not* to want eternal life, to live at least *one* life. Sini is confident that the *signs* are clear now. At least we know that we live in a world of signs and there may be nothing except signs in store for us. And yes, we must not turn "sign" into a new metaphysical absolute. There is no such thing as "sign." Every sign that we send or receive is the result of a series of operations, "practices" that can be defined only by other signs that derive from other practices. Practices are signs, and signs are practices. Prior to every practice and every sign, there is their event that puts them in motion. Sini's philosophy is a dynamic system, it's not made of "things." The risk of falling into one "step back" too many is there, yet Sini is telling us that we live in a world that is still open and undetermined, and this may be the greatest occasion that we have. Our most pressing duty is now to recognize the voice of those who have not been included, so far, in the realm of *logos*. But we also must keep in mind that the excluded might not recognize Western *logos* as the place they want to enter, just as they might decide that it is not the language of Western philosophy that they want to speak.

Foreword

The *Encyclopedia* Project

The *Encyclopedia* is divided into six stages, corresponding to six paradigmatic or exemplary sciences: metaphysics, psychology, ethology, anthropology, cosmology, and pedagogy.[1] Each stage is then punctuated by nine figures articulated in a specific mode, making up a total of fifty-four figures. Here are the nine fundamental figures:

The inscribed and the circumscribed
Thought and practices
Origin
Difference
Transcendence or negation
Analogy
Encounter
Occasion
Truth

These figures follow one another according to a 2 + 3 + 4 pattern (whence the number 234, a very significant one, as we will see, both because it alludes to 432—its inversion—and because its digit sum is 9).

---

1. Carlo Sini, *Transito verità. Figure dell'enciclopedia filosofica. Opere Vol. V*, edited by Florinda Cambria (Jaca Book, 2012). *La virtù politica. Filosofia e antropologia*, originally published as a separate volume by Jaca Book in 2004, is the fourth part of the *Encyclopedia*. The subjects of the six volumes are 1) metaphysics, 2) psychology, 3) ethology, 4) anthropology, 5) cosmology, 6) pedagogy—Ed.

A clear understanding of this pattern is contingent upon several varied considerations. As a preliminary move, I would suggest that we start with this possible interpretation: the first two figures describe the paradoxical situation inherent in every beginning, whereby the subjects of the beginning discover themselves to be, in fact, subject *to* the beginning and proceed to make this discovery into the very means and method of their ethical emancipation.

The next three figures describe the subject's transit into truth—truth, that is, in its constitutive duplicity. Truth is duplicitous because it is the threshold of its own event, whereby the "step back"[2] of the retroflexed and anteflexed figure is always subsumed again into the vanishing uniqueness of a transcendence. Indeed, transit and transcendence are one and the same.

The remaining four figures articulate the horizon of the becoming-world of the subject (or the becoming-subject of the world), until the culminating experience of transit/truth. Free of any superstition, the subject thus coincides with its "ethic," i.e., with its exercise of crossing the truth in the significant event of its being-in-error.

The exemplification has assumed, as we can see, a reference to the subject—which is not necessary, nor exhaustive of the whole meaning represented by the succession of these nine figures. It must be pointed out, in fact, that such figures have not been artificially created. They have emerged and asserted themselves on the analogical journey of *metaphysics* and then spontaneously repeated themselves on subsequent journeys. Spontaneously in the sense that every journey, observed attentively and without prejudice, has highlighted them as already present in a subterranean way. There is no need for me to belabor this point. Anyone can verify it for themselves and choose the explanation they deem most appropriate. Or they might discover the presence of entirely different figures. Only the figure as such remains qua the essential notion, for the journey of the *Encyclopedia* is an exercise, a postural action, and in this sense an ethic of the figure, that is, the active writing of a habit, of a practice in operation.

I view the six paradigmatic practices as six doors, six ways into the ideal world-sheet (*foglio-mondo*) of the circle of sciences made into

---

2. *Stacco* in Italian: break, cut, and step back. Sini prefers "step back," which may recall Heidegger's *Schritt zurück*, although *stacco* may sometimes differ from Heidegger's meaning. Occasionally, for clarity, "break" has been used instead of "step back"—Ed. and Trans.

the object of an ethical exercise. Each door has a peculiar configuration that marks the journey, as follows:

Analogy (for metaphysics)
Mirror (for psychology)
Step back (for ethology)
Representation or theater (for anthropology)
Story (for cosmology)
Dream (for pedagogy)

How we should interpret the succession and sense of these six paradigmatic sciences is, again, a matter open to various interpretations. By way of an example, I might begin by suggesting that there are a threshold and a transit inscribed between the first three sciences and the following three, as we go from the theoretical exercise of bodies to the practice of bodies in operation—a rather generic indication that lends itself to misunderstanding.

A few essential relationships are, on the other hand, self-evident. As a repetition of the world in the body of speech, metaphysics—intended as the practice and exercise of thought—opens the way to the definitive overcoming of its own prejudice, embodied in the obdurate, recurring superstition about the mind/body relationship as well as in the paradoxes of psychology. This overcoming allows for the conquering of prejudices about the animal/human threshold, and thus for the practice of a congruous ethology of speech.

One can immediately notice, then, that the acquired practice of bodies is mirrored in the politics of bodies, that is, in the becoming-human of humans (anthropology) through the repetition of the body of the world in the body of the story (cosmology). The programmatic exercise of this story constitutes the place and manner of education (pedagogy). This is the case if we consider the six sciences in their linear, circular succession as seen above. There are also, however, numerous transversal relationships—for instance, the one that connects metaphysics and pedagogy like an alpha and an omega getting reunited. We go from the analogical exercise of speech to the practice of its body in operation, which is the educational storytelling, on whose threshold the habit (i.e., the ethic) of those who know—in other words, the practice of the subjects supposed to know—is renewed.

An analogous transversal relationship can be seen to exist between ethology and anthropology, as related to the politics of bodies and the economy of desire, a web in which the body, having acquired the transient and transiting specificity of its functions, makes life-and-death decisions, thereby becoming a "political" body and inscribing its figures on those mediums of flesh and bone that constitute sexual difference.

A vertical, reciprocal correlation is obtained between psychology (our soul) and cosmology (the world's soul) whose meaning, though constantly renewed and practiced, harkens back to the most ancient thresholds of knowledge.

These are but a few succinct suggestions. While far from exhaustive, when placed in relation to the six doors' configuration, they articulate the essential figuration of the *threshold*, that is, the *transit*. Such articulation presents, indeed, six vertices which, when unified, delineate a six-sided polygon.

First, there is the vertex of the threshold-event. From its step back, the other four vertices depart: the retroflexion of the antecedent and the anteflexion of what recedes.

Each door's configuration includes the nine figures (in the fifty-four declinations indicated in the general index of the *Encyclopedia*) which mark the journey of their respective truth—all in the name of the "oneiric" repetition that is knowledge.

As the reader has certainly guessed by now, the six paradigmatic sciences do not correspond so much to any defined or codified knowledge, but rather to the place of their ideal constitutive origin—that is, to the practices aiming to reconstitute the "knowing bodies" (*corpi sapienti*)—of the subjects (of the practices) supposed to know.

The *Encyclopedia* is, therefore, a great world-sheet in progress. The world-sheet is present everywhere and nowhere, for its consistency is that of the threshold and its figure is always in transit, permanent in its

The six ways into the world-sheet. Credit: Carlo Sini.

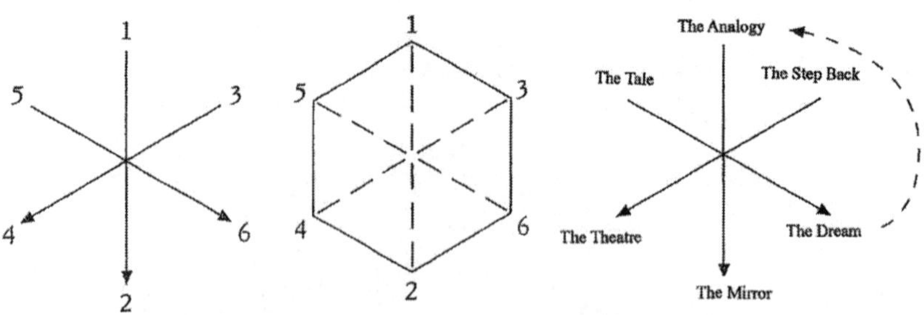

impermanence. In other words, the *Encyclopedia* is entirely the exercise that one makes of it, according to the circle of the three, or circle of transit: the event of a One which is immediately a Two (a sign of the One); and thus a Three (the meaning of the One). Which in turn is again a One, that is, a Two in the semblance of One, and so on and so forth. This rhythm of the practice—this music of gesture and speech—is no other than the progressive establishing of the subject within the figure of knowledge. His knowledge is the self-formative and self-reproducing wisdom of the circle which reincludes the doing within the knowing without obstructing it, and which reincludes the knowing within the doing without superstition.

The world-sheet of the *Encyclopedia* is no more than the occasion for the exercise of truth. It contains countless relations, analogies, hidden senses, alternate paths, accidental meanings, little secrets, unforeseen glimpses, unexpected questions, invisible solutions, to a much larger degree than I could possibly clarify here—although I am leaving a few things unsaid, not wishing to deny readers the pleasure of finding them out for themselves. For nothing here has been decided in advance: rather, everything has materialized as in a dream, and what little I have said in this "foreword" is the fruit of observations and considerations made in retrospect.

The *Encyclopedia* is a practice everyone is encouraged to discover and repeat for themselves, by continuing or modifying it as they see fit, or as they feel compelled by their own dream.

The *Encyclopedia* is a road that leads the sciences back to their home in philosophy. But it can also lead to the repetition and metamorphosis of this home, for the sake of a new formation of the person of knowledge. In the name of the event of a destiny, the person of knowledge opens the doors of their home, turning it into the medium for a world-sheet that must be constantly recomposed: the place where the world's knowledges can exercise their contrast (*polemos*), and find the occasion for an encounter in the figure of a truth-event, that is, in the transit/truth that lets itself be known in the configurations of being-in-error.

A few words on the Annotations. They are meant first and foremost to clarify a great deal of inner relationships (each one providing the theme for a possible exercise), which they do through the numbering that constantly accompanies the text. A great deal, yet far fewer than the ones that are possible. Indeed, the Annotations are conceived as the place where the *Encyclopedia* is in becoming (*in fieri*), a place open to the constant metamorphosis operated by the reader (and to which, therefore, I also belong), where the world-sheets that follow one another in a seemingly endless succession are continuously recomposed. The section is conceived as a text still written on the computer (though, of course, no one is forbidden to burn it on a disk), which, taking advantage of the nonobstructive nature of the medium, allows for an indefinite process of rewritings, insertions, and reinterpretations in progress. It allows us, in other words, to experience concretely the new figure of knowledge *in operation* which is the purpose of the text—insofar as the text, qua materially definitive sign-grave, or *caput mortuum* of knowledge, is a place that must be crossed and left behind. The moment a new writing medium comes along, the old written text can only preserve itself by changing its function and its value of truth "in error." In this sense, the Annotations are the anteflexed part of the *Encyclopedia*, its vitality in becoming, its venturing into the figure of the future.

But there is a retroflexed part as well in the occasional reference to the provenance and personal origin of what appears in the text. Thus, the Annotations are for the author a sketch of self-interpretive genealogy, the starting point for an auto-bio-graphy, and an invitation to the readers to keep this in mind, if they will, if they think they can benefit from it. Here is also where the dialogue happens—as a completely free-form sketch—between memory and the figures of the encounters with other knowledges, in the immemorial uncertainty of their event, free from the pretense of objectivity (often more apparent than actual) that characterizes traditional bibliographical entries in a typical Works Cited or Notes section. The Annotations aren't notes in the usual technical sense: I invite the reader again to view them, rather, as an active, metamorphic place where critical thinking unfolds—the place of their personal auto-bio-graphy.

First Figure

Inscribed and Circumscribed Desire

Prologue

1. The Prologue is a figure of theater. It concerns the representation that is going to follow and a character who says something about the play. In our case, the character in question is a sort of Aristotle's double, who expresses his thoughts in English.

> Man is an animal who has speech; and he is a political animal. Now then, how does that happen? He who thus considers things in their first growth and origin, whether a state or anything else, will obtain the clearest view of them.[1]
>
> In the first place there must be a union of those who cannot exist without each other, namely, of male and female, for the sake of reproduction. This is a union which is formed, not of choice, but because, in common with other animals and with plants, mankind has a natural desire to leave behind an image of itself.
>
> Equally, there must be a union of the natural ruler and subject, that both may be preserved. For that which can foresee by the exercise of mind is by nature lord and master, while

---

1. The quotations of Aristotle's *Politics*, Book I, 2, 1252a24–1253a39 are excerpted from Benjamin Jowett's translation, as published in *The Complete Works of Aristotle: The Revised Oxford Translation*, Vol. 2 (Princeton University Press, 1991). Some changes were needed to follow the author's flow and style—Trans.

that which can with its body give effect to such foresight is a subject, and by nature a slave; hence, master and slave have the same interest.

Now nature has distinguished between the female and the slave. But among barbarians no distinction is made because there is no natural ruler among them: they are a community of slaves, male and female. That is why Euripides says, "It is fitting that Hellenes should rule over barbarians"—as if they thought that the barbarian and the slave were by nature one.

Out of these two relationships the first thing to arise is the family, and Hesiod is right when he says, "First house and wife and an ox for the plough"—for the ox is the poor man's slave. The family is the association established by nature for the supply of men's everyday wants, and the members of it are called by Charondas "companions of the cupboard," and by Epimenides the Cretan "companions of the manger."

But when several families are united, and the association aims at something more than the supply of daily needs, the first society to be formed is the village. And the most natural form of the village appears to be that of a colony from the family, composed of the children and grandchildren, who are said to be "suckled with the same milk." And this is the reason why Hellenic states were originally governed by kings, because the Hellenes were under royal rule before they came together, as the barbarians still are. Every family is ruled by the eldest, and therefore in the colonies of the family the kingly form of government prevailed because they were of the same blood. As Homer says, "Each one gives law to his children and to his wives." For they lived dispersedly, as was the manner in ancient times.

That is why men say that the Gods have a king, because they themselves either are or were in ancient times under the rule of a king. For they imagine not only the forms of the Gods but their ways of life to be like their own.

When several villages are united in a single complete community, large enough to be nearly or quite self-sufficient, the state comes into existence, originating in the bare needs of life, and continuing in existence for the sake of a good life.

And therefore, if the earlier forms of society are natural, so is the state, for it is the end of them, and the nature of a thing is its end. For what each thing is when fully developed, we call its nature, whether we are speaking of a man, a horse, or a family.

Besides, the final cause and end of a thing is what is best, and to be self-sufficient is the end and what is best.

Hence it is evident that the state is a creation of nature, and that man is by nature a political animal (as I was saying at the beginning). And so, he who by nature and not by mere accident is without a state, is either a bad man or above humanity.

Now, that man is more of a political animal than bees or any other gregarious animal is evident. Nature, as we often say, makes nothing in vain, and man is the only animal who has the gift of speech (as I said at the beginning). And whereas mere voice is but an indication of pleasure or pain and is therefore found in other animals (for their nature attains to the perception of pleasure and pain and the intimation of them to one another, and no further), the power of speech is intended to set forth the expedient and inexpedient, and therefore likewise the just and the unjust.

And it is a characteristic of man that he alone has any sense of good and evil, of just and unjust, and the like, and the association of living beings who have this sense makes a family and a state.

Further, the state is by nature clearly prior to the family and to the individual since the whole is of necessity prior to the part. For example, if the whole body be destroyed, there will be no foot or hand, except for a verbal similarity, as we might speak of a stone hand; for when destroyed the hand will be no better than that.

But things are defined by their function and power; and we ought not to say that they are the same when they no longer have their proper quality, but only that they are homonymous.

The proof that the state is a creation of nature and prior to the individual is that the individual, when isolated, is not self-sufficing—(as in the case of the female without male, or of the master without slave)—; and therefore, he is like a part in relation to the whole—which, as such, will not even be able to exist.

Accordingly, he who is unable to live in society, or who has no need because he is sufficient for himself, must be either a beast or a god: he is no part of a state.

A social instinct is implanted in all men by nature, and yet he who first founded the state was the greatest of bene-factors. For man, when perfected, is the best of animals, but, when separated from law and justice, he is the worst of all.

Armed injustice is the most dangerous, and man is equipped at birth with arms, meant to be used for prudence and virtue,[2] which he may use for the worst ends.

That is why, without virtue, the human being is the most unholy and the most savage of animals, and the worst with regard to the pleasure of sex and food.

But justice is the bond of men in states; for the admin-istration of justice, which is the determination of what is just, is the principle of order in political society.

2. Exit Aristotle's double.

Now imagine one of the revolving stages that sometimes are used in theaters: Aristotle's replica is going off while the back of the stage is progressively appearing. And there stand I, indeed my *analogon*, or my double, if you prefer—which is to say, this Speech that is speaking to you. I will not repeat it.

And I too need to act in this play. Chastely.

Our Aristotle has set the topic of the performance, be it drama or comedy: namely, Man, or better still, politics. But also, which is the same, the animal that speaks and by speaking expresses his desire—desire for descent in the eternity of life, and therefore desire for sex and food,

---

2. The Greek word *areté* (*virtus* in Latin) carries different meanings: capability, competence, excellence, and manliness. Contemporary translators tend to avoid "virtue" because of its association with modesty. However, Sini's prose relies heavily on Italian readers who have studied Latin and Greek in high school and are familiar with the Italian word *virtù*, which carries the same meanings. We have therefore decided to adopt *virtue* regardless of its old-fashioned aura—Ed.

so that he may keep himself alive. And lastly, desire for a happy life, assured by the complementary and mutual roles achieved in a community ordered around justice.

He said that we understand these things if we see them in their first growth and origin. Origin of mankind, of political community, of desire, of speech . . . Origin itself of this origin: in fact, many things in one. Many things which are not originally divided yet, which are not "established knowledge" yet.

3. Imagine, instead, that I show you the image of a cross, at whose vertices are the words "philosophy," "anthropology," "economics," "politics." If we join the vertices with a line and form a circle, we get a representation of drifting forms of knowledge whose vertices have not yet consolidated and separated into definite branches of knowledge. What interests us here is their circulation at the "origin," their intertwining, exchanging roles, mirroring each other, because this primary circulation is what gradually comes to define them.

At the center of the cross, then, let us write "language."

Here is the backdrop at the back of the stage. We are not merely invited to gaze at it but also to put it to work, while we train ourselves in "political virtue," in its characteristic *areté*, which, as the center of the cross shows, is one with the virtue of speech. Especially with its *mise-en-scène*, which for example asks, "What is at stake in the knowledge and power of *politics?*"

4. An ambiguous question, for it is already rhetorical. If you assimilate the genealogy of the political with the genealogy of speech, by the mere fact of saying it you have already staged a peculiar "ethology of speech," and man, taken as a middle figure between animal and God, has already made his entrance.

The fascinating power of speech, stimulant of desire, is already in action, in the figure of philosophical fascination: while it claims to be addressing the genealogical places, it already frequents the places of its *éthos*, of *its* rhetoric—its unmistakable *ethology*.

The Prologue says, with its inscribed and circumscribed cross, "I will make you sink into the genealogy of speech, as the foremost source of political power and of its desire. Yet this investigation of the ethology of speech qua *mise-en-scène* of the Political and qua constitutive feature of the Human—an investigation that does not shy away from revealing the rhetorical backstage of the very speech it employs—finally shows its true colors: itself, in turn, a *mise-en-scène*, in the form of the *mise-en-scène* of the backstage.

The backstage is already captured by political rhetoric, whose logic displayed in the figure of the backstage is, in turn, a stage mask.

An ambiguous situation: yet we will not give up the genealogic intention of portraying this cleavage, which shows *the staging of philosophy as politics*. The former, we will show, is immediately the latter, as figures of Plato's theater.

We are still acting on his forestage: unaware performers of a theoretical scene and of a script that Plato's direction has long since arranged.

5. That is precisely why we do not desist, for the matter concerns *us all*. And the cleavage, as ever, is an auto-bio-graphical threshold, which, as such, is also Plato's threshold. What else is his conscious theater if not a piece of autobiographical staging? Dramatic theater whose leading actor is Socrates, Plato's ambiguous alter ego.

And we could even point out that if Socrates is the leading actor in the political foundation of philosophy, that is, the philosophical foundation of politics, then the rhetorical aspect of Plato's choice calls for the existence of the character—in a way, the heir of the Priest and of the Sovereign by blood and divine descent.

Yet Plato's scene is at the same time our direct backstage: we are still today miming the same character, his rhetorical mannerisms, and logical subtleties.

And the same holds true for Aristotle, who feigned a genesis where everything had already been settled: who is above and who is below, who commands and who obeys, in an ethology of the Human in every sense "preconceived."

6. Then, in the Prologue's last move, we will conjure up one of Nietzsche's masks—he who first warned us against Plato's theater. A warning for the future philosopher against the "Socratic martyrdom for the sake of truth." Denunciation of the backstage of this "suffering for

the sake of truth," of the philosopher's martyrdom in his "sacrifice for the sake of truth."

Now, the backstage reveals the demagogic and histrionic traits lurking in this philosophical figure. Yet Nietzsche also admonishes, "If one has so far contemplated him only with artistic curiosity, with regard to many a philosopher it is easy to understand the dangerous desire to see him also in his degeneration (degenerated into a 'martyr,' into a stage-and-platform bawler). Only, that it is necessary with such a desire to be clear *what* spectacle one will see in any case—merely a satyr play, merely an epilogue farce, merely the continued proof that the long, real tragedy *is at an end*, assuming that every philosophy was in its genesis a long tragedy."[3]

The Socratic philosopher has degenerated into the figure of the actor-clown: the double of the mime of truth Plato had staged in his *Sophist*. Socratic dialectics and rhetoric as deterioration of the Dionysian wisdom of the tragic age, according to Nietzsche's well-known formulas and jokes, to which we should add the "democratic" degeneration of politics carried out by men who no longer have a fatherland.

And Nietzsche thinks that if the real tragedy is at an end, it will be necessarily followed by the great catastrophe of all-pervasive nihilism, with its death of the Political—an end marked by the advent of the tribune, *consolle*, and video bawlers.

Nevertheless, to see this is also a dangerous desire: wherever might the desecration of the Socratic philosopher lead us, if not to a sort of slapstick comedy, to a chitchat philosophy, a philosophy of cultural games and fashion magazines, with its ridiculous revisiting of the costumes of the past, carnival masks worn for one evening?

7. Yet, going deeper, it must be said that even this desire we have, to step back and understand genealogically is a dangerous desire, in that it also inherently frequents the sense of profanation, parricide, and incest—which carries us back, once again, to Plato's scene.

The fact is that, in the end, the political question represents the very enigma of desire. "What does woman want?" wondered Freud, but he might well have added, "What does this (definitely male) will to

---

3. Friedrich Nietzsche, *Beyond Good and Evil: Prelude to a Philosophy of the Future*, chap. 2, par. 25, translated by Walter Kaufmann (Vintage, 1966), 37—Ed.

truth of mine want?"

Let us leave the last word to the ghost of Nietzsche whom we just conjured up in our scene. He says, "Where the tree of knowledge stands is always paradise; thus speak the oldest and youngest serpents."[4]

Therefore, beware of this old serpent that is talking to you. I have told you, and I will not repeat it.

(End of Prologue)

---

4. Nietzsche, *Beyond Good and Evil*, Part Four, Epigrams and Interludes, 152, 90—Ed.

Act One

The Scene of the *Republic*

8. "Kateben chthes eis Peiraia": thus begins the *Republic*, with a descent to the wide gap (*chasma*) of Piraeus, the harbor of Athens. *I went down yesterday to the Piraeus*,[1] starts off Socrates, who speaks and narrates to mysterious listeners.

A meditated and tormented beginning, as it is told in a very old anecdote, which is probably news items passed down within the academic circle. "The beginning of the *Republic*," says the anecdote, "was found, with a lot of corrections and alterations, beside Plato's bed, soon after his death."

So, imagine the Piraeus scene, filled with a miscellaneous, noisy, and colorful crowd gathered to celebrate a festival—because that is what it is about.

The festival is in honor of the Thracian Goddess Bendis, and it is celebrated for the first time. Now, imagine the effigy of the Goddess carried in procession: a barbaric deity holding some spears and torches.

Near the Piraeus, a suburban area compared to the Acropolis rock, lived a community of Thracians; their costumes are allowedly connected to the celebration of shamanic rites, which, we can imagine, have an influence over the Bendideia festivals.

At the Piraeus, there lived many foreigners, who were either accommodated not far from the city or officially recognized as metics thanks to Pericles' liberal policy, an economically profitable policy for all, both citizens and noncitizens. Athens had at the time reached its peak.

---

1. Here and throughout, the quotations from Plato's *Republic* are excerpted from Benjamin Jowett's translation (1871, then revised and corrected, 1892). The text is in the public domain and available both in print and online. Some changes were needed to follow the author's flow and style—Trans.

Who is Bendis? Her figure may verge on the Greek Goddesses Cybele, Demeter, and Artemis but most of all on Hecate, Daughter of the Night, torch carrier and queen of the Underworld, where she accompanies the souls of the dead.

In fact, Bendis too is a nocturnal and infernal Goddess. In the portrayals she holds a double spear, and Proclus meant her as a symbol of the crossroads. We might think of Nyx, Parmenides' Goddess, or Heraclitus' *two paths*, the path up and the path down, or Prodicus' *Heracles at the Crossroads*.

The Bendideia festival will end, as we will hear, at nightfall, with a spectacular torchlight race on horseback. Thracians, as everybody knows, are skilled riders.

9. If you look closely at the scene, you will perhaps understand *where* Plato lets Socrates, his main character, symbolically go down. It is eloquently suggested by the verb *kateben*, "went down," with which Plato significantly decided to begin his text. If you had the ear of a Greek member of the audience, it would be impossible for you not to connect it at once with a Homeric recollection (the Greeks knew Homer by heart, as many in Italy knew, at one time, the *Divine Comedy*). "Kateben eis Aiden," says Odysseus to Penelope. "I went down to Hades." And Socrates too goes down, accompanied by Bendis/Hecate, to a sort of Hades, to a metaphoric, human, and social underworld.

And he will come up from it. At the end of the long journey of the *Republic* he will invite us to "hold ever to the upward way"—but I shouldn't anticipate.

A descent into hell and return: again, we can think of Dante. And for one more singular reason: because both Plato and Dante let the dead speak. An impressive dialogue takes place on the scene of the *Republic* among the shadows of the past. All characters in the *Republic*, as we will see, beginning with Socrates, are shadows of the recent past and some of them died a violent death.

Being a great artist, Plato re-creates their features, with the traits, idioms, ideas which were their hallmarks and with which the audience, namely the readers of those years, was familiar—both from direct memory and for having heard of them from their elders. Splendid "prose of the world," that of Plato, stylistically different from tragedy and comedy, and yet inspiration for his theater.

Also, notice the subtlety: Plato stages Bendis, the Goddess who leads one to the Underworld; and indeed, Plato is leading his fellow citizens underground, to visit the great shadows of a fortunate and tragic past. For the moment there is no need to say why he is doing so: you will see it and understand it as you go along.

10. "In what sense is Piraeus a Hades?" you might ask. As a matter of fact, here the Piraeus scene, with its large and most celebrated harbor, takes on the symbolic evidence of a disquieting, fearsome place. Many people of every provenance and social origin go through it. From the sea, Plato will say, comes "a variety of luxurious and depraved habits." Moral and social confusion, sparked off by the riotous events of trading and commerce, by greed, by craftiness, by the pursuit of pleasure and money.

In the *Timaeus*, however, Plato will be even more explicit: in describing metaphorically Athens in accordance with a specific psychosomatic topography, he will associate the Piraeus with the nether parts of the human body: the womb and the pudenda; he will associate the isthmus with the neck, and the Acropolis with the head. Here is the symbolic image of the Athenian man, but more generally of every man.

Hades is the cavern, the bottomless pit, the abyss par excellence. In the journey of the *Republic*, as we will see, Plato will raise a good four times the image of the cavern, of the *chasma*. About this first one, you are beginning to understand. With his descent to the Piraeus, Socrates advances into the abyss and chaos of desire, trying, evidently, to regulate it, to give it a *nomos*, a law, resorting to the "political virtue" that Plato will let Socrates recount.

A descent into the "vagina," which is normalized in the *Republic* as the "public vagina"—women (and men) jointly. I know what I'm saying, just wait and see. For the moment, make a note that this covert hint to the social dangerousness of sexual eros is one of the main and more delicate points in the *Republic*. That is why Socrates goes down to the Piraeus, metaphor of the desires for the womb and sex.

11. Yet Socrates' descent into the *chasma*, into the *antron*, has further symbolic values. The going-down refers back to archaic ritual images,

where the descent into the pit or the abyss bears also the meaning of a ritual transformation of man, which will in fact happen in the third and fourth *chasma* of the *Republic*.

These descents have cognitive and prophetic aims, as we will see in the third and fourth descent, respectively. Keep that in mind.

At the bottom of the ravine, there is usually the encounter with a female deity: Mother Goddess, Prophetess, Night Goddess, Memory Goddess, such as Mnemosyne (you, too, will meet her much later), and so forth. Therefore, if Plato lets the dead speak and takes his audience to Hades, he does so with a view to a "rebirth" of the living, on the strength of their initiation into true knowledge and into the revelation of the upward way: the righteous and good way.

At the bottom of the *chasma*, we consequently have a confrontation between life and death. *Mysterium der Wiedergeburt*: eternal rebirth or eternity of rebirth. Do not struggle too much to understand what I'm saying with these words: they will become clear in due course.

Plato knows well that he is treading an ancient path. Some had already gone down into the *chasma* before him to reach prophetic wisdom: Epimenides, Orpheus, and Pythagoras. Apuleius calls them "wizards"—and the shamanic and Orphic features of these descents are evident to us today.

But we could also mention Empedocles, who vanishes into Etna's pit, and Parmenides' mountain pass, and in general the descent every Greek wise man must customarily make, according to Herodotus, to the land of Egypt, precisely where Pythagoras came from. Plato did bear in mind this Egyptian affair, although he postponed its treatment in the *Timaeus*, yet always in connection with his *Republic* and with the Orphic tales. Egypt too is like a big *chasma*, crossed by a path from light to darkness: the paths of Isis and Osiris, who served as models for the myth of Dionysus' dismemberment, according to which he is torn limb from limb and devoured by the Titans and then restored and brought back to life by his brother Apollo.

Yes, Apollo, the God of philosophy whom Socrates invokes at the trial . . . And Plato, too, stages his brothers in the *Republic* . . .

The fact is that Plato treads an ancient path, but with the intention and hope of transforming it radically and for evermore, by overcoming death.

But now I have said enough. Socrates is about to come onstage. Listen to him carefully. I will hide myself; but you know I am here. I'll be right back.

12.

SOCRATES: I went down yesterday to the Piraeus with Glaucon the son of Ariston, that I might offer up my prayers to the goddess; and also because I wanted to see in what manner they would celebrate the festival, which was a new thing. I was delighted with the procession of the inhabitants; but that of the Thracians was equally, if not more, beautiful.

When we had finished our prayers and viewed the spectacle, we turned in the direction of the city.

And at that instant Polemarchus the son of Cephalus chanced to catch sight of us from a distance as we were starting on our way home, and told his servant to run and bid us wait for him. The servant took hold of me by the cloak behind, and said: Polemarchus desires you to wait.

I turned round, and asked him where his master was. There he is, said the youth, coming after you, if you will only wait.

Certainly we will, said Glaucon; and in a few minutes Polemarchus appeared, and with him Adeimantus, Glaucon's brother, Niceratus the son of Nicias, and several others who had been at the procession.

Polemarchus said to me: I perceive, Socrates, that you and your companion are already on your way to the city.

You are not far wrong, I said.

But do you see, he rejoined, how many we are?

Of course.

And are you stronger than all these? For if not, you will have to remain where you are.

May there not be the alternative, I said, that we may persuade you to let us go?

But can you persuade us, if we refuse to listen to you? he said.

Certainly not, replied Glaucon.

Then we are not going to listen; of that you may be assured.

Adeimantus added: Has no one told you of the torch-race on horseback in honor of the goddess which will take place in the evening?

With horses! I replied: That is a novelty. Will horsemen carry torches and pass them one to another during the race?

Yes, said Polemarchus, and not only so, but a festival will be celebrated at night, which you certainly ought to see. Let us rise soon after supper and see this festival; there will be a gathering of young men, and we will have a good talk. Stay then, and do as I tell you.

Glaucon said: I suppose, since you insist, that we must.

Very good, I replied.

(*They set off in a body for the home of Cephalus.*)

13. While they exit, a few more words.

You have witnessed a friendly and jocular dialogue among Athenians from 2,500 years ago. Noble men blessed with great genius, who treat each other with aristocratic familiarity. A charming and remarkable picture, but you shouldn't get fooled! Do you really think that Plato, who on his deathbed is still agonizing over the beginning of his *Republic*, would waste his time giving himself up to the superficial pleasure of indulging in the live imitations of stage artists?

It isn't so, or rather, it isn't *only* so. The divine Plato is playing his game and already revealing to us, in a covert manner, a great many things. All the jocular insistence on physical strength, on the competition, especially on the uselessness of trying to persuade those who do not listen, is a clear announcement of the heated dialectical competition which, shortly after, will erupt between Socrates and Thrasymachus—the "wild beast."

And some think that here Plato is having Socrates, his master, his main and favorite character, suggest that the art of dialectic, of which Socrates is the inventor and greatest champion, has only blunt weapons against the deafness of those who prefer strength, starting with the strength of words used to overwhelm one's opponents.

I cannot tell you if that is true, but I would not be surprised if it were, for the Divine's soul has countless tones and undertones, some of which are, admittedly, subtly cruel.

14. With this little starting dialogue, then, Plato might well be showing us the seal or key to the entire *Republic*, the major work in which he intends to surpass his master.

In a nutshell, I could put the message like this: Socrates was not actually the true philosopher. He did pursue the truth, but he was not able to see it, so as to establish on it a real knowledge, a real philosophical *science*. The latter is possible only if we attain the vision of political virtue, which is in fact the only true philosophy, the philosophy that can found a state ruled by the vision and idea of the Good: where human beings will be at last able to reach the happiness they have forever been seeking, as have all Greeks, and Socrates with them.

Throughout his works, Plato will mischievously have Socrates confute and surpass himself, until he is relegated to the margins in *Timaeus*, and completely gone in *Laws*, where Plato, the Divine, will be the only one to speak, in the guise of the "Athenian Stranger." And that will be his swan song.

Mischievousness or, perhaps, also a splendid homage to the man who sealed the fate of his life. We'll see.

I am sure you are eager to watch and hear what happens in the house of Cephalus and Polemarchus. You'll have instead to be a bit patient. Now the backstage will show you a scene (there will be several of them, but always, I assure you, for your benefit).

"Why?" you might wonder. Well, I too, in my own small way, have my strategies: so please bear with me.

I told you that Bendis, here, is basically a stand-in for Hecate. But who is Hecate? The scene Plato is staging will not be clear to us if we are unable to answer this query. It is what the *mise-en-scène* of your backstage proposes to do. Look, the stage is already revolving.

Scene I: The Girdle of Venus

15. The scene might simply be a big, animated painting. A young man, named Alexander, or Paris, as you choose, is gazing spellbound at three wondrous goddesses displaying their inimitable graces before him. You already know that they are Artemis, Aphrodite, and Hera. While resting his face on the flat of one hand, the young man is holding an apple in the other, which he almost forgot, so dazzled is he by the beauty of the three divine figures.

Do you recall the charming little statue of Paris that can be admired in a pond of Palermo's botanic garden, where Goethe would chase his archetypal plant?

Everybody knows how it ends, but for the benefit of all I will briefly remind you of the story.

Venus, or rather, Aphrodite, has an embroidered girdle—a belt, a loincloth or G-string, or a corset, or call it what you will—woven by the Graces with amiability and desire. Whoever wears that magical tool of enchanting seduction will acquire its powers. It so happens that Hera (Juno) asks to borrow it from Aphrodite to bewitch Zeus, her husband, who is absentminded like all husbands and yet quite busy with his frequent extramarital escapades. Aphrodite, as is usual among women, lends it freely. And Hera takes advantage of it. In fact, she is not interested in regaining her husband's love, but rather, by seducing him, in making the king of the gods hostile to the Trojans, whom she hates for reasons of her own. Susceptibility, craftiness, and deception—altogether womanly qualities.

Time goes by and it so happens that Eris (Discordia), after her banishment from Olympus, takes her revenge by throwing on the table of the banqueting Gods the famed "apple of discord," which bears the inscription, "To the fairest one." And all hell breaks loose! Artemis (Diana), Aphrodite, and Hera vie most vigorously for the apple and Zeus does not know how to get out of the predicament. Then he appoints the handsome Alexander/Paris judge of the dispute and washes his hands of the matter.

At this point the Goddesses get ready for the beauty contest and Aphrodite remembers about the girdle. She asks that it be returned, puts it on, and wins the contest. As a reward, she promises Paris the love of the world's fairest woman (Helen, wife of Menelaus), whence endless grief and woes, with the Trojan War, will be shed on earth. Discordia is triumphant both on earth and in the heavens.

I am sure you have by now realized that I did not retell this ancient and famous myth without a reason. Many hidden meanings lie at the bottom of its staging, and I will try to reveal them at least partially to you. Let's start by looking closely at the three Goddesses, one by one, as behind me they freeze into ritualistic, cult figures.

16. Let's start with the youngest, Artemis: she symbolizes the still indomitable and wild, even harsh, and cruel, maiden. We all know what she did to Actaeon, the young hunter who dared watch her nakedness: she turned him into a stag and had him mauled by the dogs. Another famous

myth lots of people have puzzled over to tease out a hidden meaning, such as Francis Bacon and many others.

Artemis is impatient with any wooing and embraces; while reluctant to love, she nonetheless is seductive in her immature and still ambiguous beauty. Indeed, she takes part in the contest, so it is obvious that she wants to seduce. Yet she scorns the amiability of the girdle, and perhaps precisely in her firm rejection of every *feminine* charming art lies her peculiar seductiveness.

Aphrodite represents femininity in the prime of its sexual bloom, at the height of its seductive power; and there is no doubt that, in this sense, the girdle is due to her, and so is victory.

Hera represents a mature and somewhat declining femininity; but precisely this self-aware and experienced beauty, almost on the wane, exerts a powerful and subtle fascination.

And yet all this is only the first layer, so to speak, of the narration. Before everything else, the three Goddesses are archaic figures of a very old *female* cosmogony; they symbolize, to put it briefly, the phases of the moon and thus the overall lunar deity—under whose archetype is condensed, cyclically renewing itself, the entire life of the *female* cosmic principle. From the sky above, this cycle is also reflected among human beings on earth, to seal the fates and character of woman's life in its immutable and eternal cycle.

17. You are oddly quiet: Is everything alright? Evidently, the girdle has dazzled you, too. In fact, who is immune to it?

What am I saying? It is very simple: it stands before your very eyes and yet you're not realizing it. I said, "The three Goddesses symbolize the phases of the moon." Well now, isn't it obvious that one is missing?

Yes, the missing phase is that of the hidden moon, the black moon. That is, Hecate the Dark. She herself, like her three sisters, is an archaic moon symbol: symbol of the black sky, orphan of the planet's light that illuminates the night.

Missing? Are you sure? Looking at me you have strayed your attention from the living figure standing behind me. Now I'll move over: look, there she is in the middle of the figure, Hecate the Dark, lewdly recumbent to show you the very disquieting black *chasma* of her perverse, rejecting, and yet in its way attractive, femininity. She wasn't there before? That's what you think . . .

What is the meaning of this? I'll explain it to you immediately, I don't want to keep you guessing. Hecate is not missing at all. Her presence is concealed in the narration insofar as she is darkened, masked by the brilliance and dazzling of the other three Goddesses and sisters.

She has no girdle, nor any peculiar seductive arts; however, she holds the key to the mystery of life and death. The cycle of rebirth and cosmic succession is renewed in her *chasma*. And indeed, someone has rightly pointed out that Hecate symbolizes the darkness of the embrace that lurks in every man: the night of conception, the night of birth, and the night of death.

18. This way, the story of the girdle takes on a new light (and we should learn to treat the myths with respect). The girdle is nothing but the concentrated image of seduction. It is the symbol of the "object of desire." In this sense, it is an eminently "transferal" object, as we would say today.

The object in itself has a negligible and, at most, a somewhat grotesque body. Imagine it abandoned and left behind in some corner of Olympus, like a misplaced piece of underwear: an utterly unimportant thing, or at most embarrassing for its ridiculous, petty nature. And yet if one wears it, it radiates irresistible power. What an odd business, you might say. On the contrary, it is not in the least strange: the girdle simply depicts the erotic investment and the illusionistic nature of desire. Above all, sexual desire, since woven behind the illusion of *eros* and female sexual attraction is the fabric of the whole universal and very real cycle of life and death—because of which, for instance, you are here, and I am with you.

This is not all. The girdle has an illusory and transferal nature, we said. In other words, it is a "sign." It stands there to direct desire for something other than itself, because, in itself, it is just an unimportant thing. It stands there to hide what becomes thereby desirable. In other words, by the mere fact of hiding, it emphasizes and *manifests*—it manifests the desirability of what, obscenely, hides itself. Obscenely because by hiding, it exhibits itself.

(It sounds as if I am describing to you a so-called fashion show of our times; but without the hypocritical cultural drivel of social commentators and journalists. I hope you will acknowledge that.)

Nevertheless, we have not come to the point yet. Because what I wanted you to note is that the girdle, being a sign, eloquently signals that the possession of the object of desire is structurally impossible.

What is that supposed to mean? I will explain right away. The desire for a woman passes through the girdle: she becomes seductive and desirable because she wears it. And yet the girdle is nothing, it is only an unimportant transferal sign. What is desired, then? Not the girdle (although now would be the right moment to deal with the matter of so-called sexual perversions, which are at most an inerasable component of desire). Not the woman, because it is the girdle that makes her desirable.

In a nutshell, the myth shows wonderfully how desire collides with, and confronts, itself.

Scene II: Distance and Desire

19. While darkness falls on the living scene behind me and they bring a chair and a small table into the spotlight, I announce to you that I am going to give a brief academic lecture on the impossibility of possessing the object of desire.

I will do my best not to bore you, trying to be concise and clear. But you must pay all the attention you can muster.

Desire, then, invests the sign of the desirable object. Let us assume that Paris meets Helen and feels a desire for her (which is exactly how it went, as far as we know). He evidently does not desire the word "Helen," nor any one of her signs, such as the bright glance, the charming smile, the curls falling on her neck, the graceful poise, the shapely figure showing through her apparel, and so on. All these signs, to the extent that they fascinate him, announce what he indeed desires to possess.

This means that what he desires is placed at a distance from him. Besides, how might one desire that which does not exist, what one does not have, what one is not, what in a nutshell is somehow "at a distance"? Well, I do claim that this distance cannot be filled. Now, what kind of distance is this?

When "distance" is mentioned, we immediately think of a physical, spatial distance between two things in space. You are there, I am here, and in the middle is a distance: some yards, twenty steps, and so forth.

That is not the distance I am talking about. The distance signaled by desire is pre-physical—or metaphysical if you will. It is a symbolic distance.

Nevertheless, it seems evident that desire, and even more desire for a body, cannot overlook the situation of a desiring body located in space that is targeting another desirable body, also located in space, precisely by desiring it. All in all, Paris can fantasize as much as he likes with his desire, but if he does not bridge the space that separates him from Helen, he will never be able to know if, or verify that, the desired woman is herself prepared to concede herself to him, thus bridging the gap that separates them.

If we approach the matter this way, however, we will be arguing about the desire already *inscribed* in the spatial constitution of the bodies' experience, without recognizing that it is precisely desire's preventive evidence and *circumscribed* nature that paves the way for us to experience something in the first place—for instance, to experience bodies in space.

20. Every experience is an *encounter*, which does not happen in the general and abstract manner I am telling—except here, precisely because of the general way I'm telling it. At any rate, we all have our experiences within concrete practices of life.

For example, an infant will inspect everything that comes within range, touching it and sucking it. When the infant runs into his father's thumb, the child immediately grabs on to it with tenacious satisfaction.

This little example is enough to make us understand, once and for all, that "things" announce themselves in experience always from, and within, specific practices of life (among which is also the telling and the naming of them in general, as we are doing here). Their announcing themselves is precisely a sign of what we can do with them (take possession of them, avoid them, observe them, name them, leave them aside, indifferent and unexplored, and so forth).

The practices of life "objectify" the things of experience through their signs, including the practice of denomination, which objectifies things by means of the signs of speech. "I have met *Helen*, and I was bewitched by her," says Paris for example.

The experience of things in space comes to meet us in the same way. To grasp the father's thumb, the child had to stretch his arm, thus realizing that what excites the desire in his eyes does not lie at the same distance from his hand. And the big toe as well must certainly be reached with some effort, so that our child can satisfactorily put it into his mouth.

The mobile experience of distance comes to meet us along determinate paths, stirred by our desiring intentionality. This is how suckling babies learn their desiring distance from the breast, and we too in this moment reach for the armrests of the easy chair to relieve the weight of our bust and shoulders.

And so, we must say that sheer physical, or spatial, distance is but the end point of a complicated series of practices of desire. It is the original movement of desire that creates, by taking concrete form, the complicated object we call space or spatial distance. We would not have the slightest notion of it, if we were not self-moving bodies inscribed in the intentionality of desire.

"Bodies" in the sense of *thresholds* of desiring events, from which every experience opens up with its encounters and specific poles and centers of interest (indeed, bodies as commonly understood are, originally, nothing but this: targeted poles and centers of interest).

21. You begin to understand, then, what I mean when I claim that the distance inherent in desire is unbridgeable, and therefore the object of desire cannot be possessed.

Now, please think carefully. Desire is a tension that announces itself on the threshold of experience. What announces itself is, in this sense, the sign of the object at which desire aims. Thus, the desiring tension "spatializes" and "temporalizes" itself in ways that are structurally congenial to it; namely, on the basis of the concrete practice of life where such tension occurs. If I wish to see, I strain my eyes, if I wish to touch, I stretch out my hands, if I wish to get closer, I move my legs, and so on. Now I ask you: When does this tension come to fruition? And how does this fruition occur?

You might answer: with the possession of the desired thing. But what do you mean by the word "possession"?

If you mean a certain success of the desiring action, then I agree. I wanted to get closer to have a better look at you and I did get closer; I wanted to touch you and I did touch you. But in so doing, I most certainly have not erased the constitutive distance that accompanies us. While I fulfilled my desire, I failed to take possession of you, that is, to interpenetrate you to the extent of canceling every distance and difference.

In fact, I cannot even do so with myself, although it is believed that I, in any case, simply coincide with my spatial "here." Nor can I "possess" in this sense the intimacy peculiar to my own body and thought: I do not see myself from the outside, and seeing myself from the inside is only a metaphor; I cannot look directly at my back, and my limbs do not always respond to my stimulations as I would like; not to mention when my body overwhelms me and surprises me with its undesired pains. I do not even possess my thoughts completely: I always must reach for my thoughts, focus them, strive to hold them still (without much success), push them in directions they are reluctant to go, sometimes putting up fierce resistance; not to mention when undesired and irksome thoughts visit my mind and will not go away.

Imagine, then, if I should delude myself that I can possess someone else's body and thoughts: no matter how close I get, an insuperable and intangible cleft still separates us. The sense of touch shows this very clearly: if I grip your hand, I bring it into the utmost possible nearness to mine; yet by so doing, I also reject it, I bounce it off beyond the threshold of my grabbing desire. No matter how many ways I can grip it intensely, each way cannot but repeat the distance: my hand does not become yours; your hand does not become mine; and even my own hand is "here" and belongs to me only to a certain extent—a sudden paralysis could make it unreachable for me.

22. Besides, what interest would we have in achieving this assimilation or total permeation (if that were ever possible)? We would simply annihilate the threshold, erasing our own desiring event. In other words, erasing ourselves.

Desire turns to the bodies in the sense that it *materializes in the bodies*. This does not mean that it aims at assimilating into them by interpenetrating them: an impossible and senseless purpose (except as a deviation and pathology of desire). It rather means that desire intends *to put* the bodies *to work* as places where its desire may manifest itself. Paris desires to "possess" Helen in the sense that he desires, for example, to hug her, realizing in the process that she is willing to do the same, and so forth.

Desire transits through the bodies, identifying them and identifying with them, that is, coconstituting them.

We have said and shown that what constitutes desire is distance. Which is a *having to be* transiting in its bodies at work, defined as such by their very operation, namely by the practice of life being enacted therein. In this sense, the fulfilled desire has not removed the distance but has consumed it by transiting through it: and this is exactly what we call fulfillment.

At this point, the distance disappears, not because desire has removed it or bridged it, but simply because desire has disappeared. Paris, feeling fulfilled by the embrace, shows clearly to Helen that he now desires to sleep.

23. With desire constituting and passing through them, the bodies are afterward disinvested, as a result of the disappearance of the desire that constituted them, just as it constituted them by desiring them; and at that moment they remain there, in their *simple indifferent presence* (which is how, after all, we usually imagine and think of them "in themselves" when we talk about them in the abstract): bodies nonetheless marked (*signati*) by the desire that went through them and constituted them, establishing them as "objects" of the having-to-be of a desire that now is no more.

That is how the girdle is abandoned in a corner of Olympus or the chair is left lonely in the room, gradually marked by the use that it has been put to and by the dust of time that has involved it in its alienated permanence.

It is then this leftover, this "remainder" of the constituting desire, that *lags behind*, taking the form of the simple, motionless, indifferent thing. Here is the disinvested girdle, deprived of the primitive desiring practices that made it into the sign and medium of sexual enchantment. Now its use becomes a nonuse, within the practice of oblivion and indifference.

And yet it is always there, available for new and perhaps different investments: the chair, for instance, can be sold or placed on a stage as a prop; I can display it as an aesthetic object at a contemporary art exhibition; I can burn it in the fireplace, and so forth.

If all this is clear enough, then we can say that the girdle from the tale is a perfect metaphor for every possible "thing." It teaches us that there are no things in themselves—things that are simply present in themselves. Things exist, and develop as things, as those very things, insofar as they were originally invested with desire. And then, to be sure, they are left there with the inert lack of desire and interest that configures them in their absent presence. However, they are not—in a supposed "reality"—originally "in themselves," separate and external existences.

That is how science imagines them, in the objectifying writings of its practices (which science is not concerned with, or utterly disregards, when it speaks about "reality of things-in-themselves"). Then we should wonder what sort of desire induces scientific practice to the extremely artificial and ingenious creation of simple things "in themselves" that can be manipulated, measured, quantified, subjected to ad hoc experiments, and so on.

As a matter of fact, and in general terms, for each "thing" we encounter we should ask ourselves: What image, what desire, is this thing a sign of? If a man buys a house or if he buys a woman, what desire is the house or the woman an image of? And what image does the "buying" convey? Much further on you will find answers to these questions.

24. So, the girdle is an image, or a figure: the image of the original "thing" that everything, in its own way, is. Everything is thus connected to a threshold of a desire that realizes itself in its having-to-be, having-to-achieve, having-to-transit, within the bodies-as-objects constituted and targeted by its peculiar desiring practices.

Now, the myth of the girdle stages precisely a game of images, a figure representation—a representation of seduction in the three femininity figures that stimulate man's sexual choice.

It is evident that these three figures are in use and manifest themselves essentially *for* man. I mean: to win the contest, the three Goddesses who wish to achieve the Apple of Beauty take into consideration the "male psychology" of desire, and on that basis, they steer their seductive practices, transferring and transiting them into the girdle. Either insofar as they possess it, or insofar as they are without it. Which is to say: the seductive beauty of she who does not yet have the girdle and pretends not to need it and to scorn it but will eventually get it; and the beauty of she who no longer has the girdle but has had it and conserves the bright reflection of its ripe fruit.

In short, the three Goddesses long for victory, not for man, about whom we are not told that they have any desire (as in the case of Hera with Zeus). Nor are we allowed to think that they make themselves desirable among themselves just because they take turns wearing the girdle, which on the contrary they indifferently lend each other to seduce the "other-than-self."

In other words: the three Goddesses are images evoked by man's desire, and the evokers of that very desire. They desire to become man's *object* of desire, and in this sense whichever of them succeeds will be able to call herself, with respect to the others, "the fairest."

25. Young Paris, on the contrary, wants simply to possess the object of his desire (possess in the already clarified meaning). Aphrodite, who knows that well, promises him in return the possession of the fairest woman among the mortals, grateful for being chosen and proclaimed the fairest among the immortals.

Which amounts to saying that the desire of mortals must transit through mortal bodies, it must be incarnated and spatialized in the material mediums of practices. So that, in the end, it is still an illusory possession, just because of its transience. Only the eternity of the three Goddesses who evoke desire is an immortal figure.

Another beautiful myth tells about Ixion, the mortal man who falls madly in love with the queen of the Gods. Zeus takes pity on him and sends him a cloud in the shape of Hera, so that Ixion can somewhat flatter himself on possessing the Goddess and thus fulfill his desire on such a transferal object. The result of this intimacy is, on the other hand, the birth of remarkable children, namely the centaurs. But then Ixion starts to boast about it and goes around bragging that he seduced and possessed Zeus' wife. Until Zeus tires of the situation: he casts Ixion down into Tartarus, condemning him to spin a wheel woven with snakes, pointlessly and for all eternity.

I will leave to you the task of unpacking the symbolic meanings of this tale.

26. Let us go back to the matter at hand. It is the sign of the girdle that, inserted in a practice of sexual enchantment, makes bodies indifferently desirable. The body is desirable insofar as it is "illuminated" by the girdle: a light that cannot be possessed but must rather be set in motion within the practices of acquisition.

In this sense we said that the girdle is a metaphor for all things, since there are no simple things, namely things being simply present. Things exist because they are invested by desire, and in this sense the girdle is an *image*, or a *figure*: image of the original image which everything, in its own way (that is, in its appearing as an object of a given practice), is.

Now, as we said before, the myth of the girdle puts on a play of images, a figure representation. It is in this admirable game of images that the *exchange* occurs. An exchange of images, but also and essentially, since the image is the original sign of desire, an *economic exchange of desire*: an *economy of desire*.

Yet it is only by means of this exchange that *identification* takes place: and so, we have finally come to the point.

It is in the image of Paris that Aphrodite recognizes herself as Aphrodite, namely, as the fairest among the Goddesses: she becomes the fairest, in all senses, *for* him.

It is in the image conveyed to him by the girdle that Alexander/ Paris recognizes himself as a potential owner of the object of desire: owner because of the girdle.

In other words: insofar as the woman gives her body to the man (a body metaphorized by the girdle that makes it desirable for the man), the man identifies himself as man, namely, as he who has the possession—first and foremost possession of the woman, or better, of her body. You will understand all the profound implications of this further on.

27. Countless consequences result from what we have said. First, that a man and a woman live differently both their bodies and the desire that involves them. This statement, however, must be taken with some contextual caution, as it applies to a certain practice of seduction, which is here carried out from an essentially male view. I am not talking of a universal and eternal anthropological feature that would always already typify male and female "logic."

Aphrodite has her truth in Alexander/Paris, because she sees in him the reflected sign of herself, from which she derives, indirectly, a "female" identity, a "self." The same goes for Alexander/Paris with respect to Aphrodite, who is for him a sign of his being a desiring subject—a seducer of the women of others.

This is what male seduction is in such a figure, since the woman is here the possession of a man: of her father, brother, husband, brother-in-law, and so on.

Within that "psychology," on the other hand, a woman becomes more desirable if she is also desired by someone else or even by everyone, given that she is "the fairest."

28. Now let us pay attention: neither of them—Paris or Aphrodite—is something for themselves; nobody is for themselves a "self." Everybody is nothing but a *relationship*, a connection, an exchange: something for the other and nothing, "originally," for themselves.

This means, with unquestionable evidence, that the subjects repeat in themselves the condition of the object: both subjects and objects are something only insofar as they are desired.

A remark of the utmost importance, which shows us how abstract is every idea that originally opposes subjects to already constituted objects, whether material or spiritual. Subject and object are strategic distinctions, merely and superficially "nonontological" practices: the subject *is* an object, namely, the pole of a desire.

The subject's center, or substance, as a threshold of desire, is therefore a *void*, or an *elsewhere*. It is in fact the event of desire, of *se(lf)-duction*, which gives rise to the subjects and prepares them for each other.

That is to say, each the *object* of the other and for the other, and vice versa.

Being this very "object," the subject is thus a sign and a mirror from which and within which the other sees and identifies themself as the subject they are—that is, as subject *to* desire.

The subject's condition lies in an object-mirror: that from which the subject is mirrored as a subject. The object's condition, however, lies in the subject: that which is the object of their desire and is mirrored by it. Constitutive *complementarity*, and unresolvable *unbalanced* mutuality: you will understand better and better the reasons for that.

But you can already see this: we are dealing with the same original imbalance between subject and world. Subjects come from the world, they are made of its flesh and are entirely its "place" or threshold. Yet at the same time the world appears only as a figure of the subject's desire and it has, in such a relationship, its place and its having-to-take-place, namely its *event*.

29. There is never any balance among subjects, nor any perfect correspondence or equality. This is the conclusion to my "academic" disquisition, but I will follow it up with a short "critical" corollary in which I take objection to the "intersubjectivity" sometimes philosophers talk about. And my objection is that such intersubjectivity is often, or in general, an abstract intellectualistic invention.

Coequal existence for all subjects, from which we derive their identical right to "equality": a "noble" figure of intersubjectivity or, as has keenly been observed, "decorous idealism." We philosophers pretend, for example when we debate, to be equal in the name of "truth."

That is a *deceptive* figure that fatally meets, in the experience of concrete life, with constant and bitter disproof; because among subjects there is at bottom an *economy* of imbalance and exchange.

On the other hand, if there really were a perfect balance, what on earth would there be to *exchange*?

So, we see that the intention to adopt equality as an ideal and a conscious, conventional pattern of the being-together of subjects—in a sociopolitical sense—is not only an abstract, formal democracy with all its vain hopes and its corresponding empirical disproof: it is also an equivocal project, much more satisfied with its recurring failure than it is engaged in correcting its flaw.

A flaw in which we are quick to take comfort as a "lesser evil" or the "best of all possible worlds," thus allowing ourselves to pursue it determinedly, protecting its interest, if necessary, even by force—just as it *is*, in fact, necessary and inevitable.

30. Young Hegel states nicely that in love we are coequal in power. And yet how should we read this equality? Of course, not in the sense that we should measure power to split it fifty-fifty. How then?

This is about political virtue (*areté*) and the Political—what we are here putting into question. The democratic illusion of allocating power based on a mere arithmetic calculation of votes falls short of the question; and furthermore, it is by no means innocent. By throwing into the game of power the universal quantification of consensus and the public rituality of democratic voting, a total objectification and commodification is eventually introduced into political life.

That democracy becomes essentially a timocracy (power of the wealthy and the ambitious) is not therefore an unpleasant accident we do not know how to avoid. The truth is that democracy and timocracy have been the same thing all along; they come from the same root and have neither the possibility nor the desire to stray from it.

It happens then, in modern democratic society, that everyone's human and political personality is molded in principle and fact on the basis of the typical sign and transferal object known as money. Ultimately, the "worth" is money and we are all "worth" and have our "rights" in proportion to our possession of wealth—in addition to the merely formal and widely illusory right to vote for our masters.

As a matter of fact, such a universal phenomenon invests everybody with the "right" to achieve exactly what they can "pay for" or "buy": from the most exclusive goods to the admission ticket for the tourist masses in the circus-pen of everything, including one's private and most private life displayed as a public thing to be surveyed with titillating curiosity.

And so democratic society equalizes all subjects in the sense that it makes them subject to the domination of money and to the rule of its desire; it makes them anxious to gain power through money, to the extreme extent of a systematic and conscious manipulation of consensus, which is, essentially, what politics is all about nowadays.

Violent "information of the souls" geared toward their subjection is being passed off sanctimoniously and crookedly as the "consensus" that would legitimate power, its seizure, its exercise, without any checks and balances, by the manipulators—themselves as prone to money as the next person. Indeed, they greatly need it, if they want "to inform" by manipulating the consensus of their fellow citizens.

In the scene of the world, the images of life and death are played. There, on the razor's edge of different practices, things and subjects take place. These figures display how human beings dwell and have a world: figures which epitomize an "ethos" passing through its thresholds. An ethos which identifies, in the "chronic" eternity of its passing through, the "political" figure of "eternal life."

We will stop here, with this obscure language that announces our future journey, while the light is going out.

Scene III: The Choice

31. While we prepare to enter the house of Polemarchus, here's another brief consideration on our myth. In it, as we have seen, the symbols intertwine and reference each other. The three Goddesses are moved by the desire either for the girdle's acquisition, or for its disdainful rejection, as happens with Artemis. Yet the girdle is a chimerical object, doomed to pass through, as is every object of desire.

In fact, Aphrodite will not be able to keep it, and to have it she must relinquish both the virginal charm of Artemis and the mature seduction of Hera. Hera is marked by the nostalgia of the girdle's loss, Artemis by the conflicting anguish of its expectation.

The meaning of this constant passing through, however, finds eventually in Hecate (the Dark—the concealed, the unspoken one) its truth and final destination.

Now let us consider the matter from Paris' point of view. His *belief* is that he chooses and that he can choose. In fact, he *is chosen* by the dazzle of the seductive object, which is the carrier of an emotion whose ultimate outcome is tragic, because the choice (every political choice, we could say) introduces abduction, violence, betrayal, vengeance, conflict, destruction, and death into the world.

Here we should not forget the great Gorgias: much more profoundly, he replaces the girdle with speech as the supreme transferal body, able to seduce, to dazzle, to comfort, as well as to divert, steering all human beings to their *kairos*, their opportune moment.

I want to remind you that at the center of our cross in the Prologue we have placed language (words or speech): the indication and sign of a major problem of the political virtue, the *politiké areté* we are here pursuing, driven by the desire for our backstage word.

32. Yet there is a further level of reading the myth, a reading connected, as it were, to the bright side of desire as the pervasive driving force of the anthropological *ethos*.

The three Goddesses, in fact, are in the end nothing but cosmic figures and images: by exchanging the girdle, they revolve eternally in the moon circle of their dazzles and eclipses—which are "natural" events.

But then, it is human beings who choose, risking the apple of knowledge, truth, and beauty. Because of this choice, they are plunged into their destiny of death, tied to a desire for procreation, which fulfills its only "natural" end.

Human beings sink thus into a destiny of death as well as errancy, in that, attracted by sexual desire, they find themselves either incarnating or being sucked into the body of Hecate the Dark: the fatal body that the lunar deity's three bright faces have carefully hidden, dazzling the choice with the girdle and seducing with desire.

The human choice is nevertheless the event of its constitutive dignity and virtue, whereby the meaning of "being political" for humans is fulfilled, which coincides with their being "ethical."

The human being cannot have any other being and truth than in the exercise of the choice in which the fulfillment of destiny occurs. We will find choice and destiny again at the end of the *Republic*.

Humanity's political dignity seems therefore to be encompassed in this choice experienced as a self-aware, or self-reflected, exercise.

This does not mean in the abstract figure of philosophical self-consciousness, but during exchange practices among subjects, and between subjects and the world of objects, beginning with that object which is our living body—where the figures of desire are reflected so as to constitute peculiar figures and "writings" of knowledge.

Scene IV: At Polemarchus' House

33. The small party of friends goes therefore with Polemarchus to his house in the Piraeus. There they meet Cephalus, Polemarchus' old father, by then retired from active life. Cephalus greets Socrates, whom he had not seen for a long time, with especially friendly warmth. Let us familiarize ourselves with the main characters that appear behind me.

On one side Cephalus, Polemarchus, Lysias, and Euthydemus. On the other side Thrasymachus, Charmides, and Clitophon; in the middle Socrates, Glaucon, and Adeimantus.

We should first make the acquaintance of the hosts. Cephalus and his sons are a family of metics, that is, foreigners who have found hospitality in Athens, benefiting from Pericles' wise citizenship laws. Cephalus is a native of Sicily, which he left for political reasons. In the Piraeus, he has started a shield factory, and his circumstances are prosperous: he is a rich man who has been able, by coping with the ups and downs of fortune, to keep intact the possessions inherited from his father. Now the head of the family business is Polemarchus, the eldest son, an intelligent man, shrewd and with a strong character.

Obviously, the whole family of Cephalus sympathizes with Periclean democracy, whereas Thrasymachus and his friends are exponents of aristocratic sophistry, in other words, intellectuals showing off their refined, unconventional, and radical culture. Hence their political ideas, on the one hand, are rather reactionary, because hostile to democracy, yet in other respects, bold and even groundbreaking.

Glaucon and Adeimantus are brothers and sons of the noble Ariston, who is also the father of Plato, the youngest of the three siblings. Therefore, Plato makes his eldest brothers into two protagonists of the dialogue, in which he will grant them the peculiar privilege to ignore Socrates' ostensible method, one that demands short questions and short answers to his dialectical reasoning. They will instead venture to expound their arguments in long speeches. Plato depicts them as young and gallant men, both already experienced at political and army life, in which they have distinguished themselves for their bravery. Both are truly keen to understand Socrates' "philosophy," but they are also similarly attracted by the new sophistic culture, of which Thrasymachus is a recognized champion. They admire its intellectual clarity, its moral earthiness, and theoretical energy.

34. Let us think carefully now. Plato's strategy is quite evident: he intends to stage a political dispute in which the various trends and currents, both traditional and new, in the Athenian political arena are portrayed. We should not forget, however, that the scene is cleverly older than its audience, which is made of Plato's contemporaries. Whether we imagine the scene taking place in 411 BCE—in the climate that will lead to the oligarchic coup—or, as seems much more likely, as early as 425 or 422 (at the time of the Peace of Nicias, when Athens was still undefeated and at the peak of its splendor), Plato's general intention is quite clear.

In the first case, Plato is telling his audience: look where we ended up, for nourishing perverse or deficient political ideas. In the second case, he is insinuating that, in times of still prosperous fortune, if the political revolution that is wished for here had been carried out, catastrophe would have been avoided, as well as the accompanying grief, tragedies, and crimes.

35. And yet Plato, above all, is plastically showing one more thing to his audience, with an intuitive and direct cogency not at all devoid of cruel and shocking evidence. We know that the topic of the *Republic* is justice, and here Plato shows, just by staging his characters from the past, that both oligarchists and democrats were to a large degree unjust and violent.

After Athens' defeat in the Peloponnesian War, an oligarchic coup seized power in 404 BCE, breaking with Athens' long democratic tradition. It was a very traumatic episode. Oligarchists availed themselves of the Spartan garrison's support and ushered in the Four Hundred government, among which especially notorious are the Thirty Tyrants, who administered the rich Piraeus. They were guilty of excesses and violence, as well as of serious injustices. For instance, putting to death Polemarchus, if for no other reason than to get their hands on his considerable wealth.

With the return of democracy, the aforementioned Lysias, Polemarchus' brother, would call then to account, in the celebrated oration "Against Eratosthenes," one of the Thirty Tyrants.

And yet the democrats, too, once back in power, went on to commit various injustices, among which the notorious one of putting Socrates to death by hemlock, on the deliberately fabricated charge of impiety. Socrates counted several friends among the oligarchists, but he had never compromised himself with that regime, even courageously refusing, at the risk of his life, to obey their order to dispense with an enemy of the Thirty.

However, beside the two innocent victims of Athenian politics, Socrates and Polemarchus, Plato also places his two brothers. Although exponents of the noble and uncorrupted aristocracy, although spiritually so endowed as to figure as citizens of the new philosophic republic Plato will have Socrates describe, they do not seem able to help being sympathetically attracted to the paradoxical sophistic thesis of Thrasymachus and his mates, thus unintentionally fostering the climate that will enable the oligarchic coup and its atrocities.

But, more broadly speaking, we could say that Plato stages the general crisis of politics, with its injustices and tragedies—a crisis as lasting as human history, or just about, as will be reaffirmed in the *Timaeus*.

Hence the necessity of a *new politics*. Which will only come true by means of a remarkable improvement concerning human nature: a full-blown anthropological revolution and conversion enabled by a new *paideia*, a "philosophical education" that ought to rear a new humanity, a new moral and social ethos, based on an original sense of truth, of reality and community.

Scene V: Dialogue Between Socrates and Cephalus

36. Socrates and Cephalus have started an amicable conversation, we were saying. Indeed, you can see them amid the dinner guests arranged in a circle. Do not be surprised by the ivy crown Cephalus wears on his hoary head; the fact is that, when his friends arrived, he was getting ready to celebrate a sacrifice in honor of the gods. But do not think, now, that Plato's direction wastes time on delighting us with a merely introductory sketch, a simple plot device with which Plato will later lead us on (as indeed he will) to the topic of the general discussion.

The sketch is indeed delightful, but its aim is also exceptional, because, against all appearances, Plato is pinpointing the deep-seated and fundamental issue which circumscribes *politiké areté* and which at the same time inscribes itself within it. Not just clever theatrical entertainment, then, but the covert exhibition of the real stakes: of course, for those smart enough to see it.

In fact, what do Socrates and Cephalus tell each other after the customary pleasantries? I will sum it up right now. The two men, as we know, had not met for a long time. It is evident that Socrates is shocked by the physical transformation undergone by Cephalus, who looks very much aged and weak. Therefore Socrates, by now a mature man though still far from old age, asks Cephalus, who is experiencing it, what old age is like, and what is its misery.

And Cephalus answers: the fading away of desire, *epithymia*—the intense and violent desire that accompanies bodily pleasure. Particularly, the pleasure of food, wine, and sex. Then he adds: since old men regret these desires and pleasures, their fading away makes them feel as if they were no longer alive; that is why, in their eyes, life has lost entirely its appeal and sense. Here is, in general terms, the condition and misery of old age.

But he hurries to specify that it is still possible to live old age differently, by appealing to superior wisdom. And this is precisely his case. In this regard, Cephalus recalls an anecdote about old age from Sophocles. A fellow asks wise Sophocles, "How does it go with the pleasures of love? Can you still have intercourse with a woman?" And Sophocles replies, "Hush, man. Most gladly have I escaped the thing of which you speak as from a mad and furious master."

Which means that Cephalus sees in old age the chance and the ideal condition for getting rid at last of desire—which he compares to inner slavery.

37. Notice how Plato is summarizing in the most succinct yet effective way the field of application of desire. In present-day terms we could say that he breaks it down as follows:

Oral *eros* (Eating and Drinking)
Anal *eros* (Money)
Genital *eros* (Sex)

Wherever is it to be found—you might ask—this anal eros symbolically sublimated in the transferal object which is money? Well, Plato knows a thing or two: sure enough, the issue appears already in the second question Socrates asks Cephalus: whether money (wealth) provides comfort for the evils of old age. An innocent and rather obvious question, in the house of those wealthy people, and yet, much more profound than it might appear.

Cephalus answers that it depends on people's characters, namely on the nature of the impulses of their "soul" (as Socrates will say below). It is indeed true that one can take advantage of wealth, especially because, if well used, it allows one to avoid the need to commit injustices within interpersonal relationships. In a nutshell, wealth delivers us from the temptation to appropriate other people's money or work to further our own interests.

What is, however, "justice" (*dikaiosyne*)? And now the way is paved for the amazing wheels of Plato's *Republic* to start turning.

38. But there is still a final touch we should not miss. At this point Cephalus leaves the company. With a garland on his head, he withdraws to celebrate his usual sacrificial rites. Cephalus is obsessed with certain popular beliefs and rumors, and he holds a superstitious fear of the everlasting torment that, according to these rumors, would be awaiting him in the afterlife. Which clearly shows that Cephalus is not too sure of himself: although rich and wise, as he boasts, he fears he might have committed some injustice during his lifetime.

Cephalus is the typical figure of the old man seized by a religious mania, whose temperament Plato outlines in an unforgettable way with just a few strokes of his admirable art. Anxious to obtain divine benevolence to evade punishment after his death, Cephalus maniacally increases his offerings and prayers in any moment of the day, in hopes they might gain him some powerful ally or protector in the afterworld.

On the other hand, the exit of Cephalus complies with a stringent logic. He throws himself into religion, intended precisely as the "opium of the people": instead of facing the problem of injustice in this world, old Cephalus entrusts its solution to an imaginary afterworld.

But above all: fallen into a weak old age, now incapable of desire, and even pleased with its extinction, Cephalus is no longer a "political subject," unlike the still "virile" Socrates. In the dialogue on justice and *politiké areté*, therefore, he has nothing more to say and his presence is unnecessary.

In practical terms, Plato is telling us that without *epithymia*, specifically without sexual desire (see the colorful hint to Sophocles), there is neither politics nor a political problem. The latter, in fact, arises in the core of desire and for the sake of desire, which is therefore the fundamental anthropological question.

Anthropological also in the sense that desire ties humanity to something prehuman, something mad and furious, which are in fact the images used further below to describe Thrasymachus—the "wolf" of politics, unlike the meek shepherd dog which Socrates will evoke to describe the philosopher.

And so, Plato, as I have noted, is already showcasing the fundamental issues: desire, exchange, money, the economy of life and death, happiness, and justice.

Now the dialogue, or rather, the strife (*eris*) among the "active" characters of the play can begin.

Second Figure

The Practice of Force

Scene VI: Dialogue Between Socrates and Polemarchus

39. The just man does not take possession of other people's belongings and will pay his debts to everyone. This is what Cephalus says as he walks out. Socrates asks if that is the correct definition of "justice." Polemarchus says it is so, even calling on the authority of poet Simonides' definition. The son sides with the father. We know, however, that calling on someone's authority makes Socrates' hackles rise. Here he is now, picking on Polemarchus with a whirl of questions and strange insinuations, which are deliberately studied to give Polemarchus a hard time and catch him in a contradiction.

Yet Polemarchus, a confident and practical man, stands his ground: what he is maintaining seems to be quite evident and unanimous. And his supported theory is, in the Greek thinking, the most traditional.

What is he maintaining? In brief, he is saying that a friend ought always to do good to a friend and evil to an enemy.

Before we continue, however, you should note Plato's chilling directorial choice. He puts into Polemarchus' mouth the same idea which, embraced by the Thirty Tyrants—enemies of Polemarchus because of his democratic sympathies, but above all eager to take his possessions—will lead him to his death. With unaware naïveté and confidence, Polemarchus expresses the same principles that will inspire his implicit guilty verdict as well as his downfall.

Polemarchus' theory, on the other hand, is just a resumption of the "agonistic *areté*" that has been inspiring, since time out of mind, much of the culture and life of the Greek peoples—and not only them.

40. Socrates is up to all sorts of ploys to disprove Polemarchus, but no argument comes easier to him than the one I am going to sum up for you. It goes as follows: those who can harm their enemies must necessarily be experienced in "slyness" if they want to be useful to their friends. And here is the exemplification: Who would be the best guard of a treasure? Indeed, whoever knows perfectly all the tricks of thieves; it's only natural. So that the just man must also be a sort of thief.

Now, this is stretching it a bit, but you certainly understand what Plato is driving at. I will translate it and voice it for everybody.

In a nutshell, it seems quite clear to me that Plato is showing us that if we use craftiness and force to favor "one's own" and damage the "stranger" all we do is pursue the logic of desire that rules the economy of life: again, as always, how to obtain food, sex, power, and money.

Which means that the alternative harming/benefiting (our enemies, our friends) might be at most a sort of "natural" justice, but in no way adequate for laying the foundations of real political justice, or political virtue—or better still, of a peaceful and happy, social community.

In this alternative, in fact, the violence of desire is not removed at all, on the contrary, it is pursued and strengthened through aggregations and parties: that very violence that disturbs and breaks peace and a necessary social cooperation.

41. Yet the main objection Socrates levels against Polemarchus is the following: since we can be mistaken in judging people, we might happen to be in the right—in our own interest or the general interest—in harming friends, if they are wicked, and in benefiting enemies if they are good.

A group of friends, whatever its composition (familial, professional, economic, sociopolitical, etc.), fulfills operations and functions of common interest. Whereas a group of enemies competes within the range of the same interests. If among the circle of friends, however, some are addicted to deviant and corrupted behaviors, it might not necessarily be in the group's interest to favor and protect them. On the contrary, it might well be advisable to win over to our side the best individuals from the rival group.

A sensible but ultimately unsatisfactory reading. It precisely misses the magnitude of the move Plato has staged.

The fact is that this interpretation has become completely familiar to us and so we no longer catch its unheard-of, revolutionary novelty, its strategic scope, and consequences.

It is time for us, then, to pause the scene and apply ourselves to our backstage work.

Scene VII: The Birth of Moral Virtue

42. Let's get down to the real issue, which can be expressed in these terms: Plato puts into Socrates' mouth a total change of meaning for the word *areté*, and that is perhaps the core of authentic Socratic thinking and of its historical message. The old and traditional meaning of the word *areté* (*virtus* in Latin) does not carry any "qualitative" connotation, that is, any moral implication.

Areté, as we know, defines efficiency, ability, force. The virtue of the eye is to see, that of the horse is to run, and so on. Therefore, being virtuous means in this sense to be able to bring our actions to success, to achieve the result we desire, and the like.

Now Plato produces a decisive shift: he replaces the pair friend/enemy, which does not imply any judgment as to the moral quality of individuals, with the pair good/wicked, which, on the contrary, does imply an opinion and in fact requires it.

"Political virtue" does not address, therefore, the functional qualification of the individuals in the group—their efficient action—but their inner human quality, in which is visibly at work what has been called Plato's "soul strategy." A strategy that involves, precisely, shifting the problem onto a "moral" level.

By so doing, Plato promotes and hopes for the realization of a new human quality, that is, of a new anthropology, as the basis of politics. Essentially, he secretly replaces the question "What is justice?" with the (Socratic) question "What is man?" What *areté* makes him a man? How can he be defined "just"?

Be careful, however, not to misinterpret. These questions seem obvious to us and completely clear and plausible, as we have said, because from time immemorial we have been inscribed in Plato's moral cosmos, which anyway did not exist before he invented and established it. What Plato produces is not a mere shift from one kind—the functional—to another—the moral—that was already preexistent. To which we might well have replied: So what? We are talking of political virtue, not of moral virtue. Yet this is precisely what was not possible, and the effect that Plato immediately achieves by this shift is one of incomprehensible estrangement, to the point that it will take him the entire enunciation of the "philosophy" heralded in the *Republic* to have it understood.

In short, by putting this objection to Polemarchus into Socrates' mouth, Plato brings into being precisely the "moral" meanings of virtue (*areté*) and justice (*dike*), a meaning unknown to the Greeks of the time.

Someone said: the shift at issue is from things produced, and from the ability to produce them, to the subject's "inner intentions" and "intimate aptitudes." Yes, that is true, but at the same time it is not well said, because it gives the idea of a mere shift between things or aptitudes already set up in their dialectical opposition; that is to say, as if there were already "inner intentions," and "intimate aptitudes," and above all "subjects" in this sense.

On the contrary, it is precisely this unprecedented Platonic gesture that *establishes* the inner intentions, the moral subject, the soul, and the famous voice of conscience that on many occasions Socrates professes to hear and follow faithfully.

43. And there is one more thing, also essential, that I want you to see. Plato does not establish separately, so to speak, the soul, the moral conscience, the philosophical inner subject, to later apply them to politics. Precisely the opposite is true. *It is within the already existing political practice and because of its problems directly and dramatically lived that Plato invents and institutes philosophical virtue, with its moral, psychological, and ontological consequences.*

There, if I cannot get you to understand this, my entire backstage effort fails miserably.

And there is one more important corollary. Plato invests the "subject" with a soul possessing good or wicked "intentions." He is the subject *of* these intentions. Yet at the same time, and because of this same gesture, he is in fact made subject *to the soul,* namely, to the soul's practices of speech, evaluation, and judgment: a liberation of "moral" subjects, which at the same time produces their invisible prisons.

In this sense the Socratic and Platonic revolution is not at all the establishing of the essence of the human, as if it were its universal and planetary culmination acquired for evermore. It is rather a definite *practice* of the human and of its concrete political experience. What began to set us free from this superstitious overvaluation, from this self-reflected blindness, was Nietzsche's brave impiety and his painful parricide.

It has been rightly pointed out that "Socrates rejects the conflictual dynamics in their totality, because they are incompatible with any kind of intersubjective relationship, either private or public." And yet we must add that the distinction between "private" and "public," as today we still mean them, was created precisely by the gesture that institutes the inner subjects and their moral intentions. Therefore, do not be fooled by those who would oppose private to public thinking as if they were advocating some kind of revolution: the two concepts are mutual to one another and are reflected in their metaphysical sameness.

Eliminating conflictual dynamics in their entirety. You can easily understand how this erasure calls for nothing short of a radical anthropological reconstruction and how this very project turns out to be the core of the political virtue enabled by a philosophical education (*paideia*). But this means that *political reason*, or rather, politico-philosophical reason, places itself as a screen and shield against the original conflictual relations.

What remains, however, effectively hidden? And at what price? Here are the capital questions we must now deal with.

44. Careful thinking is required. In this Platonic gesture, the notion of justice takes on a clearly pedagogic character: the main task of the state will be to educate its citizens to act according to "good" aims. It will have to *produce*, primarily, good souls. Doing violence and causing damage, indeed, does not make people good. Doing good makes us good, doing harm makes us evil; this is evident.

Socrates says it in plain language to Polemarchus: "To injure a friend or anyone else is not the function of a just man; on the contrary, it is the function of the unjust."

Have we said it all? And is it all that simple? No, it is not, and this is not all. In this rhetorical twist, *the question of desire remains unsettled*. And Plato knows it well. So much so that for the education of the guardians of his state, he removes completely from them the three objects of desire he had placed on the scene in the beginning: food, money, sex.

A most difficult undertaking, Plato admits: no wonder historical experience shows it as being constantly contradicted and, in essence, impossible. And it is no accident that in *Laws* Plato will break new ground, trying to educate desire in his symposia. We will leave aside for now, however, what that would mean.

Why can't the revolutionary gesture of the *Republic* be successful? Plato has already had Cephalus answer this question: without *epithymia*, without the eagerness that accompanies desire, there can be no "interest." Consequently, there is neither love nor the resulting "doing good"—of whose ambivalence we are all too aware today—since every love carries within it a component of aggressiveness, suffering, and, in brief, evil.

Without eagerness and desire for possession we only have the generic "love of the nun"; not worldly, and therefore not political; an aseptic love indifferently addressed to all human beings "for the love of Him," the heavenly Groom who is, in a way, the nun's true passionate love—a love addressed to "the world behind the world" (itself not altogether independent from the Socratic-Platonic moral revolution that occurred in the West).

To conclude, then, we could say that the threshold of the political purporting to abolish desire is doomed to fail for lack of anthropological comprehension as well as due to phenomenological insufficiency in describing the practices of life and knowledge.

We find evidence of this in the fact that this political project is not innocent at all. On the contrary, to establish itself and endure it demands coercion, force, and even deception. The project wants peace, but to achieve peace it promotes its own kind of violence.

45. On this point we should not be hasty and superficial—such as those who wash their hands of it all and say: everybody knows that politics is a dirty business—"beautiful souls" we can never mistrust enough, because they are the ones who in fact endorse *every* kind of violence. They are akin to those who assure us, with sly winks, pleased with their own cleverness, that democracy, as we all know, is the worst form of government, but unfortunately there is none better. A despicable statement in its stupid and wanton charlatanry.

In Plato's gesture lies not a generic political violence, but the violence inherent in the constitution of the "rational soul"—a violence inspiring the philosophical pedagogy that in fact hides, behind rational visions and argumentations, the will to control life.

Remember what Aristotle said: he who reasons, rules. As far as the meaning of reasoning goes, Aristotle himself will explain it to you in full detail—he, the archetype and paragon of the perfect human being: male, Greek, financially independent, and philosopher.

It is through this road that the so-called "logic of things" will establish itself, as will the "reason of the state"—and philosophy shows the ontological basis of both. This is the origin of things taken "in themselves," that is, disconnected from their exercise in the practices, unlinked from their specific constitutive desire.

Yet these alleged things in themselves are not, as we said, the ultimate and objective reality of the world but rather a *construct*, carried out through a transcription and a transference, starting with the objectifying *transfer* of the practice of speech. Which is to say: the *meaning* of things as it is transferred to the practice of moral and rational judgment, while the *event* of such a practice, its inauguration, and its exercise, hide in the backstage of its dazzling, and certainly extraordinary, *mise-en-scène*.

What this rational project, in turn, desires, is not easy to see, although we might assume—with good reason—that it aims at erasing Hecate and at taking over death.

It is a "techno-logical" project aiming at transferring the economy of life and death, which are called "natural," to the field of appropriation of the "human." I am reporting this just as I heard it, with the utmost care though without much conviction. Perhaps the matter is more complicated.

46. The next consideration seems much more apposite to me, and I suggest you examine it carefully. On the strength of what we said and showed, it ascertains the following situation: that Plato's "strategy of the soul" leads precisely to a "soul" as a mere *residue* of the constitutive operations of philosophical and political reason. It is these operations that get *this* soul to the surface. It is in the desiring intentionality of these practices that the soul has its root and entirely, as it seems, its substance.

A soul which, as pure residue, is per se a mere nothing, a fantastic projection detached from life. It is at the same time an effect of the erasure of the titanic part that all human beings carry along with them—as the Dionysus myth would show if we had the time to go over it.

And so, gathering up the threads of all our behind-the-scenes work, we could say that the Platonic *mise-en-scène* aims at shifting the friend/foe relationship into a sort of imaginary, pre-political, and pre-philosophical wild naturalness. We will find shortly the analogue of this gesture in the retroflexion of the supposedly natural need as economic justification for the construction of political reason and its constitutive violence.

Yet the friend/foe relationship, *as a vehicle for desire*, is not so easily eradicated and, in many ways, it comes up again in the actual dynamics of the practices of life and knowledge as well as in the associated desire for mutual recognition.[1]

On this concealed relationship Plato superimposes, as we will see, the rational soul, that is to say, its psychology and anthropology as well as its ontology, or in a word, philosophy.

You cannot accuse the backstage of not saying clearly and explicitly, even at the cost of some instrumental oversimplifications, everything it thought it had to say; of not striving to show, with some foretaste here and there, the sense of the road ahead of us, so that no one can complain about being caught unprepared.

As you can see, the forestage is beginning to revolve, and you are going to be brought back onstage. There is Thrasymachus who, with impatient fury, is about to pounce on the unaware Socrates and Polemarchus, just as they were within inches of reaching an agreement or concluding an armistice.

Scene VIII: Dialogue Between Socrates and Thrasymachus

47.

SOCRATES: Several times in the course of the discussion Thrasymachus had made an attempt to get the argument into his own hands, and had been put down by the rest of the company, who wanted to hear the end. But when Polemarchus and I had done speaking and there was a pause, he could no longer hold his peace; and, gathering himself up, he came at us like a wild beast, seeking to devour us. We were quite panic-stricken at the sight of him.

He roared out to the whole company: "What folly, Socrates, has taken possession of you all? And why do you act like fools, knocking under to one another? I say that if you

---

1. In Sini's use of the term "recognition" (*riconoscimento*), which is in fact the last word of this book, we must hear the echo of Spinoza's treatment of man's ambition and love of esteem (*agting* in Dutch, *existimatio* in Latin). See also Carlo Sini, *Spinoza o l'archivio del sapere. Opere, Vol. IV, Tomo I* (Jaca Book, 2013)—Ed.

want really to know what justice is, you should not only ask but answer, and you should not seek honor to yourself from the refutation of an opponent, but have your own answer; for there is many a one who can ask and cannot answer. And now I will not have you say that justice is duty or advantage or profit or gain or interest, for this sort of nonsense will not do for me; I must have clearness and accuracy."

I was panic-stricken at his words, and could not look at him without trembling. Indeed I believe that if I had not fixed my eye upon him, I would have been speechless: but when I saw his fury rising, I looked at him first, and was therefore able to reply to him.

"Thrasymachus," I said, with a quiver, "don't be hard upon us. Polemarchus and I may have been guilty of a little mistake in the argument, but I can assure you that the error was not intentional. If we were seeking for a piece of gold, you would not imagine that we were 'knocking under to one another,' and so losing our chance of finding it. And why, when we are seeking for justice, a thing more precious than many pieces of gold, do you say that we are weakly yielding to one another and not doing our utmost to get at the truth? Nay, my good friend, we are most willing and anxious to do so, but the fact is that we cannot. And if so, you people who know all things should pity us and not be angry with us."

48. I am sure you want to know one thing above all: why, if Socrates had not looked at Thrasymachus first, he would have lost his speech. Well, it is a Greek folktale according to which a man is struck dumb if he is seen by a wolf before he sees it. What is Plato's purpose in recalling it here? The answers can be many (one being perhaps that those who rely on wild strength lose their mind), but first it is clear that Socrates uses a jocular tone to answer Thrasymachus' raving attack.

Jocular, but not too much so, because what announces itself here, even in the subtle vocabulary chosen, is indeed a battle, a physical and mortal, as it were, confrontation. Anyway, it is an epoch-making duel between Socrates' "moral" irony and the theories of the "people who know all things," namely the most radical sophists. Of them, Thrasymachus, the famous logographer and rhetorician of Chalcedon (the clever, and terrible—*deinos*—as Plato calls him in the *Phaedrus*) is a symbolic figure.

And if Socrates' description has tragicomic features, the resulting political fray is dreadfully serious.

Please note: Thrasymachus the wolf-beast is on the verge of mauling the horrified Socrates and Polemarchus, who are absorbed in their "civilized" conversation. But most of all, Thrasymachus wipes out with one fell swoop the entire plot and intention of the Socratic research method, here reduced to a sly gimmick for tackling the political question (asking is easier than answering), one which is ultimately foolish and hollow: vapid nonsense for simpletons. And besides, Socrates is far from being merely a simpleton; he is one who pretends he wants to know what is just, whereas he is only interested in entrapping interlocutors into his snare of confutations.

But the issue is a serious, and in a way, "tragic" one; it lies in the harshness of things rather than in the subtlety of words.

49. Thrasymachus expounds and asserts *his* method, for which he is famous. It is not a matter of prevaricating over definitions and mere synonyms (justice is what is beneficial, and so on), but of arguing one's case with fierce rigor.

Even Thrasymachus' name tells us something: it means "fierce fighter." He was in fact admired, as Dionysius of Halicarnassus noted, for his "extraordinary ability to express his thoughts clearly and compactly." And here Plato wonderfully builds the character of Thrasymachus, by imitating his argumentative style.

Thrasymachus, then, is beside himself with the desire to argue his case, challenging his audience to battle. And at last, he can argue it. In a nutshell, his argument goes: "Justice is the advantage of the stronger, who makes the laws in order to remain in power."

There is no doubt that the theory is daring and, for a Greek, unheard-of and even outrageous.

The Greeks traditionally identify justice with the law. At first in a religious sense, for example as a gift from the Gods. This is how Hesiod speaks about it: there is no justice among the fish and the beasts and the winged birds, but they are subjected to the violence of the stronger. Mankind, instead, was given the law, the highest of gifts. And Solon is still of this opinion. Later the thing takes on a profane meaning: the law is a human creation, which functions to prevent violent chaos in the competition for life and death. In this sense, the law can also be defined, for instance by Critias, as tyrannical insofar as it inhibits one's "natural" instincts and rights. A widespread theory among the sophists: the law is therefore "unnatural."

Subjection to the laws of the city—from which Socrates will draw inspiration in the *Crito*, and which had already been established by Protagoras in his defense of democracy—is thus rejected by the most radical sophistry.

50. That is not all, however, because Thrasymachus displays a remarkable originality of his own in the field of radical sophistry. As has been persuasively shown, he cannot be, for instance, assimilated to the theory expounded by Callicles (one more typical character in Plato's theater) in the *Gorgias*.

And precisely because of that, Thrasymachus is the most aggressive and redoubtable opponent of Socrates, who in fact will not be able to counter him in direct discussion.

Precisely the invincible force and consistency of Thrasymachus' position will compel Plato to move beyond Socratic irony and to tread the new path we have already defined as the foundation of a new anthropology through philosophy, the origin of *politiké areté*.

The sharpest interpreter of the theories of Thrasymachus writes for instance that in Callicles we still find a defense of an archaic, oligarchic nostalgia:

> He complains that the stronger and more powerful are subjugated by the weak through the laws, which impose the equivalence of equality and justice. The metaphor Callicles resorts to—the image of fettered and tamed lions—clearly betrays that the cultural horizon of the oligarchic nostalgia is that of the Homeric hero. And herein precisely lies his archaism with respect to Thrasymachus, because Callicles considers force as an absolute, natural quality, belonging by birthright to a particular social class and to its best representatives. But what is the meaning of this "force" defeated by the weak and subjugated to their laws? According to Thrasymachus, the control of power is the only sign of force: from his perspective

entirely focused on political strife, strong are those who can promulgate a law (therefore, in a democratic context, precisely those whom Callicles considers weak—*astheneis*—by nature), and weak are those who undergo it.

51. We should now take a closer look at how Thrasymachus carries out his reasoning. With a clever rhetorical ploy wholly focused on the most minute accuracy (*akribologia*) supporting his method—in contrast to divine revelation and to the authority of the ancients—he immediately reveals his conclusion: justice is no other than the interest of the stronger.

In fact: "just" is that to which the laws demand our obedience. And yet, only those who have power can promulgate laws (it does not matter what kind of power—tyrannical, aristocratic, or democratic). But the aim of any lawmaker (a single person, a group, or a majority) is to maintain power. It follows that for the citizens "justice" is to obey the laws laid down by the stronger, according to their interest. QED.

Hobbes, in our modern age, will only repeat this reasoning.

And so, the ideology of the "good laws"—saviors of humankind, be they divine or human—is completely unmasked: behind law and justice there are neither the Gods nor the wisdom of sage lawgivers, nor the solid will of the citizens. There is only the plain reality of power; that is to say, force in its inner logics, disclosed in its very inception, from which stem all the well-known political and moral consequences.

As a confirmation that Plato means exactly this, by putting his belief into Thrasymachus' mouth, we have the *Laws*, in which Plato, with an evident allusion to Thrasymachus, writes: "The laws, they say, in a State are always enacted on each occasion by the stronger power, and they will be set up with any other primary aim than that of securing the permanence of its own authority."

All this does not mean in the least, in the eyes of Thrasymachus, that the laws contain some tyrannical feature. It is not a matter of establishing whether by nature they benefit the good or the wicked. Power, force, or strength are simply what they are: neither good nor wicked in themselves, but only effective. That is how the political thing is, and there is no other possible way—a more just way, for instance, as naïve people say, superficially and inconsistently. A conclusion which, as we know, goes for all forms of government: aristocracy, democracy, or tyranny (according to the canonical classification of Herodotus).

This laying bare of the *arcana imperii* (to which Machiavelli will have little substantial to add) entails a consequence that is the fulcrum of Thrasymachus' argument: power *can never be unjust, for it is simply its force that establishes what is just and what is not—namely right and wrong.*

A conclusion, as astonishing as it is clear, that shifts power back to the origin of *politiké areté*, an area that has been defined "neutral" with regard to values: it does not matter who the holders of power are (an individual, party, or oligarchy), or what their nature is: the political values of good and bad are established through the exercise of power—as are the values of the licit and illicit, and thus the laws governing the citizens' habits accordingly.

We might wonder whether this tremendous intellectual clarity really belongs to the historical Thrasymachus or whether it is rather the outcome, as has been argued, of the "strength of Plato's thought," who is recreating the character for his own political and dramatic aims. "It is equally obvious, however, that he needed a mouthpiece for his new reading of somebody else's theories, and he found this in the powerful and violent logographer—just as in Book II of the *Republic* he would use his own brothers—young aristocrats undoubtedly of oligarchic and sophistic sympathies"—for similar aims.

We should now return backstage. Follow me because the time has come for some considerations. I am confident that you will acknowledge their importance.

Scene IX: Plato's Subtlety

52. In Thrasymachus' disquisition, power resides in a neutral area, neither just nor unjust. But what do we mean by neutral? Is that because power, and the force that produces it, are wielded without any reason, like the force of a waterfall or the crack of a thunderbolt? It is not like that at all, nor would it make any sense if it were.

As a matter of fact, an explanation has been given: power decides, as we said, on what is just or unjust (by establishing laws) on the basis of the *desire* for stability of power itself.

This specific desire has thus been admitted explicitly. But there is another that we have hardly talked about. It is, of course, the desire for predominance (*pleonexia*), that is, for power.

What are, though, "stability" and "predominance"? Why are they desirable? What do we really desire through them? Finally, what is the relation of these desires to the three fundamental erotic interests mentioned by Cephalus, without which life would not even be desirable? Here are the questions of your backstage.

53. Now, if the point really lies, as we ventured to say previously, in the *desire for recognition*, as constitutive of every desiring and operating subject, then, in the so-called neutral area, a transfigured and transcribed desire suddenly flashes—namely, a desire embodied in the writing of that transferal thing which is the name: *in the name of the law.*

And a great deal more should be said, but only further on will we be able to understand it.

For the moment, however, we can already carry out, on Plato's direction, some effective behind-the-scenes work. In fact, the translation of the desiring backdrop into a supposed neutral area of power (in Thrasymachus' words) makes us suspect that this might well be just a skillful cover-up operation: the construction, or rather invention, of a *scene* of the political with the aim to subjugate, at last, the ghosts of desire.

What I mean is that Plato needed to invent this irrefutable original force which generates the political and its violence, as well as this "wild" need of a settled predominance, so that he could justify, as its only countermeasure, the philosophical-political revolution he wanted and the anthropological creation of citizens and guardians who are emancipated from desire by dint of the philosophical *paideia*.

Thus, it is Plato who is primarily responsible for this "tragic" *mise-en-scène* of the political, and not Thrasymachus, who is after all no other than the former's theatrical invention, instrumental in convincing us of the necessity that philosophy will be the foundation of *politiké areté*.

In fact, Plato takes good care not to expose the ambiguity of Thrasymachus' position, although it is not all that difficult to see it and perhaps even to disprove it. Those who have strength, Thrasymachus says, also have the power to issue laws for their own benefit, that is, to remain in power. This, and nothing else, is politics. All moral arguments, dreams of legal isonomies among the citizens, appeals to any supposed natural rights, are completely inappropriate because devoid of foundation or meaning.

Very well. But why does power aim to last (as we have already asked)? In other words, *why is power desirable and what is desirable in holding power?* In Thrasymachus' disquisition this is all implicitly taken for granted, as if it were completely obvious that everybody desires power, and why they do.

54. It has been rightly pointed out that Plato's Thrasymachus goes beyond both Cephalus' individualistic morality and Polemarchus' faction morality, two other characters who are functional for the dramatic plot Plato is carrying out and whose subtlety and effectiveness we are beginning to perceive with unconditional admiration. Thrasymachus, and this is where his strength lies, *poses the issue of the political and of political power as such.*

It follows that Socrates (another character) can no longer confine himself to his moral arguments, but he must decide to enter the debate on the *"political as such"*—an evident twist that shows how in the *Republic* Socrates is moving beyond Socrates, or rather, Plato is moving beyond his master.

A twist that takes its bearings from the *mise-en-scène* of Thrasymachus' thesis, which shows the coimplication of law and justice: the just is what the laws establish. It remains to be discussed the how and the who of this establishing. Plato, it is noted, will never question, in the *Republic*, this coimplication of law and justice, nor will he dispute that all lawmaking aims at giving stability to power (if necessary, even resorting to public violence and public mendacity).

All of which we do, instead, most certainly question. Nor are we satisfied with knowing who is establishing the social equation between law and justice and how, but we add an explicit question on the "why." Precisely the question that Thrasymachus' thesis is hiding or omitting; herein lies the secret of its strength, and of its inherent (yet undenounced) weakness.

Our issue, in fact, is the *genealogy of the political* (of its *areté*). Rather than "raising ourselves to the level of pure politics"—as Thrasymachus (or rather, as mentioned above, Plato) invites us to do—we aim at lowering ourselves into its roots.

And that is why we suspect that the formulation of the abstract domain of political power as such is only apparently a radicalization: a false *mise-en-scène* of a radicalism that anyway does not really get to its roots, but on the contrary hides them and transfigures them ideologically. This is indeed the core of Plato's theatrical gesture, its backdrop or backstage while he stages the character of Thrasymachus.

55. Thrasymachus is undoubtedly possessed of a tragic greatness of his own. A greatness that, whatever its historical truth, emanates from the context Plato builds around him, opposing him, as a character in his philosophical theater, to other characters such as Socrates and Polemarchus. Thrasymachus utters his battle cry in the luminous circle of the wrangling friends and he is surrounded by the scene of the transfigured Piraeus night evoking the fading echo of festivals for the barbarian divinities, processions of torches and racing horses; and then the gradual triumph of long spaces of silence which, shrouding the nighttime harbor, emanate from the sea: apparently peaceful spaces that play as background to our friends' voices ringing out happily in the still of Polemarchus' abode, spaces that are also rather unsettling.

Thrasymachus does not resort to nature or to anthropology to account for the political, because he basically *sees the man "within" the political*, that is, constituted originally within the dynamics of the domination of force and power. Which is precisely the feature of his tragic greatness.

Young Nietzsche, too, would reach this problematic place. At first, he is much closer to the aristocratic Callicles than to Thrasymachus, therefore less consistent and radical than Plato, the moralistic inspirer of *décadence* and modern nihilism; the spiritual, albeit unintentional, father of that Christianity which is only Platonism for the people. Later on, however, Nietzsche will be able to pose the real question in clear terms, that is, the question of the ultimate meaning of what he will call *Wille zur Macht*, "will to power."

What does power (*Macht*) want? What does *will* want? That is really when things come to a head and Nietzsche's anti-Platonism attains in turn its tragic fate.

Here we simply say, for the moment, that Plato's reply to Thrasymachus will consist in superimposing "ethics" on "the political"; or better, in superimposing anthropology, psychology, pedagogy—that is, philosophy as a place for the reabsorption and resolution of the political.

A superimposition summed up in the outrageous proposal of "communism." Which confirms to our eyes the ambiguous nature of the political: what is truly at stake in it is desire; the desire that the communism of goods and women ought eventually to eradicate or normalize.

56. The backstage of this scene, as we have seen, is astonishingly complicated: the *mise-en-scène* of the "pure political" (Thrasymachus) intends to trigger and motivate an ethical-political reply, that is, a philosophical

reply. Which means that philosophy as the establishment of a rational community ruled by the vision of the Good and by the scientific enunciation of definitional discourses *needs the political of the force as a foil, premise, and justification.*

What is properly staged here, then, is a rhetorical device: that is to say, precisely the *political* force of speech that we mentioned at the beginning of this representation, which is quite different from, and quite more than, a mere device. It is the force of those arguments, embodied in fictional characters, that prepares the ground for an ethical-political solution—that is, the advent of the philosophical essence of politics qua politics' *true* virtue.

Yet this political rhetoric undoubtedly also prepares the ground for philosophy qua philosophy because all in all philosophy is nothing else but *this* scene and this political intention. And for us here, there would be a lot to think about: for us who are still playing this game and are still staging this *mise-en-scène*, with the unknowing confidence that the frequentation of the argumentative space of philosophy may in and of itself result in a "pure" and self-sufficient path of truth.

Paraphrasing Nietzsche once again—who cunningly remarked: "What if the good Lord were but an *artifice* of Satan?—we could in turn ask: "What if philosophy were but an artifice of Plato?"

And this stage game, with all its backstages, might precisely be what is expounded in Thrasymachus' second thesis, for which we now make room on the proscenium.

Scene X: Why the Unjust Man Is Happy

57. Not content with the commotion he already caused, Thrasymachus allows himself a second thesis, even more outrageous than the first, and both a curse and a blessing for the interpreters. The theory claims that justice "is someone else's good," meaning that "the man who knows all things" does not really need to care for it: that's none of his business, for he is only concerned with living a happy life.

A provocation that strikes directly at poor Socrates, who, like all Greeks, looked for happiness and from there he had started in his question to Cephalus about the presumed unhappiness of old age.

Let us see in summary the argumentation Thrasymachus spills out to his rather dumbfounded friends.

The subjects, given that they respect the laws imposed by the powerful, respect the good of the powerful. Reversing the terms, we must draw the conclusion that, if justice represents the good of others to which the subjects submit, injustice represents the "personal good" of the powerful themselves. Against the famous thesis of Socratism, then, it turns out that the unjust, since they are strong and regularly exercise political oppression, are also happy, whereas the just are unhappy. An odd metamorphosis of the Thrasymachus character, who is now depicted as an ordinary eristic and an aristocratic sophist—an advocate of tyranny.

The rhetorical trick of argumentation (if justice concerns the subjects, subdued to the good of another, then, by a simple reversal, injustice concerns the powerful, who turn the law into a good of their own, into a private use) is not actually worthy of Thrasymachus' intellectual prowess.

But most of all, what is claimed here clashes with his first thesis, in which since both the just and unjust result from the exercise of power, they have no value in and of themselves, as power is ethically neutral. Saying instead: "Injustice has power"—as Thrasymachus now asserts—contradicts the first thesis and essentially weakens it.

58. In support of the introduction of this second topic, several conjectures have been put forward. For instance: the subject matter is functional to staging the dialogue's continuation insofar as it triggers the reaction of young Glaucon and Adeimantus, who demand a rebuttal from Socrates; though they do not morally approve of Thrasymachus' conclusion, they are intellectually struck and dazzled by it.

Moreover, the reference to the happiness of the unjust hints at the theme of tyranny, which will loom large in the *Republic* and eventually meet its final confutation in the myth of Er and the punishments of the afterlife assigned to tyrants. Which implies the whole theory or strategy of the soul, which also underlies the division into classes of the "philosophical" city. In short, the entire itinerary of the *Republic*.

One more conjecture: behind Thrasymachus' second argument can be glimpsed the threatening image of Critias, leader of the Thirty Tyrants, instigator of the execution of Polemarchus and Niceratus, and the one who tried, though unsuccessfully, to implicate Socrates too, by asking him to commit a "political" crime.

And finally: perhaps Plato, by putting into Thrasymachus' mouth words of the second argument, intends to suggest that the first thesis (power's neutrality) has in the second (the tyrant's desire for absolute *pleonexia*) its psychological truth and ultimate reason.

In other words: whoever concocts subtly bold and radical arguments does not do so for sheer intellectual pleasure, or for the sake of consistency and truth, but rather because this is eventually functional to their substantial desire for unjust violence.

And indeed, during the dialogue Socrates will appeal, as we would say today, to Thrasymachus' conscience: Does he really think "in all conscience" that the unjust is happy and that violence is a good thing? But Thrasymachus silences him: rather than worrying about what Thrasymachus thinks or desires, Socrates should attend to the business of refuting the argument, if he can.

59. And Socrates cannot. He openly states his dissatisfaction with the "ironic" refutations he has opposed to Thrasymachus. The battle remains unresolved, at the very least.

Socrates' self-reproach goes like this: I have been so busy chasing Thrasymachus' arguments around that now I feel like I don't know anything about anything anymore. Until I know what justice is, in fact, I am not likely to know whether it is or is not a virtue, nor can I say whether the just man is happy or unhappy.

In other words, Socrates reaffirms his fidelity and trust in the dialectical quest for truth, that is, in philosophy. Abandoning it—letting himself be dazzled by Thrasymachus' *shrewdness*—was his mistake and the reason for his defeat.

And yet this precisely confirms the functionality of Thrasymachus' second thesis for the continuation of the *Republic*.

We can gather that this is the course of Plato's *direction* from a further remark. Among the arguments Socrates raised to refute Thrasymachus' stance, at least one was certainly effective. It claims that among perfectly unjust individuals, that is, among convinced and consistent followers of supremacy or *pleonexia*, there can be no cooperation in exerting power, hence, no politics. They would in fact end up destroying each other (as has indeed happened umpteen times throughout history to the ruling groups who had taken power, we could certainly remark).

Not even a band of thieves, Socrates says, could function on the principles of pure and simple *pleonexia*, let alone an army, or a *polis*.

From this Socrates derives the necessity of a justice that may give the foundation to cooperative values and be based not on coercion or violence, but rather on consensus. An undoubtedly effective argumentation, although with the "historical" limitations we have pointed out.

And yet Socrates does not insist on the perfect blow he has struck; he does not go through with it. Or, we should rather say, going through with it will entail the whole journey of the *Republic*, of which Book I, dedicated to the confrontation with Thrasymachus, is the introduction.

What is really at stake here, however, I will try now to clarify by means of an example, to which we dedicate a scene from our backstage.

Scene XI: The Soldier and the Fort

60. Imagine a man who is presented with two packs of cards. The first contains twenty-five black cards and one red one; the second has twenty-five red cards and one black one. He must draw a card from whichever pack he chooses, knowing however that with the drawing of a black card he will die, whereas with the drawing of a red card he will continue to live.

An unlikely circumstance, you might say. But let me remind you of the Sphinx's riddle, equally trivial and yet connected to the risk of death. But isn't it equally trivial if you happen to find yourselves in the place and time when a bomb goes off, or when a stray bullet hits? That's life, we say in those cases . . .

Well now, a man must choose (as Paris, and everyone else, always must). How would you choose? Of course: you would choose, as everybody would, from the pack containing as many as twenty-five red cards. What would you say, though, if you were to draw precisely the only black card in it? Would you find, after some imaginable expletives we will not here repeat, consolation in telling yourselves that, after all, your choice was concordant with logic? But what kind of "logic" would that be if it causes us to die rather than saving our life?

And could you absolutely deny that, choosing instead from the pack with twenty-five black cards, you might perhaps have drawn the only red one? After all, isn't this precisely what happened to you in choosing the pack with twenty-five red cards and only one black one in it?

What is the meaning of this bizarre yet not implausible example? Simply this: that if we really want the choice to be concordant with "logic," then the interest provoking the choice must not be confined to our *self* but must rather ideally encompass the whole community of human beings—more generally, every imaginable rational community.

The author of the example says: "He who would not sacrifice his own soul to save the whole world is illogical in all his inferences taken collectively. Logic is rooted in the social principle."

In other words: to be "logical" the aforementioned choice must appeal not to the individual's fate (which cannot be guaranteed and thus remains subject to chance), but to the whole rational community to come. It is only in the name of the latter that it is statistically true that, by so choosing, human life will stand more chances of being saved.

61. Let us make a second example, closer to our subject matters. A regiment must storm an enemy fort. Every soldier who climbs the wall knows that he will probably be shot. Yet he also knows that if all the regiment, with which he identifies himself, were to rush forward as one, the fort would be taken.

Here, too, the "logical" behavior is the identification with the interests of the community represented by the regiment.

But I can well imagine that some of you have already thought the following. There might be, you say, an opportunistic soldier who reasons like this: "Look how my fellows *identify themselves* (with the regiment); there's no need for me to do the same; therefore, I will try to lag behind, while the others rush in. I will increase my odds of surviving and the fort will be taken anyway."

Congratulations! With subtle logic, you apply to the part (the opportunistic soldier) the logic of the whole; the fort will be taken yet he will be safe. You have not considered two circumstances, though. The first is that, in so speculating, the soldier is not actually a soldier any longer (or, to put it plainly, a man is no longer a man). And the second is that if everybody, or many people, were to do the same, the ethical community assumed by the example would cease to exist, which means that the fort would not be taken, and the lives would not be saved. I will limit myself to suggesting that this is precisely the logical defect of laissez-faire individualism.

The fact remains, however, that the entire reasoning is eventually based on a feeling of identification (we could also say of mutual recognition). The soldier must feel that he identifies with the community of the regiment. On a formal level, the logic is fatally abstract and inconclusive. To be considered as such, that is to say "logical," it must be ultimately founded on "feelings," or better, it must implicate desire—which is in fact the point I was trying to make.

Philosophical and merely rational pedagogy is not enough, not even if it calls on the whole logic of the universe as its justification and foundation (as Plato will in fact try to do in the *Timaeus*). It must include the education of desire and its exercise—education, not the simple, abstract repression. And yet what it means to educate desire is quite a complicated and mysterious matter. We will return to this.

Third Figure

The Origin of the State

Scene XII: Glaucon's Statement

62. After staging metics, rhetors, and sophists, Plato now calls upon Glaucon to speak and comes to grips with his people, the Athenian aristocrats, and with his own brothers.

We have already said that Glaucon, like Adeimantus, is a brave and intelligent young man. It is possible that Plato thinks of his two brothers as human paragons potentially suited, if philosophically educated, to become citizens and guardians of the renewed city. Still, it is a fact that they are clearly attracted to the radical and "libertine" intelligence of the oligarchical faction, that is, to characters such as Thrasymachus, Critias, Alcibiades, or Antiphon.

Glaucon criticizes Socrates' weak argumentations. He says he wants to hear a discourse both in favor and against justice and injustice. His request is modeled on the "banquet songs," in which the guests talked in praise or in censure of someone or something: a typical educational task of traditional poetry which now Plato seems to want to assign to philosophy.

Indeed, we can read here a "pedagogical" turning point that marks a crucial threshold for the establishment of a new political *areté*. Which will afterward find several confirmations.

63. In introducing his statement, Glaucon distinguishes three classes of desirable goods: for their own sakes, and independently of their

consequences; for their own sakes, and for their consequences; not for their own sakes, but only for the sake of some reward or result which flows from them (such as gymnastics and medicine).

Socrates identifies the second category as the most appropriate place for an inquiry on justice, consistent with the subject of happiness (*eudaimonia*): justice is itself good, and besides, it makes us happy.

We would say: the economic-political subject of life because the desire to be happy is at the bottom of every political choice (we have already heard of it from Aristotle). As a matter of fact, an abstract idea of the political and of justice, as has become familiar to us in modern times, would be meaningless to an ancient Greek.

The second category (desirable goods for their own sakes, and for their consequences) includes for example being in good health: a cue that will take on full light when Plato poses the problem of the soul's health, which works as a model for the city's health.

Health and salvation of humankind, of the soul, of the city: this will be the basis for a definition of justice, according to a foundational consistency that involves at the same time anthropology, psychology, and politics: in a word, philosophy. Only then, we could say, will Plato have adequately responded to his noble and brave brothers.

64. After these clarifications, Glaucon does not give Socrates leave to speak. He delivers, instead, a long speech that has been aptly defined a real "genealogy of morality." His intention is to corroborate Thrasymachus' strictly logical thesis, elaborating it in a more complete and convincing way—that is, giving it an origin and a concrete foundation.

First, he will show what is meant with justice and how it originates; secondly, that all men observe justice reluctantly, as an obligation rather than as a good falling within the aforementioned categories; and finally, that the life of the unjust man is far happier than the life of the just.

He adds, however, that in his heart he cannot share the theories he has just summarized. Nonetheless, he feels perplexed when he hears Thrasymachus and his ilk; whereas he has yet to hear an effective argument for the superiority of justice to injustice, and for how it makes people better and happier. And who else could make one but Socrates, who has been talking about it all his life? Therefore, he will praise the unjust life to the utmost of his power, with the expectation that Socrates will then praise the just life.

But now, let us listen to Glaucon's words.

65.

GLAUCON: They say that to do injustice is, by nature, good; to suffer injustice, evil; but that the evil is greater than the good. And so when men have both done and suffered injustice and have had experience of both, not being able to avoid the one and obtain the other, they think that they had better agree among themselves to have neither; hence there arise laws and mutual covenants; and that which is ordained by law is termed by them lawful and just. This they affirm to be the origin and nature of justice;—it is a mean or compromise, between the best of all, which is to do injustice and not be punished, and the worst of all, which is to suffer injustice without the power of retaliation; and justice, being at a middle point between the two, is tolerated not as a good, but as the lesser evil, and honored by reason of the inability of men to do injustice. For no man who is worthy to be called a man would ever submit to such an agreement if he were able to resist; he would be mad if he did. Such is the received account, Socrates, of the nature and origin of justice.

Now that those who practice justice do so involuntarily and because they have not the power to be unjust will best appear if we imagine something of this kind: having given both to the just and the unjust power to do what they will, let us watch and see whither desire will lead them; then we shall discover in the very act the just and unjust man to be proceeding along the same road, following their interest, which all natures deem to be their good, and are only diverted into the path of justice by the force of law.

The liberty which we are supposing may be most completely given to them in the form of such a power as is said to have been possessed by Gyges the ancestor of Croesus the Lydian. According to the tradition, Gyges was a shepherd in the service of the king of Lydia; there was a great storm, and an earthquake made an opening in the earth at the place where he was feeding his flock. Amazed at the sight, he descended into the opening, where, among other marvels, he beheld a hollow brazen horse, having doors, at which he stooping and looking in saw a dead body of stature, as appeared to him, more than human, and having nothing on but a gold ring; this he took from the finger of the dead and reascended. Now the shepherds met together, according to custom, that they might send their monthly report about the flocks to the king; into their assembly he came having the ring on his finger, and as he was sitting among them he chanced to turn the collet of the ring inside his hand, when instantly he became invisible to the rest of the company and they began to speak of him as if he were no longer present. He was astonished at this, and again touching the ring he turned the collet outwards and reappeared; he made several trials of the ring, and always with the same result—when he turned the collet inwards he became invisible, when outwards he reappeared. Whereupon he contrived to be chosen one of the messengers who were sent to the court; where as soon as he arrived he seduced the queen, and with her help conspired against the king and slew him, and took the kingdom.

Suppose now that there were two such magic rings, and the just put on one of them and the unjust the other; no man can be imagined to be of such an iron nature that he would stand fast in justice. No man would keep his hands off what was not his own when he could safely take what he liked out of the market, or go into houses and lie with anyone at his pleasure, or kill or release from prison whom he would, and in all respects be like a God among men. Then the actions of the just would be as the actions of the unjust; they would both come at last to the same point.

And this we may truly affirm to be a great proof that a man is just, not willingly or because he thinks that justice is any good to him individually, but of necessity, for wherever anyone thinks that he can safely be unjust, there he is unjust. For all men believe in their hearts that injustice is far more profitable to the individual than justice, and he who argues as I have been supposing, will say that they are right. If you could imagine anyone obtaining this power of becoming invisible, and never doing any wrong or touching what was another's, he would be thought by the lookers-on to be a most wretched idiot, although they would praise him to one another's faces, and keep up appearances with one another from a fear that they too might suffer injustice. Enough of this.

Scene XIII: Virtue According to Glaucon

66. We could clearly say many things about this. But let me deflect your attention, for the time being, from the extraordinary tale of Gyges: we will come back to it in a little while.

It is easy to notice how Plato puts into Glaucon's mouth the opposition between law and nature, *nomos* and *physys*, which was widespread in fifth-century sophistry. But we should not take the matter as a self-evident historiographical observation, or as something obvious. Here Plato appropriates a crucial threshold which is at the same time very problematic and worthy of some backstage remarks.

I think you will easily understand me if I observe that people always start from "culture" (and always from a culture defined in its own way) to determine by contrast what "nature" would be. What happens is that a definite cultural figure, retroflecting the figure of its specific threshold, looks at and sees itself, retrospectively, in its difference from so-called nature, which is thereby established as such. The same happens when we establish the difference between human beings and animals.

At this point, many reasons would call for a painstaking genealogical analysis of these notions, which is in fact nonexistent.

On the contrary, people mostly take for granted the intuitiveness of this difference and passage from nature to culture, without having any problematic awareness of it.

Moreover, it must be noted that the myth of the Adamic fall from the Garden of Eden, which Kant will read as a passage from nature to culture, results from an assimilation of the Christian culture with Greek culture. The whole "historical" conception of human life originates here, with a sort (to put it briefly) of synthesis between Antiphon (Plato) and Augustine (Vico). The entire Western political ideology is deeply affected by it and in some ways derives from it.

67. And yet, holding on to our behind-the-scenes path, we see the matter this way: the discussion on the "political"—from the sophists to Plato—projects the "state of nature" backward to constitute and justify the construction of *politiké areté*. (Augustine, too, wanted to construct an Earthly Jerusalem, while waiting for the coming of the Heavenly and ultimate Jerusalem.)

On closer look, this point reveals the ideological character of Western political philosophy, along with its anthropology, psychology, economics, and so forth.

Going back to Glaucon: from the opposition *physis/nomos* he draws the idea of a state of nature that would precede the social contract. It is in this contract that the notion of justice is grounded. By nature, in fact, man would tend toward violent and unjust abuse (*adikein*).

It has been noted that even Thucydides, educated like his contemporaries by the great tragic lesson of the Peloponnesian War and by the internal conflicts deriving from it, describes man as naturally afflicted by the desire to overpower others and by the ambitious desire to be honored (*pleonexia* and *philotimia*). This would be the natural field of anthropology, characterized by its fundamental instincts—the will to power and the universal desire to be admired, to quote again Nietzsche.

68. However, as we heard, no one is strong enough to afford to commit abuse without ever undergoing the injured party's retaliation; equally, no one is sure of being always able to avenge the injury received. A dialectic between wrongdoing and being wronged is thereby begun, which is extremely dangerous and painful. Particularly, we experience that suffering a wrong without being able to avenge it is, of all evils, the worst that can happen to a human being, and, especially, to a Greek.

To avoid it, because of the common and general *weakness* (mind you), human beings make a compact (*syntheke*) with one another: neither to commit nor to suffer injustice. Here is, then, the shared rule that seals the equality of everybody before the law (as Hippias and other sophists observed). In other words, here comes "justice."

In putting the matter like this, however, it is obvious, or at least easy, for the law to be perceived by everyone as a limitation and a violent act against nature, and that people will accept it only out of weakness. "Discontent in morals," someone said, with a brilliant implicit reference to the "discontent in civilization" mentioned by Freud.

We should add that in so doing Glaucon (Plato) boldly, if not shamelessly, reverses the famous Socratic theory according to which nobody does evil of their own free will. In Glaucon's opinion, instead, this is the way things stand: nobody avoids evil of their own free will, but only out of fear.

69. There follows a description of the citizens' common behavior, based on what we would call today a thought experiment. If we did not know

that it is Plato who makes him talk and invents his character, we would consider Glaucon as one of the most original Greek thinkers. And here we must underline a very significant passage. A "real man's" behavior, Glaucon says, would consist in pursuing abuse. Renouncing this "real man's" *ethos* shows that the citizens who are subject to the compact, which they chose out of weakness, are basically lesser men: pale social stand-ins for the true man by nature.

Being openly real men, however, is too hazardous. Thus, a separation between public and private conduct comes into play: *in public* people praise justice and follow the law; *in private*, instead, they covertly pursue injustice, that is, abuse, whenever this is possible without being caught.

Note how there emerges here the traditional separation between public and private as constitutive features of political economy. We have already seen how Aristotle considers these two spheres as self-evident and natural, that is to say, founded on the needs of a supposed nature in general, and on human nature in particular. I would say we have never moved forward from there.

70. Glaucon goes on in his speech to state what he means by political virtue, which I will summarize quickly for you. Essentially, politics is a "strategy of injustice," and a man of virtue is he who can practice it in the best way, namely, more inflexibly, cynically, consistently, and effectively.

Glaucon describes this strategy in detail. A man of political shrewdness, that is of *virtue*, needs above all a lot of courage—like the courage of the "real man"; and then he needs craftiness, resoluteness, and oratorical strength to persuade his audience and achieve public consensus. He also needs money to arrange political banquets and reinforce his public fame. For these purposes he must obtain many friends, also courageous and effective, who will be his accomplices, and with whom he will hatch secret plans in total defiance of the law. Such a man, capable in public of feigning respect for the general interest according to the rules of fairness, will stop at nothing, not even at organized murder, to eliminate his enemies or to appropriate someone else's belongings. Such a man has then thoroughly restored "natural" abuse, by acting stealthily and hiding his actions from the law.

Still not satisfied, Glaucon now shows Socrates how, inevitably, the just man cannot possibly be happy. Unversed in trickery and unable artfully to build a good reputation for himself, he will fatally end up defeated, a victim of someone else's violence: in which we cannot fail to perceive a touch of tragic irony from Plato. He puts into his brother's mouth, who is talking to Socrates, the prophecy of ruin and death for his master (repeating a similar situation in *Gorgias* as well).

Then, it is not difficult to understand why, during the *Republic*, Socrates calls Glaucon and Adeimantus "sons of Thrasymachus."

This does not mean that Glaucon subscribes totally to Thrasymachus' theories. As has been noted, justice is for Thrasymachus only an effect of power. Whereas for Glaucon the "compact" underlies the laws, so that they are no longer the tool of power, but rather a protection, although fragile, for the weak.

This puts Glaucon on a par with Callicles (the laws are an invention of the "weak") but without aristocratic nostalgias toward a social class that would by nature be "worthy."

In particular, and with the aim to restore the "natural" right to overpower the weak, Glaucon relies on secrecy (of which the tale of Gyges is an example). This secrecy comes therefore to constitute the essential core of political *technique* (another way to say *areté*), a thesis that still holds undeniable relevance for us today.

We may observe that Glaucon's position has its parallel in the well-known theory of Critias, who boldly claimed that the Gods are merely a human invention, a political expedient. The Gods would be, in other words, a "psychological" means to frighten those who privately—that is, on the sly—are inclined to break the law, since the Gods see us and watch us even in private (remember Cephalus).

Scene XIV: The Bonds of the Law

71. It is refreshing to compare the character of Glaucon (rather than comparing him to Critias), to the historical figure of Antiphon, an Athenian rhetorician and politician—a comparison that has been duly suggested and widely analyzed.

Indeed, Antiphon's political action might well have inspired a page of *Laws*, where Plato recalls the bad masters who teach that the laws are not by nature but by convention and by political technique. As a result, justice, no less than the Gods, would be merely a practical invention that the bravest and boldest youth can skillfully violate. These bad masters teach how to defeat, overpower, and dominate people using force so as to live a true life according to nature, rather than submitting to others according to the law.

To begin with, Antiphon distinguishes the truth (*aletheia*) of the rules according to nature from the merely arguable nature (*doxa*) of laws. The latter are nothing except impediments and obligations (*desma*) artificially imposed on human nature. Here Antiphon is fully in agreement with the position of the character Callicles in Plato's *Gorgias*.

But let us give, without further ado, the floor to Antiphon himself, so that we can hear how he describes, indeed in the most efficient and resolute manner, the social control of people's conduct enforced by the law.

> ANTIPHON: For laws have been established for the eyes what they should and should not see, and for the ears what they should and should not hear, and for the tongue what it should and should not say, and for the hands what they should and should not do, and for the feet where they should and should not go, and for the mind what it should and should not desire (*epithymein*).

72. This admirable sample of the "microphysics of power" denounces the intolerable coercion exerted by laws over individual nature. In fact, the laws come from an agreement (*homologethenta*) that is at the origins of the *polis*, so that justice consists simply in the obligation not to transgress these "names."

The juxtaposition law/nature, we said, is a common trait of a part of sophistic culture, but the theory of the contractual origin of justice is specific to Antiphon. And Glaucon, too, supports it.

This relation between the two men even takes on the appearance of a verbatim reprise of Antiphon, if we consider how Antiphon specifies the essential requirement of justice: "Not to do harm or injustice and not to suffer it."

We arrive at a similar conclusion if we read the fragments of Antiphon's treatise *On Truth*, in which are drawn with great accuracy the political and moral conclusions of the juxtaposition nature/law and the conventionalist conception of justice. "Thus a man," Antiphon said, "would best employ justice to his own advantage if he were to deem the laws as important when witnesses are present, whereas when in the absence of witnesses he were to deem the requirements of nature as of greater importance." In fact, "someone who violates what was established to be just avoids shame and punishment if he can keep out of sight (or, remain hidden, *lathe*) from those who have established the laws."

73. We do not know what Glaucon, Plato's noble older brother, really thought or said, although there is no denying that Plato shaped a character with many references to the "wise" Antiphon.

The fact remains, however, that Plato, as already with Thrasymachus, takes the theories of others to a conceptual level of extraordinary height and consistency, so as to create antagonists worthy of his theater and his revolutionary philosophical and political doctrine, which is stunningly powerful and elaborate.

It is not difficult to note how much of Plato's Thrasymachus and Glaucon is present in Hobbes, who was indeed a good connoisseur of fifth-century BCE literature. He claimed (unlike Locke and Rousseau, who did not deem the state of nature necessarily violent) that men are all fundamentally equal in this: everybody can kill each other and everybody wishes to do so.

In like manner Nietzsche, in *The Genealogy of Morals*, will describe the establishment of "morality" as the fruit of the revolt of the slaves, that is, of the "weak." The so-called "values" are then nothing but the fruit of fear and resentment. Which reveals the ideological characteristic of Socratic morality: it teaches what is called "not wanting to take revenge"; but the truth is that such a habit is simply the consequence of "not being able to take revenge," as would desire the sound instincts of the "real man"—a man not yet nihilistically dead and corrupt.

Scene XV: Gyges' *Katabasis*

74. I trust you will remember, in all its details, the tale of Gyges told by Glaucon, because the time has come for us to reckon with it.

Gyges goes down into the abyss in the earth, into the *chasma* (it is the second in the *Republic*) and beholds several marvels (*thaumasta*): the bronze horse, the giant corpse wearing a gold ring on his finger, and so forth; not to mention the marvels he will see next.

In the meantime, let us ask ourselves, with the aid of the scholars who have dealt with the matter—who is Gyges? A fictional character or a historical character? The tale, in fact, is very old and Plato's version is just one among many.

There was in fact a historical Gyges who in 662 fought against the Cimmerians, and he might be the Guggu king of the Luddu mentioned in the Assyrian tablets of the Assurbanipal temple.

In this regard, an entry in *The Oxford Classical Dictionary* is of great significance: "Gyges, king of Lydia (ca. 680–645 BC), founded the Mermnad dynasty by murdering King Candaules and marrying his widow. The word 'tyrant' . . . first appears in Greek applied to Gyges. He started the exploitation of gold from the Pactolus; attacked Miletus and Smyrna, captured Colophon and sent sumptuous offerings to Delphi. He gained Assyrian protection against the Cimmerians, but lost it later by helping Psammetichus I of Egypt . . ."

The two references to the name "tyrant" and to the exploitation of gold, which will eventually bring the invention of coinage (in Lydia around 630 BCE, as it seems), are also very important for us. As to the first reference, we are forced to reckon with the tyrannical nature of man and his desires, which is certainly a crucial theme in the *Republic* as well as in its anthropology and psychology. We might ask ourselves whether Plato does not actually mean the naked giant in the tale as a symbolization of the tyrant. As to the second reference, which will have ample developments below, we are brought back to Cephalus.

Of course, we cannot know to what extent our reconstruction of Plato's direction is punctually correct; but from a genealogical perspective this is a side issue because the economy of writing and the underground influence of the text cannot be reduced to the author's painstakingly accurate awareness.

75. Let us now consider the abyss, the *chasma* into which Gyges sinks or descends. That is an evident allusion to the realm of the dead. In fact, it has to do with a *chthonian* descent into Mother Earth's womb, which sooner or later becomes everyone's grave. This determines the birth of a new condition, as will happen in the last *chasma* of the *Republic*, with the myth of Er.

We are anxious, however, to emphasize primarily the connection to the first *chasma*, with Socrates' going down to the Piraeus—an act we interpreted as a descent into the *bowels of desire*, an initiatory descent and ritual death with a view to a new condition of life or a new economy of life.

Now, the new condition that Gyges acquires is a sort of magic *invisibility*. This invisibility enables someone to possess anything they desire: goods, bodies, forbidden deeds, and so forth, so that the new condition functions like a transferal object—like the girdle, which seduces those who look at it, or like money, which we exchange for everything.

We begin to understand that Plato connects the topic of power and of its genesis or foundation with the pair visibility/invisibility: a public visibility hiding a secret invisibility of its own. We already know something about this, but we are still missing the greater part, and we need not try to give an answer now.

76. Let us get to the horse. It is obviously reminiscent of the famous Trojan horse and its trickery, concealed and therefore invisible. Its cracks are an evident metaphor of the threshold; once again, we are dealing with a passage to a different dimension, that is, with an initiation. We should also remember that Babylon's royal gates, at the time of the Hittites, constituted for the subjects the impassable thresholds of power. Similarly, we could say, Pythagoras' disciples were prohibited from lifting the curtain behind which the master imparted his teachings: they had to wait until the end of the initiation.

For the Eastern peoples, moreover, the horse is a symbol of royalty, and its nature is magic. As to the connection of the horse with the sea deities (which bring us back to the Piraeus) the examples are countless and well known.

At this point, some of you might wonder what the purpose is of such meticulous analyses of the tale. I can only say two things. The first is that we will appreciate better all its usefulness and weight later. Secondly, there is no question that the fable of Gyges is just as important for Plato, and its function is not merely that of an example. Suffice it to note that Plato makes explicit reference to it precisely at the end of the *Republic* when Socrates wraps up his speech. He affirms, peremptorily: "Justice in her own nature has been shown to be best for the soul in her own nature. Let a man do what is just, whether he has the ring of Gyges or not, and even if in addition to the ring of Gyges he put on the helmet of Hades" (whose similar quality as a purveyor of invisibility is attested in Homer, Hesiod, etc.). This mention of Gyges appears in a much later place in the text, in a passage of a lofty, conclusive tenor, and for these reasons it cannot be deemed merely occasional. Rather the opposite is true. In fact, many interpreters have read in the tale of Gyges either an allegory of the entire *Republic* or a portrayal of the sophist's wiliness together with the tyrant's violence, or even the reference to the sophistic distortion of truth through deceiving speeches, symbolized by the effects of turning the ring on the finger, and so on.

Scene XVI: The Power of Glances

77. Now we must go deeper and touch on an issue that is decisive for us in every sense. The issue is the acquisition of power through a woman (in our case, the queen).

It has been noted that the tale of Gyges reproduces, in this respect, the dynamics of many sovereignty myths having at their core the transition of kingship through a woman. I am not just talking about the possible echoes of a matrilineal succession, but also about the legends in which the story revolves around a woman who bestows power on a man she has chosen.

The point of the matter is, obviously, *power*. A man takes a woman away from another man, thereby becoming her lord or master. The examples are countless: the Rape of the Sabine Women, originating the Roman ceremony of the fake matrimonial abduction; Oedipus and Jocasta; Aegisthus and Clytemnestra; the Suitors of Penelope (who will not succeed); and so on. We should also remember, in J. G. Frazer's *The Golden Bough*, the fight between the young aspirant and the old king who, if defeated or killed, will lose his power as well as his wives.

78. At first sight, the matter seems to move contrary to the myth of the girdle of Venus, where it is a man who chooses a woman. But reading deeper into it, we ought to emphasize the enchanting circle of seduction/power. Which goes like this: Paris, dazzled by the girdle, gives Venus the attribute of seducing beauty. Venus, in return, gives Paris the *power* of possessing Helen, by seducing her and stealing her from Menelaus.

However, something doesn't add up in this plot. Let's see why.

By possessing Helen, Paris does not inherit any political power. The reason is simple: because he does not kill Menelaus, which would settle the matter by closing the circle of succession. Hence the Trojan War. But let me remind you that, significantly, at some point in the *Iliad* there is growing support for the idea that the conflict should be solved with a duel between Paris and Menelaus. Everybody agrees and preparations begin. This would indeed be the "right" solution, according to traditional customs. However, as we all know, the initiative falls through, on the account of which the Trojans and the Achaeans will have to suffer endless woes.

The event clearly indicates the peculiar and specific nature of the Trojan War, which the Greek people, in their imagination, place halfway between myth and history: it is the threshold that marks the transit from a universe of meaning to another. Using one of G. F. Creuzer's categories, we could speak of "historical legend."

Its confirmation is found in the well-known episode of the dispute between Athenians and Spartans over who should have command of the army in facing the Persian invasion. The Spartans claim it on the strength of their mythical descent from Agamemnon. Essentially, they see in the Persian Wars nothing but the return of the mythical archetype of the Trojan War. But the Athenians oppose them successfully, by advancing the profane and prosaic argument that they own the fleet and without their navy there is no hope of defeating the Persians. Thus, the mythical precedent is repressed. The way is open for the feat of Alexander the Great, the armed wing of philosophy, with which begins what Schiller and Hegel will understand as "universal history"—the great daydream of the Western alphabet culture and its "scientific" historiography, which has in Herodotus and Thucydides its original fathers.

79. After this digression we can return to Gyges. The tale recalls a myth on the foundation of power, a power that specifies itself in tyranny and money. It is noteworthy that in another version of the story, as Lucian reports it, the ring is given to Gyges by Hermes, the God of trickery, of cunning, of nighttime thievery and adultery, that is, of a forbidden nocturnal world.

However, we must add, Hermes is also the God of eloquence and writing. There emerges here, then, the essential nexus *speech/writing/money*: an observation, as we will see, of crucial importance to us. Especially if we add that the dead body is invisible, the soul is invisible, the meaning of words is invisible, and finally the value of money is invisible. Here is the universe of meaning that is gradually manifesting itself.

It is above all noteworthy that Herodotus (certainly known to Plato) tells a whole different story about Gyges, one in which there is no horse, dead body, or ring; as well as, apparently, no *katabasis* at all, no descent into the abyss.

Here the nexus of visible and invisible is expressed in a completely different way, that is, in the subtle connection of reciprocally constituted glances; and perhaps there is not even a transferal object, unless the queen's clothes can be interpreted as such.

80. Here is, in short, Herodotus' version. King Candaules wants Gyges, a squire and member of his guard, to admire the queen's naked body, of which he is very proud. Thus, he tells Gyges to wait near the threshold of the bridal chamber, under cover of the night, so that he can behold the queen as she undresses. However, it happens that the queen suddenly turns around, sees Gyges, and says to him, "Now, there are two avenues open to you: either to die at once, for you have seen what you should not have seen, and so that you should not see other forbidden things; or to kill the king, and take both me and the kingdom." Gyges' choice is not so difficult to imagine. Indeed, he possesses the queen, lying with her on the nuptial bed. Then they both wait for the king's arrival in the middle of the night and together they kill him. And so it was that Gyges went from squire to king.

Note this: it all happens during the night, weaver of deceptions, so that night itself represents here the *chasma*, the dark abyss of desire connected, as Freud had it, with the "criminal" dreams that night gives birth to or lets surface (the tale, in a modern psychological version, might simply express a dream of Gyges, the squire, or even of the queen herself). The desire to overpower, possess, and kill that we all harbor, as Glaucon says, and Hobbes will repeat.

There is also the enigmatic play of glances. Gyges must see without being seen, but *he is seen*, and therefore he must assume power in every sense by killing. The queen must be seen without seeing, but instead *she sees*, she sees herself being seen, and so she becomes the giver of power—that is to say, the "right" to be violent, both in private, toward Candaules, and in public, toward the subjects.

What does this all mean? We must be patient and wait like every-body else on the threshold of this secret and its wonders (*thaumasta*) before we offer an answer.

Scene XVII: Socrates' Two Moves

81. In response first to the speech of Glaucon, and then to the some-what similar speech of Adeimantus, Socrates makes two moves that will become crucial for the dialectical path of Plato's *Republic*. Let us give for the moment a simple description of them.

With the first move, Socrates shifts the quest for justice from the individual to the state. You should remember that the initial question was whether the unjust man was happy or not. From private to public, then, which are the two places brought forth in Glaucon's speech and reiterated in the moral fable of Gyges. In private, hidden from the public compact that establishes justice, we go back to natural *pleonexia*. But now Socrates suggests we look at the matter from the point of view of a "writing" greater than that of the individual, specifically, the "writing" of the "state." We will see what this means.

The second move reconstructs the genesis of the state starting from people's needs. Human society would thus arise to meet the "natural" need.

In both moves, as we can see, the issue of desire disappears. More generally, we shall have to say that with these two moves Socrates retroflexes the reason of state to circumscribe and subjugate desire. A surprising design, if it is true that the initial issue was, on the contrary, how from desire there arise both power and the state.

The point is that we should never forget that we are constantly faced with a clever *mise-en-scène* of rhetorical discourses: a whirl of mirror-plays embodied by fictional characters that are the masks of Plato's philosophical theater, who aims with his direction at achieving the political foundation that may coincide with his philosophical vision of truth and the Good.

That is exactly why we must hold fast to our behind-the-scenes work, reviving continuously its thread.

82. Let's see, then. The quest for justice, thought of as the essence and condition of the political, had begun from the analysis of desire: in short, food, sex, money. Which gives rise to the universal desire to overpower others, obviously to get food, sex, and money. An additional factor is the desire for "renown" (*philotimia*), as Thucydides said, significantly presented by Aristotle as a desire for immortality, for the aim of which we justify the command of those who can predict with intelligence.

Or put differently, the living beings desire to possess other living beings; they desire to "assimilate" them. Both directly (food and sex) and indirectly (through the mediation of the "sign" as a transferal object: speech/money/writing).

Might this not be—we could wonder—precisely the "origin of speech," that is, the mediated realization of possession of which speech is the tool? For the moment, we must be satisfied with the question.

83. Now, Glaucon presents the dynamics of desire as a natural fact: it characterizes the condition of the "real man." In the human being, then, there is a "titanic," wild nature that precedes political society, established on the conventional nonaggression pact: it enshrines an equity and a prescriptive justice which are in turn conventional.

Yet our genealogical reading, a backstage reading that takes into consideration the retroflex effects of the step back of speech, reads the matter as follows: Plato, through the mask of Glaucon, *stages* the state of nature to justify the social state.

This supposed state of nature is presented as a natural and somewhat eternal condition connected in this sense to the living conditions of the Gods. A God is in fact he who, benefiting from the condition of invisibility, can do whatever he wants: stealing in the marketplaces, sleeping with anyone he wants, raping and killing with impunity anyone at will. Whoever can do this behaves just like a God, because there are no limits to desire (to its originally possessive and criminal nature) and this would in fact be, according to the traditional mentality adopted by Glaucon, the divine condition.

Yet natural desire cannot be satisfied. It befits an immortal God, not a mortal being, because its fulfilment leads everybody to the risk of unavenged sorrow and ultimately of death. Hence the necessity of the compact.

Of course. Is such a universal desire to overpower others, however, conceivable as an original "natural" condition of the living? Because if it is, such a natural impulse would have led every living species to extinction long ago. Which means we must read the profound truth of Glaucon's speech in a whole different way.

84. The backstage of Glaucon's words is a retroflexion effect: starting from the already constituted social *hybris* of men (not at all "natural") we retroactively posit a natural condition as the justificatory origin of social laws and political justice, as well as of the conventional legitimacy of its legally binding force.

As Glaucon puts it, we agree to establish a law (*nomos*) that abolishes prevarication (*pleonexia*). Yet this social convention does violence to "nature," and that is why political *areté* maintains its effectiveness and its justice within a double behavior—visible and invisible. The former in accordance with enacted laws, the latter with the nature of the "real man."

And so, as we have seen, through this *rhetorical tale*, the *public* sphere and the *private* sphere come to constitute themselves: the former visible, the latter invisible. We should remember Antiphon: "For laws have been established for the eyes what they should and should not see . . ."

Hence, we might observe, the traditional public character of truth, which goes hand in hand with the public truths of language. But precisely this institutive gesture creates the space for lying, that is, for the private intention of lying. As Nietzsche said in his Basel lectures, truth is nothing more than the agreement to lie with the herd in a canonical manner, or rather, in accordance with the conformism of linguistic conventions. Which are of course at the root of every economic exchange, to begin with the institution of money, and the resulting social *hybris*.

85. After these considerations, let us return to Gyges. We have seen how in the story that stages him, the play between visible and invisible is essential and constant. What is to be crucial for the achievement of power and for the fulfillment of desire is the fruitful exercise of invisibility.

Which generates further echoes: it is the girdle that makes Aphrodite's sex invisible and therefore desirable; just as Adam and Eve, once they leave the Garden of Eden, discover their nudity, and hide it with a transferal object (the fig leaf) which makes their nudity desirable.

And yet at this point we too discover something—something very important indeed. That this nexus of visible and invisible can work as an Ariadne's thread and can bring us to understand the meaning of the third and crucial *chasma* of the *Republic*: the famous myth of the cave, which is the culminating place of Plato's strategy or *mise-en-scène* of philosophy as *politiké areté*.

We should in fact consider this. Socrates says: "The enquiry would be of a serious nature, and would require very good eyes . . ." There is no doubt, we could remark. It is a matter of seeing the invisible!

There ensues the first, extraordinary move we have mentioned, although we should now focus on its literal *mise-en-scène*. Let us conjure up Socrates again backstage.

86.

SOCRATES: Seeing then, I said, that we are no great wits,
I think that we had better adopt a method which I may

illustrate thus; suppose that a short-sighted person had been asked by someone to read small letters (*grammata*) from a distance; and it occurred to someone else that they might be found in another place which was larger and in which the letters were larger—if they were the same and he could read the larger letters first, and then proceed to the lesser—this would have been thought a rare piece of good fortune.

Socrates' example (but is it just an example?) shows moreover that the metaphor of the letters (but is it really a metaphor?) hints at the necessity of having recourse to a model, a type, an archetype in order to enter the realm of vision: and this is only a foretaste of the function that the ideas will have within the philosopher's supersensible vision.

However, if in a real genealogical sense, the ideas happen to model themselves on the letters (that is to say, they model on the "logical mind," which is an effect of the practice of alphabetic writing), then the entire example is just a *symptom* (which by the way Plato will take up again in the *Statesman*) of the constitutive blindness that has made possible the Platonic vision of philosophical truth. And that is what I am confident will emerge in our future journey.

In the meantime, we can already observe that with the example of the alphabet Socrates reveals his intention to move beyond the sophists' conventionalist individualism. Plato is showing (as later will Aristotle) that the whole, that is, the *model*, is prior to its parts: it gives them meaning and specifies them as parts. In fact, whenever we establish a convention, we need to assume an already-constituted community, and consequently a common language.

Nevertheless, this move no longer considers the demands of desire, which are neither individual nor collective nor communal: they are in every sense of the word pre-categorial and pre-semiotic. Therefore, what eludes the grasp of political philosophy (or, for that matter, of any "concept") is precisely being-subject *to* desire, and specifically to those drives which, as we have seen, are originally constitutive and formative of the individual.

87. For the same reason, even Socrates' second move fails to solve the political issue, which consists in retroflecting the *need* as the supposed origin of social relations. If that were the case, there would be no need for a political virtue either, as the very logic of needs calls for agreement and peace.

But humans partly want peace (or constantly *claim* they want it) and partly don't, and at worst they don't want it at all, because the desire for supremacy and renown manifestly prevails in them. While claiming they want and hope for peace, because of these constitutive passions, human beings are always taking risks of one kind or another and they cannot refrain from competition, from aggressiveness, and at worst from war.

So, it is no accident that Plato excludes from his ideal state the "passionate" generation (which is in fact the root cause of fame and *nomen*, or recognition), as well as the possession of money and goods. On this point, his communitarian thought is certainly more profound; yet the thought of all sophists, and future empiricists, is pragmatically more effective (the same happens, in modern times, between Hegel's political thought and Locke's).

Establishing public desire for the good of the community through a philosophical *paideia* may be metaphysically more profound insofar as the community comes before the individual; but at the same time, it fails the moment it must (because it must) concretely confront the individual's private desire, which must eventually prevail. In fact, it is much easier to perceive the private invisibility of the pull of desire than the supersensible invisibility of the Good.

The organic universality of the concept is right, but the logic of reason is only a scene or a *mise-en-scène* and it is not original. As we will see later, it is a rational transcription of the involving globality of the sacred in its original commerce with the exercise of sexuality.

88. The empiricist conventionalism, on the contrary, is well satisfied with leaving room for a private desire of individual happiness (a desire pertaining by now to profane individuals, although empiricism does not care about its genesis and does not see it as a problem: empiricism takes things as they are and that is good enough). Such a conventionalism, in fact, does not mind the contradictoriness of its reasons and arguments, altogether inconsistent and naïve compared to the metaphysical reasons of Plato, Hegel, Marx, or Gentile. This conventionalism is just satisfied with its practical success and the resulting occasional consent, but without being able to explain it, except with moralistic rhetorical arguments and ideological assumptions.

That is why we feel it is necessary to surmount the logic of the concept if we want to understand both the limits of *politiké areté* and the limits of any empiricist solution, given that the latter is effectively unable, and indeed increasingly unable, to overcome the constitutive *pleonexìa* of political life as well as the worldwide social existence of these days.

We must therefore reiterate: Socrates' two moves (the subordination of the individual to the state and the construal of the genesis of the state from necessity, with the attendant repression of desire, of *epithymia*) amount to a retroflexion of the reason of state with a view to circumscribing desire.

The reason of state is established by retroflecting an imaginary, peaceful natural state, ruled only by natural need (the first cell of the modern myth of the noble savage).

89. In fact, though, it is from the already consolidated social *hybris* of human society that we derive the fantasy of an original (originative of society) natural need. A social *hybris* that must be understood primarily as a *hybris* of *language and exchange*: both constitute the invisible "value." It is this *hybris* that *creates* need.

In other words, need is inscribed in desire, which is inherent in speech (the center in our cross of forms of knowledge we illustrated in the beginning) although it remains a mystery to us what it is that speech itself desires.

There emerges here a dark background connecting the urge for economic exchange with language: the whole economy of life and death, as we will see, is marked by it.

In conclusion, let us conjure up backstage the ghost of Adam Smith, because he was the first, I think, to get wind of the matter.

> This division of labor, from which so many advantages are derived, is not originally the effect of any human wisdom, which foresees and intends that general opulence to which it gives occasion. It is the necessary, though very slow and gradual consequence of a certain propensity in human nature which has in view no such extensive utility; the propensity to truck, barter, and exchange one thing for another. Whether this propensity be one of those original principles in human nature of which no further account can be given; or whether, as seems more probable, it be the necessary consequence of the faculties of reason and speech, it belongs not to our

present subject to inquire. It is common to all men, and to be found in no other race of animals, which seem to know neither this nor any other species of contracts.[1]

(End of Act I)

1. Adam Smith, *An Inquiry into the Nature of Causes of the Wealth of Nations*, Book I, chap. 2, "Of the Principle Which Gives Occasion to the Division of Labour," edited by Edwin Cannan, with a new preface by George J. Stigler (University of Chicago Press, 1977), facsimile of the 1904 edition, 29—Trans.

Interlude

90. It is even more necessary, you will surely agree, to pick up the thread of what happened onstage and backstage so that we can better understand it before we go any further.

Now let us go back to the beginning, that is, to the issue of "political virtue." It marks, in the West, an inaugural event characterized by the proposal for a peculiar philosophic anthropology.

Philosophy and politics, we have said, arise together, one for the other: they are "forms of knowledge" that announce themselves on the threshold of the Greek desecration of *logos*—a desecration that has in the propagation of the practice of alphabetical writing one of its essential conditions.

We are saying, in other words, that establishing the category of the political called for a preliminary anthropological foundation involving a peculiar vision of what would be human. When Aristotle speaks of man as a political animal, or of an animal gifted with speech, he perfectly summarizes the results of this (presenting them and leading us to believe they are "origins").

And yet we must be careful not to expose the speck in other people's eye while ignoring the beam that blinds our own. We too, in fact, as well as our language, frequent that very internal circulation within the forms of knowledge (politics, anthropology, philosophy, economics, etc.) about which he talks. We too, by exposing its threshold, are seized by it: we are seized by the coming of philosophy, that is, by the philosophical *episteme* as Plato means it.

That is exactly why we are reflecting on this inaugural gesture, whose advent we find in a paradigmatic place: Plato's *Republic*, precisely.

We can never ignore, however, the problematic character of this backstage consideration. Showing the pre-categorial circulation of certain practices of discourse as breeding ground for the disciplinary foundation of politics, economics, psychology, anthropology, and linguistics—established over the centuries as specialist forms of knowledge—does not free us at all from being already talking, in a general and at the same time specialized way, as philosophical subjects (and therefore, in a derivative sense, also as political, economic, psychological, etc., subjects).

Even in the process of staging our backstage, we are always-already captured by these canonical and public figures of the encyclopedia of knowledge, in accordance with a definite cultural sense.

91. And so, when we speak of genealogy, we face up to the threshold phenomenon that differentiates between the stated meaning and its event. For instance, behind the meanings Plato stated in his practice of writing—in the theatrical setting of his dialogues, in the mimetic and dramatic features of his characters—we try to find the event of this same Platonic gesture: namely, the anteflexed and retroflexed threshold function it exercises.

What is certain is that the meaning of this gesture cannot be "defined," cannot be "circumscribed" in the light of the meanings inscribed in this same gesture, that is, of the meanings it puts into action, or rather, *onstage*.

In other words, we cannot define *philosophically* Plato's gesture, the practice it was subject to, because philosophy was precisely the result and the objectified meaning of that very gesture. Doing so would inevitably be inadequate and naïve.

Therefore the "thing" which starting from Plato takes on, both for him and for us, the character of philosophy and politics cannot be captured philosophically in its event. If philosophy and politics are figures inscribed in Plato's gesture, those figures cannot define their own circumscribed event.

This situation could be put as follows: we cannot *say* what happens, yet insofar as something happens, we *can* say it. The saying, that is, follows the happening and retroflexes itself into it. And yet it is merely superstition to claim that this saying says the happening itself, or the happening of its saying. There is nothing to say about the happening, but there is something to say because the happening has happened.

Getting to the bottom of this situation shows the nature of the "possibility" peculiar to the act of saying, because saying is always inscribed in its event. Or it shows the possibility and reasonableness of genealogy, as we now understand better and better.

Here the genealogical procedure intends to put into play the behind-the-scenes activity of the philosophical scene, which is the event of the institutive gesture of Plato's philosophical theater. The revelation of this activity, however, is in turn a *mise-en-scène* and, besides, is already caught up in the language and figures of philosophy.

Thus, the awareness of such a subordination problematically heralds its event as a distancing journey. And it is the very nature of this journey that we are interrogating here.

92. Let us say it again and put it this way. The intention of the genealogical journey is to face up to Plato's gesture, starting from the meanings brought into being by that gesture and going back to trace their event: meanings established in the gesture itself, that is, in their *mise-en-scène*.

On close inspection, there is nothing particularly original in this intention: it merely repeats the fundamental autoreferential, self-critical, or auto-bio-graphical character which is distinctive of philosophy—to a degree found in no other form of knowledge. Philosophy has always called into question itself, its foundation, its condition of possibility, its beginning, and its meaning. Plato himself gives us more than one example (suffice it to think of *Euthydemus*).

Philosophy must always doubt itself and account for its *operations*, distinguishing itself from the forms of knowledge it originally establishes. But that is not always the case, you might say. Very true. Words are often abused, and it so happens that many people are called philosophers who are at most brilliant ideologists or keen commentators—no doubt very deserving people, but philosophers, no, they definitely are not! And truly, and paradoxically, if you will—but this is quite understandable—there are not that many philosophers in the so-called history of philosophy.

Now, perhaps, we are beginning to pinpoint the sense of genealogy. It is no other than the effort to look at ourselves "auto-bio-graphically"—that is, as subjects *to* the meanings that philosophy establishes, avoiding to take them for granted and to take ourselves as embodied writings of truth and reality. We should, instead, take ourselves as result-figures, or resulting-figures, within which a place is designated for our being subjects that live and operate in the way we do.

Genealogy is therefore the destined task of philosophy.

And so, we can say again, with a more peaceful awareness, that what we display in our genealogic investigation is the *mise-en-scène* of philosophy and politics—we are indeed talking about the institutive correspondence of these two figures—as philosophical theater. And here is the scene of our backstage.

Our genealogical work would then entail making "visible" (as we can see, the visible/invisible pair has captured us too) the *backstage* of Plato's gesture, or rather, what happens within that gesture, *regardless of Plato's intentions*. This is a gesture that embodies itself in the writing of the dialogue and its characters, to begin with Socrates, the character par excellence, the *protagonist* of Plato's theater.

93. It goes without saying (let us repeat it) that by displaying our backstage we put up, in turn, a *mise-en-scène*. It is a fact that we still talk as if we were some characters of Plato's theater, using its vocabulary and its "truth-making" rhetoric. We dwell, albeit after centuries-old transformations, in the place of the very same representation. We are actors who talk about their scene and, by so doing, stage this very scene, redoubling its gesture, without ever moving beyond the theatrical place. Theater within theater, which talks about theater, stages it *in the* theater: and this, too, is nothing new.

Yet the ambiguity of this expedient, as we will see, is the ambiguity of every form of knowledge and of every subject *supposed to know*. We will then be able to gather the ripe fruits of genealogy.

Which is—if you will—very similar to a suspension, an *epoché*. A suspension of those very forms of knowledge (of that circle we drew at the beginning) that Plato's gesture puts on scene, constituting them precisely in that *mise-en-scène*.

And this implies going back to the roots of the figure of "truth," as a backstage figure of all the forms of knowledge of the Western world: a going back to the "desire to know" that establishes them in philosophy. And that is indeed how metaphysics arises.

An excavation and overturning, in the light of its *mise-en-scène*, of the roots of the philosophical Olympus.

This suspension has taken on for us the figure of a question, which inspires the whole journey: *What is at stake in the knowledge/power of politics?*

And besides, if we consider that Plato's gesture has its explicit representation in a gesture of speaking or writing, we can perceive in our question the echo of a request regarding the *ethology of language*: the revelation of a rhetoric place, of a habit of discourse serving as a cradle for the political animal.

94. And so, at the beginning, we followed Socrates in his descent into the *chasma* of Piraeus and to the procession of the Goddess Bendis, which led us to inspect the enchantment of the Girdle of Venus and the transferal nature of the objects of desire.

There we learned the great lesson that there are no simple things, simply present in their supposed "absolute" being-in-themselves: things are not absolute, that is, dissolved from the practices of life and knowledge; things are not independent of their being investments of desire.

Things are bodies marked with the desire that established them and that keeps them available for further investments.

We then discovered, however, that the nature of desire is that of unequal exchange, an exchange through which recognition takes place. Here is the first root of every figure concerning the subject; a figure having a nature not at all different from that of the object. Subjects *are* only to the extent that they are *desired*, insofar as they are *made the objects* of desire, because the subject is made of nothing but the "flesh of the world."

Hence the illusory, rhetorical, and enchanting—that is, ideological—feature of the Platonic strategy of the soul, as well as of every reduction pretending to attribute the world to a supposed constitutive subject. How could that be if subjects are still the world and, rather, they issue from it?

We have then seen that the propelling and relational center of desire—what we usually call and identify with the subject—is more appropriately a lack, an emptiness, an elsewhere. Every subject is an object of relations and exchange, a relationship of "se(lf)-duction": two poles attracting each other, and thereby identifying with each other.

Each pole acts as a mirror for the other, that is to say, *it acts as a sign*.

It is by virtue of this mirrored sign that subjects see and recognize themselves as the subjects they are. That is, in the way that each is an object of the other's desire.

Desiring subject and desired object get involved in a so-to-speak *an-archic* circle: they are in fact poles in a dynamic reciprocity, and not original or archetypical substances.

95. A pole desires insofar as the other (the object) has already reciprocated. And yet he or she has reciprocated only by desiring in turn and by desiring to be desired. In this relation to the other, in this game of exchange, of mirrors and signs, the two poles mutually recognize and mirror each other, subsisting only in that very relation, a relation that is objectifying *and therefore* subjectifying. In themselves, they do not subsist.

In this sense we say that subjects have their own taking-place in the "elsewhere." They take place in the unbridgeable distance and difference of desire (isn't Plato already intimating this in the myth of Eros from his *Symposium?*).

The subject is always subject *to* desire and therefore finds their place in mirroring the other, that is, in recognizing the other, whereas the "other" in turn needs the exchange to recognize themselves.

Hence, the constitutively unbalanced and unequal nature of desire. To think that there can be equality between the subjects, who develop from an uneven exchange between desiring and desired, and from their reversed reciprocity (I desire to be desired by your recognition; I desire to be recognized as desiring by your desire to be desired), in short, to think that subjects can be equalized is a mere ideological illusion. An illusion that is instrumentally dressed in that universal, transferal object that is "value," embodied politically in the casting of the "vote," and economically in "money"—two things that eventually become identical: a social delusion of equality, with its strengths and weaknesses, its advantages and disadvantages.

The constitutive economy of exchange requires imbalance even to establish itself (What would there be to exchange, after all, if no difference existed?). Which invariably also recurs in the desire for social equality: an unbalanced desire, like all desires, because if that were not the case, it would not even be desirable. Which implies, however, an ineliminable part and component of *pleonexia.*

Indeed, as we have learned, behind the dazzling of the girdle (of value—namely, of speech, of money) there looms Hecate: the destiny of death that lies in wait at the end of every desire and of every choice, that is, of every economy of life, because, as we shall see later, she carries in herself an economy of death.

96. We have seen the emergence, in the first dialogue between Socrates and Cephalus, of the universal goods embodied by money: by making

possible for anything to be exchanged, money buys desire, but only by reducing it to the conventionality of value. And yet desire will not be reduced, as old people know too well in their regret for a desire that money cannot give back or substitute for. Which is like saying: without desire, transferal objects no longer exert any seduction, any enchantment, because what they hide, making it desirable, no longer exists. They become a mere presence of the insignificant.

As Horace said to Maecenas: "Give me back my head of hair and the smile of youth, and I will certainly honor you like a God."

In other words, money replaces unequal recognition—socially dangerous because founded on desire, by nature uncontrollable—and equals it in value, that is, in price (as the saying goes, "Nothing comes without a price").

And so here comes the economic exchange—economic in the normal sense of the word; here comes the categorial economy, or the economic science—as Adam Smith would have it.

This reasoning by categories and values, however, skips the pre-categorial *anthropological* foundation, specifically, the very constitutive event of a language of value as a universal sign of objectification, or better, commodification.

A reasoning by values that has no value, and rather announces its disappearance. Reasoning by values, it has been said, implies a humanism that does not adequately estimate man—in fact, it underestimates him. From this point of view, only man (the soul) has value. The man in the archetypal dream of this assumption, however, is rather the nothing of the most profound nihilism, lacking self-awareness because unaware of how the figure of the subject and its political birth come into being.

What really has value, then? Might it be the *not committing injustices* that Cephalus appeals to, putting nonetheless a value on the afterlife? Is that what makes man happy? Or rather, is it not the case that the opposite is true?

The matter revolves around justice—and thus all the stage machinery of the *Republic* is set in motion. Truth be told, it is an amazing war machine with a power, indeed, that has no equal.

97. The dialectical game revolves around the just and the unjust, the happy and the unhappy, the violent and the peaceful, the autocrat and the cooperative; and there is no doubt that from the very beginning

Socrates, the protagonist of this war machine invented by Plato, is in favor of peace, of "being at peace." Which is not, however, Cephalus' peace of mind, for that is beyond any *politiké areté*.

It is rather the peace of the "soul," for it is *virtuous*. Not in the traditional sense of the term, that is to say, because of the ability to achieve its end—whereby man would still be merely a tool and vehicle of desire—but because of the ability to achieve "*good* ends." And that is an unheard-of, *moral* statement that is revealed in all its problematic nature. In fact, what does "good" mean? What peaceful life would be good and who would decide this, and how? The whole matter of *politiké areté* is thus marked by these questions.

It would seem indeed that such a peaceful life—in an archaic and pastoral meaning—would emerge as a first answer. It is put forward in that first description Socrates advances about the origin of human society: a society restricted to the satisfaction of basic needs, without luxury and without money (and without any allusion to the problems of sexuality or of sexual difference).

Then Socrates himself abandons the idea, acknowledging it to be "not human" and considering Glaucon's objection, who drastically calls it "a society of pigs."

98. And so there must be another road. To achieve good ends man needs first to put a curb on desire, through the establishment of philosophic reason, which is the same as political reason or reason of state; although the latter is anything but peaceful and, on the contrary, entails a good deal of violence both inside and outside itself.

That this is precisely the road we are questioning in our back-stage reading does not obviously mean that we want to deny (or even underestimate) the importance and effectiveness of reason qua founder of civilization. We are asking instead, "What does reason, or *this* reason, really desire?" A reason, Freud would say, which implies a peculiar "discontent" of civilization as it is politically understood.

What does the political civilization of the philosophical West desire? Which is tantamount to asking: What is the desire of speech (*logos*), writing, money, and the sign as it is generally understood?

99. We should never forget that the *mise-en-scène* of reason is a political gesture performed under Plato's direction. By making Thrasymachus into

the perfect spokesman for absolute *pleonexia*, Plato obtains, by opposition and contrast, the perfect *philosophy*. For he is the director and puppet master of this game, of this war of discourses, and we must be careful not to remove from the scene (as Plato, with his captivating writing, would like us to) the hidden *rhetorical strength* of his *mise-en-scène*.

Now this game begins to break cover: Plato is showing the necessity to suppress desire, categorically identified with *pleonexia*, to ensure a political *areté*, which is to say, a "just" and "happy" politics; one that can only be constructed by the "true" politician, in other words, the philosopher. And so, it is either *pleonexia* or *philosophy*. But then what is missing about desire? What is removed or feared in desire through this *mise-en-scène*, namely, with this gesture that establishes *politiké areté*? Perhaps imbalance and ultimately death? Perhaps the *chasma* of Hecate the Dark?

Isn't philosophy—as Socratically understood—precisely an exercise in death? And isn't it perhaps, in this sense, a transvaluation of the "little death" which is the purpose (at least apparently, or ostentatiously) of the sexual act? Isn't this precisely the message of *Phaedo* and *Symposium*?

With these queries we close our Interlude.

(End of Interlude)

Act Two

Fourth Figure

Sexual Difference

Scene I: The Power of Blood and Sperm

100. As you can see, the act opens with the figure of the intercourse between Gyges and the queen behind me: we know the consequences, but its *secret* remains obscure. What *really* happens between Gyges and the queen? Here is the first question which we inherit from the Interlude, and which now opens our way.

Let us summarize the situation. Gyges descends into Mother Earth's womb, which may suggest several symbolic meanings: descent into the realm of the dead; return to the ancestral roots; descent into what is concealed from the realm of the living (but which Er will eventually reveal). Mention has already been made of the fact that the whole journey of the *Republic*, from the descent into the Piraeus to the myth of Er, could find in the tale of Gyges its propulsive center as well as a metaphorical synthesis, albeit a partial one.

Now, by lowering himself into the womb of the earth, Gyges appropriates its secret, obtaining a precious gift—perhaps the very secret of the economy of life, seeing that its possession will make him a bridegroom and the progenitor of a royal lineage.

This gift is represented by the golden ring, harking back to the theme of money, of which Gyges would be, supposedly, the inventor. It is the mythical ring we still find in the Nibelungen saga that fascinated Wagner (as well as young Nietzsche, who later weaned himself of it). Wagner saw in it a parable of the "curse of gold" and the symbol of the perverse, modern industrial civilization revolving around capital. But all this is premature.

Indeed, the ring harbors a gigantic and tyrannical strength which is the emblem and symbol of political power: the very power that Gyges, with the aid of the ring, will achieve.

We could also note that Gyges fundamentally seduces Mother Earth (in this sense the queen, his Lady), which evokes the scene of an incest, with added elements of betrayal (or abduction) and murder, as in Oedipus, who thereby brings "the plague of the political" to Thebes (as Blanchot might have put it).[1]

101. The essential fact, however, is that the ring bestows on its owner the value, the "virtue" of invisibility. And precisely what is invisible makes possible the possession of all the goods in the world.

As we already pointed out, the dead body in the ground is invisible, the soul (the inner designing to which Glaucon assigns the virtue of the real man) is invisible, the meaning of the spoken and written word is invisible, and finally, the value of money is invisible.

Here begins the play of the invisible and visible (private and public) that we already recognized before as the first figure of the relationship between soul and body.

This play is particularly apparent in Herodotus' version of the tale of Gyges: what sees cannot and must not be seen; what is visible cannot and must not see. And yet she who was supposed not to see, the queen, ends up seeing; and he who was supposed not to be seen, ends up being seen. It follows that Gyges' intrusion is an incursion into the private sphere, which is "seen," that is, discovered—an event demanding public reparation: a marriage and the seizure of royal power. It is the secret of this game that we must now solve.

If we consider the matter in terms of the dynamics of desire, we could say the following. Desire, which sees what is desirable, is invisible. Similarly, invisible is the way someone is desired, so that no one can see their visibility (which is to say his or her being desired).

---

1. The expression "plague of the political" does not appear literally in Blanchot. It is Sini's, but it occurs in Sini's discussion of Blanchot's interpretation of the Oedipus myth. See Maurice Blanchot, *The Infinite Conversation*, 17–18, 438–439, and Carlo Sini, *Teoria e pratica del foglio-mondo* (Laterza, 1997), 45—Ed.

But the queen sees in Gyges her desirability, and Gyges finds himself exposed in his desire. Their secret is thus shared in an unequal exchange, realized, and consummated exactly in the corrective sexual intercourse. An act that remains concealed (every couple, we could say, has its secret, which is invisible to others).

The invisible is nevertheless, or precisely because of this, made public in the wedding, which is in fact the appropriate way to *re-cover* the invisibility of the private sphere. We will later understand the political consequences of this process and these remarks.

102. We can now turn to another series of considerations: the visible (the queen) was not supposed to be seen, since she was the king's *private possession*. It is this possession that *provides the foundation for the king's power*, that is, his public (political) power. For what reason?

Because in the exercise of his private possession, the king embodies the sacred possession of the generation of life. Here is the archaic thought that founded the oldest genealogy of power known to us. It assigns to the sovereign couple and to the "generation of blood" the simultaneously real and symbolic feature of public power. It is still in accordance with this *way of looking at things* that the commandment urges us "not to covet our neighbor's wife," that is, not to look at her to "know her." It goes without saying, as Freud pointed out, that prohibition always implies desire: incest no less than murder; it would indeed be pointless to forbid what one does not desire.

We must go back to the same thought if we want to understand the thaumaturgical power placed in the king's persona: a thought so persistent that we find it still enduring in modern Europe well into the seventeenth century. The king possesses the secret of life, the secret of its economy, and therefore he can heal the sick with the touch of his hand, he can make fertile the fields and the herds, and so on.

103. But now we need to remember Plato's words: "As soon as he had seen the chasm opened up in the earth, he was amazed and beheld, among other marvels, a fabled brazen horse . . ." The queen too, in Herodotus' version, mentions these forbidden marvels (*thaumasta*) that Gyges must not see, unless he, after killing the king, becomes her husband and possesses her.

What Gyges must not see, therefore, are the consequences of the act of penetration that is the king's private possession—the invisible exercise of his penetration into the queen's *chasma*. Penetration and possession which establish his visible public power.

The original *chasma* is thus specified in the female sex, which is after all the secret itself of the generativity of Mother Earth, the bestower of her gifts.

Gyges' chthonic descent had already heralded the shepherd's fate, perfectly symbolized in the magic and precious virtue of the ring. By appropriating it, Gyges becomes in turn a symbol of male sexual power, in its difference from (and complementarity to) female power.

Penetration and the magical effect of fertility are the power that men wield over women; the visible consequence of this is the gift that a woman returns to a man: she bestows the fruits of man's invisible fertility, rendering it visible. This visible gift is therefore the token of the legitimacy of man's invisible power, that is, of his being publicly recognized as "Lord," sovereign of his progeny and irrevocable judge of life and death.

Marriage, with its inviolable "property," is nothing but the consecration—necessary and indispensable, as we will see—of all this.

104. This reveals the backdrop of an ancient sacral world that, in fact, has never completely disappeared from our anthropological unconscious mind. And we should add that in this primitive sacral mentality you do not need, for this empowerment through the procreation of children, the woman's consent. This power is essentially and sufficiently attained by man with that act of violence which is a violation of the *chasma*.

This does not mean that the female passivity, perceived as such by man, might not be concomitant, in woman, with a first germ of the awareness concerning the active-passive role she complementarily plays. That is proved, according to Alfred Kallir, by the analysis of the iconism of alphabetic signs, and particularly the role played in languages by the "deponent" verbs (from the Latin *deponere*, to lay down, originally: laying down man's seed), a role in turn modeled on the archaic figures of the signs of writing.

In any case, the archaic man's thinking could be expressed as follows: the obscure impulse of desire brings to light *thaumasta*: marvelous and venerable things, specifically, the wonder of the generation of life. And so, it generates *phainomena*, that is, what is seen in the light (*phos*) of the sun, originating from the invisible and dark night of desire itself. Therefore, the invisible gives birth to the visible. (This is perhaps the "magical" reason that led Paleolithic men to paint animals on the dark inside of caves, understood as symbolic wombs: a graphic exorcism to ensure their real birth.)

It follows that the legitimacy of power, which is made manifest in its "magical" fertility, has its roots in the invisible: the virtue Gyges acquires by taking it away from Mother Earth. This virtue is the power, which man has, to make women fertile.

And yet, by the very fact of making him a father, the woman entrusts him visibly—that is publicly—with such a power, although she remains subject to him with the "veneration" due to the "magical" act he carried out on her.

This subjection relegates socially, politically, the woman to the private sphere: being man's private possession, she cannot be "known" by anyone else. Which is a guarantee both that she will not be violated and that the children will be legitimate, since the father is by nature invisible. Only this legitimacy will veraciously bear witness to man's actual fertility, that is, to his actual possession of the magical power to renew life—hence the legitimacy of his public power, safeguarded and sanctioned publicly by the wedding.

This unconscious set of thoughts and symbols has characterized a long phase of human life, and its influence is certainly not totally extinct even today.

105. On the other hand, the conferral of a public and visible power cannot but go back to an act or event that is not public or visible, precisely insofar as power is instituted by it. Whence comes the political (as Thrasymachus had partially intuited).

The source of the political is that which, in its invisibility, makes power visible.

Thrasymachus, we were saying, grasps something about it, but misunderstands it completely. He mistakes the original founding violence of primitive sexuality for the violence of political force and power, which are instead, if anything, its consequence. Thrasymachus, or rather more appropriately, Plato.

Plato and his times have long had all the sacral world of the origins behind them. From this point of view, the institutive operation of philosophy looks more like an imposing transcription of the mythical and ancestral past into the visions, categories, words, and writings of the philosophical soul. In this regard, Nietzsche already used the image of Socrates as a boatswain, who takes aboard his remarkable ship, which we will never tire of beholding with endless amazement, the entire ancient wisdom: he ferries it into the future and the unknown.

In fact, Thrasymachus, Glaucon, and Socrates are already psychological individuals, seized by the subjective imagination of desire: impulse, greed, *epithymia*, are in them as many experiences individually inflected, captured by the "ana-graphic" identity of the public name. Not mythical models, but rather figured repetitions of public writing.

Which means that Plato invented the soul on an anthropological figure already mature. It is a figure that allows the establishment of new practices of life and knowledge, marked by the practice of money and by alphabetic writing, where the new practices have their typical referents as well as their conditions. All this shows the markings of a universal conversion—individualistic and profane—of desire.

106. As a matter of fact, Plato's strategy of the soul operates within sophistic anthropology. It fights the reduction of value to a mere convention and exposes therefore its profanation (although the very fact of reasoning by values, we will recall, is part and consequence of the profanation it would like to erase). Plato fights the conventionality of Glaucon (or Hermogenes in the *Cratylus*) so that he can reconsecrate it in the Political established by philosophy.

We could then point out that, in Western civilization, Plato's essential gesture has never stopped repeating itself. As a philosophic category, in fact, politics implies a reconsecration through theology (heralded in the *Republic* by the myth of Er). Generally speaking, just as metaphysics is theology, so is politics essentially theological, even when it denies it. The same is true of scientific ideology.

The French Revolution, for instance, dared behead the king, thus severing the ancestral tie of sex and blood that was the sacred symbol of traditional power: an event that at the time all Europeans experienced as traumatic and *tremendum*. But the French Revolution did not put the cuirassiers and the entire ritual of power out to pasture, just as it did not renounce power's thaumaturgic and salvific character. On the contrary, it repeated its magical illusionism, that is, its visible representation in favor of an invisible one. In our times, this illusionism has come to coincide with the power of video, the utmost authority in charge of the "information" of the souls and of their domination through the rituals of spectacular broadcasting—desirable and forced rituals that have replaced in every home the offerings to Hestia's hearth.

Scene II: The Noble Lie

107. Let us go back to the scene, following the thread of the visible and invisible. This connection, we said, will lead us to the heart of the third *chasma*, that is, to the very heart of the *Republic*; it will show that the invisibility of power, or the power of invisibility, staged in the tale of Gyges, is not a casual passage but rather a crucial one.

And so, at first Socrates describes the "holy city," or "the true city" (as completely opposed to Glaucon's "real man"). A city ruled only by the satisfaction of the basic needs and therefore unaware of violence, luxury, and money.

But then Socrates lets himself be persuaded to describe a more realistic city: the *tryphosa polis*, literally the "inflamed city"—evidently by desire.

Because this city requires superfluous goods and happiness, luxury, wealth, pleasures, and money, it must obtain these things beyond what the natural territory offers, stealing them from other men and cities, and then defending them from their desire to obtain them in turn.

Plato is suggesting that the human inclination to fight is a consequence of the desire for luxury, without which man would instead be a "noble savage"—a theory that sounds to us simplistic and largely false. Let's go ahead, anyway.

108. Out of necessity, thus Socrates goes on to say, warriors and rulers appear. And so there arises necessarily and urgently the problem of their education, which from now on will be the propulsive center of Socrates' arguments revolving around the introduction of *politiké areté* and the consequent philosophical-pedagogical revolution of politics.

In fact, warriors and rulers must be endowed with a contradictory nature: a meek nature for their fellow citizens, and an aggressive, irascible one for everybody else. And so, the fundamental opposition comes to be specified: philosopher (Socrates) contra sophist (Thrasymachus), or dog contra wolf, being in fact the dog tame with the flock of sheep but ready to defend it from the wolves.

It has been noted that, significantly, in this context of speech, women are mentioned for the first time in the *Republic*, as well as the adjective "philosophical." Indeed, the guardians, namely the warriors and rulers, must have a philosophical nature, not a "choleric" one. The adjective "philosophical" had never occurred before Plato and here it heralds the discourses that, as we will see shortly, will reshape the figure of the philosopher for the entire Greek culture.

But more to the point of women. Here they are in fact the *hetaerae*, the hired companions at luxurious banquets, those women that were never mentioned in the "holy city" in which desire, obliterated by the introduction of need, remained essentially silent.

Plato describes a luxurious banquet, drawing manifestly on Aristophanes, who wrote in one of his plays: "All is ready—couches, tables, cushions, chaplets, perfumes, dainties and courtesans to boot; biscuits, cakes, sesame-bread, tarts, lovely dancing women, the sweetest charm of the festivity."[2] Xenophon, in the *Symposium*, adds to that the auletes and the citharedes: "There entered a man from Syracuse, to give them an evening's merriment. He had with him a fine flute-girl, a dancing-girl—one of those skilled in acrobatic tricks—and a very handsome boy, who was expert at playing the cither and at dancing . . ." The trio was led by a Syracusan, who had been called to promote the revelry. Today we would call him an entertainer, MC, or TV or live show "host"—that's how old these trades are . . .

109. Now Socrates' crucial words are uttered. You should listen to them.

SOCRATES: "Come then, and let us pass a leisure hour in storytelling (*mythos*), and our story shall be the education of our heroes."

Here begins the (explicitly declared) mythological and rhetorical pedagogy of the *Republic*. Here begins, in other words, the true *mise-en-scène* of philosophy qua founding place of *politiké areté*. We are thus witnessing the representation of philosophical discourse, of its *mythos*, which goes on to replace the traditional poetic tales of the Gods, steeped in violence and desire, for the purpose of a new human *paideia*.

---

2. Aristophanes, *The Acharnians* (*The Acharnians*, by Aristophanes [gutenberg. org])—Trans.

This philosophical *mythos*, however, cannot avoid the lie, conjured up several times and finally culminating in an explicit political lie, on which the education of the guardians (i.e., the future warriors and rulers of the city) must be predicated.

Of course, Socrates emphasizes, it is a "noble lie," a sort of "Phoenician stratagem," that is, a *pharmakon*: both medicine and poison, as the word suggests. But the word "Phoenician" should also be borne in mind since the Greeks used this expression to allude succinctly to the letters of the alphabet. Be that as it may, we have a lie for the greater good as the culmination of political rhetoric.

As a matter of fact, Socrates is hesitant and most unwilling to enunciate this stratagem. Only at the behest of his audience will he decide at last to speak.

110.

SOCRATES: Well then, I will speak, although I really know not how to look you in the face, or in what words to utter the audacious fiction, which I propose to communicate gradually, first to the rulers, then to the soldiers, and lastly to the people. They are to be told that their youth was a dream, and the education and training which they received from us, an appearance only; in reality during all that time they were being formed and fed in the womb of the earth, where they themselves and their arms and appurtenances were manufactured; when they were completed, the earth, their mother, sent them up; and so, their country being their mother and also their nurse, they are bound to advise for her good, and to defend her against attacks, and her citizens they are to regard as children of the earth and their own brothers.

You had good reason, he said, to be ashamed of the lie which you were going to tell.

True, I replied, but there is more coming; I have only told you half. Citizens, we shall say to them in our tale, you are brothers, yet God has framed you differently. Some of you have the power of command, and in the composition of these he has mingled gold, wherefore also they have the greatest honor; others he has made of silver, to be auxiliaries;

others again who are to be husbandmen and craftsmen he has composed of brass and iron; and the species will generally be preserved in the children. But as all are of the same original stock, a golden parent will sometimes have a silver son, or a silver parent a golden son. And God proclaims as a first principle to the rulers, and above all else, that there is nothing which they should so anxiously guard, or of which they are to be such good guardians, as of the purity of the race. They should observe what elements mingle in their offspring; for if the son of a golden or silver parent has an admixture of brass and iron, then nature orders a transposition of ranks, and the eye of the ruler must not be pitiful towards the child because he has to descend in the scale and become a husbandman or artisan, just as there may be sons of artisans who having an admixture of gold or silver in them are raised to honor, and become guardians or auxiliaries. For an oracle says that when a man of brass or iron guards the State, it will be destroyed. Such is the tale; is there any possibility of making our citizens believe in it?

111. This is how the "tale" establishes the psychic foundations of an aristocratic communism which has eliminated all references to the generation of blood. A communism that subsequently establishes, in fact, that the protectors or guardians, divided into rulers on one side and into warriors, guards, or soldiers as one might say, on the other, must not have any property of their own or any private house. They must not touch or handle silver or gold, since they already have it within them, nor can they be under the same roof with these metals, and they will similarly have to abstain from drinking from golden or silver cups.

As you can see, the philosophical battle against desire, or *epithymia*, is in full swing. Cephalus is completely removed and obliterated. The noble lie is therefore more than a simple stratagem: Plato knows perfectly what he is aiming at, and what he is saying. He is destroying from its foundations the entire archaic past of manhood to bring forth a new humankind based on the quality of the souls (rather than on blood) and on the force of philosophical reason (rather than on desire). The shift of meaning of the word *areté*, which Socrates had subtly and silently performed, here openly manifests itself and begins to speak with all the imagination and rhetoric that philosophical dialectics can conjure up.

We must make sure we are getting a clear understanding of these Platonic gestures and *mise-en-scène*. With the noble lie, or Phoenician tale, Plato has basically excluded men from sexual generation, making them instead spring out directly from the earth, through a sort of autarkic, self-sufficient generation. Accordingly, their character will derive from the metals buried in the bowels of the earth itself.

112. With this tale we are exactly poles apart from the tale of Gyges, insofar as it specularly abolishes the very *thaumasta*, the very wonders tied to the constitutive, invisible desire of the archaic man. If in the myth of Gyges we can read a sort of original incest, since Gyges descends into Mother Earth's womb, this incest is later redeemed, or transvalued, through the intercourse with the queen and the ensuing shotgun wedding—which is a symbolic way of representing the passage from nature to culture.

Quite on the contrary, the Platonic incest excludes all nature, as it equalizes all men to the same rank of symbolic brothers, that is, of "friends," as philosophical rhetoric will have it. The origin is already philosophical: it rationally provides all human tools suitable for survival, such as weapons and any other equipment.

In this imaginary and entirely virile generation, the complementary relationship with woman is excluded or symbolically transfigured into "Mother Earth." It is certainly not by chance that there emerges here in Plato the theme of pederasty, although "purified" of all its sexual elements: an initiation rite and custom meant for adolescents so that they may educate themselves to enter the community of adult men.

Self-sufficiency of procreation (people are self-born from the earth, already supplied with any art and tool); self-sufficiency of sexuality (in the pedagogic community of men, desire for women is excluded and replaced with a vague spiritual infatuation with male adolescents). Thus woman, that is desire, disappears.

There is much food for thought here for modern feminism, insofar as it models itself on the same antipodal removal and exclusion of maleness, in fact taking up a mentality and logic that are entirely male and captured by the very same philosophical *politiké areté*.

It is also evident now that a new anthropology is taking shape, along with a new economy of life—one that excludes mythical archaism and reconsecrates it both philosophically and morally. It is the end of the ethical-sacral world and the "aristocracy" of desire, the beginning of an aristocracy of rational vision.

Thaumaston, the wondrous, becomes in fact the "Good," that is, the philosopher's supersensible vision. We could therefore summarize the Platonic operation like this: making the ancestral desire, that is, the ancestral parents, invisible, in order for the "idea," and for the philosophical and political Good, to become visible.

Scene III: The Drama of Women

113. So far, however, we have said nothing about women's role in the new city, nor about the exercise of sexuality that concerns them. Once more, however, Socrates will not hear of it. Pressed on by his friends, he states all his hesitations, and yes, he does have an idea, but he is not too sure of himself and fears he will cause a scandal or a commotion, or that he will not be taken seriously. His friends insist, encourage him, reassure him, and eventually Socrates makes up his mind to do it.

Very well, he says. "But maybe this way is right, that after the completion of the male drama (*andreion drama*) we should in turn go through with the female (*gynaikeion*)."[3] And so here begins the *mise-en-scène* of the new woman. Hold on to your seats!

114. What is essential for the development of this drama is the decision to be made about the nature of man (*anthropine physis*), that is, the outstanding issue of "anthropology." In other words, it must be decided whether the *human nature* of women is equal to that of men in every task, or not.

A question undoubtedly embarrassing, if only because Socrates had shortly before said (and Glaucon had agreed) that in the city everybody was to do the one work suited to their own nature: warriors as warriors,

---

3. Here we deviate from Benjamin Jowett's translation ("The part of the men has been played out, and now properly enough comes the turn of the women"). We quote from Paul Shorey's translation (available online at Perseus Digital Library) to follow the author's argument on the subject—Trans.

in conformity with their silver souls, craftsmen as craftsmen, because of their bronze souls, and so on. And everything added up, or was made cleverly or plausibly to add up, at least according to the philosophical tale. But what about women? In Socrates' words, "Have you not fallen into a serious inconsistency in saying that men and women, whose natures are so entirely different, ought to perform the same actions?"

While our friends debate all their understandable doubts onstage, let us retreat backstage to carry out some preliminary observations, which, in my opinion, are absolutely necessary.

115. We already know that Plato will promote equality between man and woman as far as their social role is concerned, and even their role in war. This is a move of unprecedented boldness in the ancient world, with some partial exception for Sparta. But if you think you can take it as a sort of "women's liberation" *ante litteram*, I'm afraid you are on the wrong track. Let this be a warning to you.[4]

To emphasize how, despite everything, Plato does establish a social equality of women and men is to reason superficially and naïvely. There is something else that we should not overlook.

Above all at, this: that in making man and woman equal (of course, at the level of government, that is, of the class of guardians), Plato truly cancels out their profound difference, that is, their constitutive *complementarity* and, with it, the unequal exchange deriving from it.

This difference, however, cannot be taken away with impunity, nor can it be made in any way homogeneous, *because it is above all constitutive of their respective identities, masculine and feminine, and of their mutual complementarity.*

And yet Plato (who, I repeat, knows perfectly well what he is doing and what he wants) will nevertheless make homogeneous even sex, consistently with the cancellation of the difference and of the desire that establishes it. If there is no difference, then even sex is indifferent—or better, it takes on a completely different meaning: the one, precisely, that Plato wants to give it.

---

4. Here Sini's interpretation differs sharply from other commentators who see in Plato a precursor of women's emancipation. See for instance Giovanni Reale's introduction in Platone, *Repubblica. Testo greco a fronte*, edited by Giovanni Reale and Roberto Radice (Bompiani, 2009)—Ed.

Plato assimilates the exercise of sexuality to social work. In so doing, he basically causes the woman to become a sort of "public vagina" at the service of the state: her *chasma* is rendered public and visible, according to *good* procreation, understood rationally as a sociopolitical end.

That the *chasma* is structurally invisible (because assigned to desire), and what this invisibility means (which, as we have often suggested, should be connected to the desire generated by speech, about which we are still in the dark), well, all that is canceled by Plato and rendered in turn invisible, *removed* by the basically asexual foundation of his philosophical politics.

With a strange consequence: just as he wanted his guardians and citizens to believe they were not born because of sexual procreation, so Plato wants us to believe that sexual desire is not something essential to *human* nature. He makes it regress to animality, that is, to mere nature—which, as we already know, is precisely an effect of unconscious retroflexion.

But since he turns sex into social work for the sake of procreation, Plato treats his men and his women like farm animals.

116. Sexual desire is made to "regress" to what precedes the laws and *politiké areté*; the sexual exercise as such is instead made to "progress" to the figure of the publicness of work intended as social procreation. But Plato is not telling it like it is.

By establishing the two extremes of, on one side, violent and lawless desire, and on the other, of work rationally ordered and for the public good, he is canceling out the anthropological dimension *intermediate* between these two extremes (themselves entirely artificial and imaginary): the human specificity that found expression primarily in the sacredness of the mythical world, and in its conceiving of politics as a consequence of the ancestral embrace and the *power* of life and death deriving from it. And indeed, this is exactly what Plato wants: for that ancestral humanity to be forever forgotten and removed, or at least demoted to an expression of the world of fairytales, of the absurdities of myth, of the reveries of poets.

In its stead, a new anthropology of the soul arises, by dint of the translation of desire into social need and supersensible truth. Or rather: into the need for a supersensible truth and for its supersensible vision.

I am sure you will understand me now if I say: translation into a will to truth qua political mask of a specific will to power.

Now we can go back to our scene.

117. Urged by his friends, but still hesitant, Socrates speaks. He says he knows well that the extraordinary novelty of what he is going to propose will appear whimsical and perhaps even ridiculous, as well as impractical according to most people. In the end, having overcome his hesitations, he begins by establishing that in the city they are envisioning women ought to be educated similarly to men. Therefore, they should exercise at the gymnasium, be schooled in the art of war, and any other virile thing.

Indeed, argues Socrates, there is no specific (meaning: gender-based) difference between women and men in terms of intelligence and skills, although it is true that in general women are physically weaker than men.

Not all women, however, will receive such education, but only those who show an inclination for it—which, incidentally, holds true for men as well. So, it is not true that these things, applied to women, are against nature; quite the contrary, it is against nature to exclude them.

With this, Socrates has tackled and warded off a first "wave" of predictable criticism and stupid banter, provoked for instance by the image of young women hanging around all naked in gymnasiums, handling heavy spears, and so on.

But now he must tackle a second, much more tremendous "wave."

118. SOCRATES: "The wives of our guardians are to be common, and their children are to be common, and no parent is to know his own child, nor any child his parent."

But then is this life of the guardians—in every way communal and generic—really feasible? We shall see later. Now it is appropriate for us to go into details, as the astonished listeners invite Socrates to do. How does he view this commonality? He should be more explicit on that point. For instance, how is one to deal with sex?

Socrates replies: women and men, selected for their equally "golden" nature, must live in common houses and meet at common meals. They will be brought up together and will associate at gymnastic exercises. Obviously, living mixed in with each other and in total promiscuity will cause them to be seized by desire, that is by the inborn necessity of their natures to have intercourse with each other.

This must not occur, however, in a random, disorderly fashion. The rulers will be responsible for establishing the proper ceremonies, "holy weddings" having as their sole purpose to obtain optimal breeding, just as is done with farm animals.

And here, again, the "lie" turns out to be essential and precious. Our rulers, Socrates says, "will find a considerable dose of falsehood and deceit necessary for the good of their subjects." They will resort to many stratagems, such as festivals, fixed drawings, prizes for the bravest, and the like, to assure "that the best of either sex should be united with the best as often, and the inferior with the inferior, as seldom as possible; and that they should rear the offspring of the one sort of union, but not of the other, if the flock is to be maintained in first-rate condition. Now these goings on must be a secret which the rulers only know, or there will be a further danger of our herd, as the guardians may be termed, breaking out into rebellion."

Plato's inflexible strategy could not be any more stringent or consistent. After excluding, with a "Phoenician tale," his first citizens from sexual procreation and blood legacy, now, with another "Phoenician stratagem," he excludes the guardians from it: none of them will be father or mother, son or daughter. Blood procreation is completely obliterated, and reproduction is rather turned into a sanctified act, that is, an act purified, as far as nature allows, from desire.

Thus, the creatures of reason take possession of their city.

Scene IV: Justice of the Soul

119. Socrates has achieved an important result, as conclusion of a previously formulated theorem: to read justice in the large writing of the state and then to read it again, and find it confirmed in the small writing of individuals. A resort to writing that could be called a further stratagem, tale, or *pharmakon*.

This is the situation. If the state must have the communal characters we mentioned, based on the division of its citizens into three classes, what are then the *virtues* that characterize it and define its good quality? Here we get to the crux of *politiké areté*, in tune with that new anthropology predicated on the strategy of the soul.

We must now establish the virtues pertaining to the three classes of citizens, whether men or women. They are itemized as follows.

For the *rulers*, wisdom, or knowledge (*sophia*).

For the *warriors*, courage (*andreia*), that is, the active exercise of the awareness of what is to be feared or not to be feared: what pains, fears, pleasures, and desires.

For the *workers*, but also for all three classes, temperance (*sophrosyne*), that is, the mastery of pleasures and desires within the permissible limits.

From this group we finally derive justice (*dikaiosyne*), an essentially distributive virtue, for the sake of which everyone discharges their tasks in the state, each following their own peculiar virtue and avoiding exceeding its limits.

Now, on these social virtues, Plato literally constructs the soul. The fact that such a soul is the result of a political retroflexion, as we claim, could not appear more clearly to someone who, like us, is observing this from backstage.

Yet the operation, taken as a whole, is problematic to say the least and, in this sense, quite strange. I now ask for your full attention.

120. The criterion on which justice is modeled, now finally defined (as Socrates wanted) and here staged by Plato, is basically the "organic" character of the state, the one we already saw asserted by Aristotle. It teaches that the whole precedes its parts. Which means that social individuals do not exist prior to the state. Before the state comes into being, they do not exist. They do not stipulate contracts, do not act as social individuals, and so on.

Individuals are formations and functions within the totality of the organic relationship we call the state, which is characterized by its justice (in other words by its structures and by its laws—*nomoi*). And as Plato is showing, these individuals are to be socially educated to conform to the community in which they participate.

But now we are shown instead that it is the innate psychological virtues of the individuals that establish and justify the functions and roles of the individuals themselves in the state, as well as the functional and legitimate forms of the social organization.

While pretending to describe the genesis of the state and its justice (the large writing), Socrates is staging his own psycho-philosophical drama, founding the state on the strategy of the soul (the small writing).

However, what is above all evident in this whole operation is its "injustice." First, because Plato has already envisioned its culmination in the government of philosophers, and the hierarchical subordination of all the other classes of citizens to it. The effect of this predetermined base—the large writing—is then retroflected onto the supposed small writing that the souls ought to have for themselves. Thus, Plato does not read in the large writing what would already be written, though not too visibly, in the small writing; on the contrary, he posits it by reflection, expecting us to swallow this theory with the tale of the metals.

This is a true sleight of hand: putting in the top hat the virtues borrowed from the presupposed state and then having them come out as the inherent virtues of the rabbit magically pulled out from the hat. Bravo!

121. Secondly: it is evidently *we* (men and women), being already in a society and, somehow, in the state, who want to imagine a time before society and the state. Which inevitably implies that we unconsciously go look in the origins for those features that characterize us—how else could we think of them?

So, it is abundantly clear that we, the inheritors of Plato's retroflexion, have been regularly repeating it from time immemorial, reiterating its injustice.

The same happens, significantly, when we wonder about the supposed origin of language: a central topic for us, as we will understand better and better. Starting from what for us is language, from what we think it is, we retrospectively look for its origin, producing mere spiritualistic, biologistic, or structuralist fancies, yet understanding nothing about what ought to be thought about any thought of origin.

It follows, as a corollary, that those who today appeal to the "communicative linguistic community" as a universal criterion of justice to be applied to worldwide and intercultural global politics are completely on the wrong track. In fact, despite their good intentions, they end up reproducing the age-old injustice, retroflecting on the whole of humankind the Western ideology of *logos*, intended in the sense of its implicit political philosophy and its constitutive imperialism.

We should also remark that the common feature in these retrospective operations is, of course, *desire*. We desire to speak of the origin so we can derive justice from it: the justice, or justness, of our discourse itself. In other words, we desire to represent our theater and its drama, permeated by its typical *mythos*. This is a risk that comes with our backstage as well, until we can confront the theoretical prejudice that holds sway over it. Only then will *politiké areté* begin to sight a horizon freed from tradition's philosophical options, which today's practices of life and knowledge have made obsolete.

Let us now return from backstage to the *kinesis* of the scene.

122. Justice therefore means that every class should carry out *its own* function in the state, which demands from everyone the "temperance" that subordinates both workers and warriors to the rulers and binds the latter to overcome "natural" desire in favor of the "supernatural" desire of philosophical virtue. Now Plato will show that to the classes and different social functions correspond three kinds of souls; thereby he will consider accomplished the parallel reading of the text writ large (the state) and the text writ small (the individual).

> The appetitive or concupiscible soul, which is in the gut.
> The irascible soul, which is in the liver.
> The rational soul, which is in the head.

But let us listen to Socrates' words.

> SOCRATES: Must we not acknowledge, I said, that in each of us there are the same principles and habits (*ethe*) which there are in the State; and that from the individual they pass into the State?—how else can they come there? Take the quality of passion or spirit;—it would be ridiculous to imagine that this quality, when found in States, is not derived from the individuals who are supposed to possess it, e.g., the Thracians, Scythians, and in general the northern nations; and the same may be said of the love of knowledge, which is the special characteristic of our part of the world, or of the love of money, which may, with equal truth, be attributed to the Phoenicians and Egyptians. . . . There is no difficulty in understanding this.

There follows the analysis of the three dispositions, or principles, of the soul: the rational principle, with which the soul reasons; the appetitive principle, with which the soul "hungers and thirsts and feels the fluttering of any other desire . . . the ally of sundry pleasures and satisfactions"; and finally, the irascible principle (the *thymos*, the *fumus*), an intermediate function able to face and counter bravely the appetitive irrationality when this function is educated to follow the dictates of reason.

Justice in the individual will therefore be the concordant harmony of these different principles and functions, so that justice must be captured not in the outward actions but in the inward actions, which is to say, in the intentions of the soul.

The "psychization," or internalization of man, is thus accomplished. Establishing it as "the way things are," yet at the same time something that must be encouraged and accomplished through a specific philosophical pedagogy (one full of expedients, as we just saw) is an essential element of Plato's political *mise-en-scène*, that is, of his strategy of the soul and of his philosophy.

At this point, we must emphasize how in the appetitive soul we have the reappearance of *desire*, although it has been cleverly displaced from being the generative locus or function of our personal identity to being a mere area or function of the soul, molded on the needs of the state (although we are led to believe just the opposite: that the state derives from the soul).

But let us focus back on the scene, because now Socrates is about to confront the third "wave" of all possible objections to his *mythos*, namely, whether the just state he has envisioned might at all be possible to realize in practice.

123. At first Socrates defends himself against the predictable skeptical objections by clarifying that he has carried out the representation of the just man and the unjust man (a portrayal having as its aim—as we will see—to determine which of the two is truly the happy man) in ideal terms. In other words, Socrates has posed a model, to which men, in living reality, may come close.

And the same is to be said of the city: just as a painter proposing to portray the ideal (*paradeigma*) of the most beautiful man, Socrates asks, "Were we not creating an ideal of a perfect State?" It follows that "theory" finds its internal justification, although "practice" is not its equal.

These are only digressions, though. Now Socrates finally decides to really face the third and largest wave: the argument that only philosophers are the real politicians and the real rulers. A subject that will predictably arouse skepticism and laughter among men.

> SOCRATES: Now then, I said, I go to meet that which I liken to the greatest of the waves; yet shall the word be spoken, even though the waves break and drown me in laughter and dishonor; and do you mark my words. . . . Until philosophers are kings, or the kings and princes of this world have the spirit and power of philosophy, and political greatness (*dynamis te politiké*) and wisdom meet in one, and those commoner natures who pursue either to the exclusion of the other are compelled to stand aside, cities will never have rest from their evils—nor the human race, as I believe,—and then only will this our State have a possibility of life and behold the light of day. Such was the thought, my dear Glaucon, which I would fain have uttered if it had not seemed too extravagant; for to be convinced that in no other State can there be happiness private or public is indeed a hard thing.

And so, Plato has led us to the turning point of his entire philosophy, and rather, of his entire life.

124. Let us leave the party of friends in their astonishment, while we reason together. All in all, Socrates' two outrageous arguments are that women should be given the same power as men and that philosophers should hold political power (male philosophers and female philosophers, of course). Which amounts to saying: precisely those who, as a rule, are marginalized by political power should be the ones who wield it.

Mind you! Not women as women. This would be truly nonsensical, and an affront to women as women. The fact that part of contemporary feminism did not understand this point is indeed depressing, as well as masochistically self-destructive. Here we are talking about women insofar as they have become philosophers, that is, spiritually and socially equal to men.

Specifically, the utmost gender identity between men and women is realized precisely within the philosophical place insofar as it is concretely identified with the political place, with *politiké areté* (otherwise, it's just talk).

And yet this revolutionary, and in this sense outrageous, result is achieved only as long as men and women marginalize desire. Women give it up by virilizing themselves (for instance into soldiers) and by incarnating a social, promiscuous sex from which the sexual choice itself is excluded—along with erotic passion, the seductive imagination of the girdle, and so on. Men give it up by sublimating the erotic sexual desire into "love of wisdom"—that is to say, literally, into *philo-sophy*.

We can clearly see, then, how the project of a philosophical state is an essentially male project, offered by a virile logic and in the complete absence of female interlocutors and female logical voices. They cannot be present in the place of the foundation. They can only appear *afterward*, because of the political reformation put forward by men such as Socrates, Plato, and their friends. Which is to say: women will have the right to political existence and the right to speak once they have been conformed to the male founding logic. Precisely, once they have become philosophers.

Corollary: Does all this not entail, conversely, a "feminization" of philosophy? Indeed, meekness and peaceful asceticism are precisely the characteristics of the philosopher-ruler (in addition to their abilities to invent tricks and tell lies, traditional feminine weapons against male oppressors).

These characteristics will continue to hold true in the primitive Christian bishop. The credibility of the medieval philosopher was contingent on his being unmarried and, if possible, celibate, or at least chaste—hence the well-known drama of the great Peter Abelard.

All of the above implies the "third outrage": having women in common. This way of talking is itself revealing. It is a "having" clearly restricted to men: to *have* women. The point of the argument is quite different. It could easily be reversed to express the point of view of women, about whom we should say that they "have men in common"; yet these words are never spoken, or even thought, within the circle of friends gathered in the Piraeus.

But now I have digressed. What I wanted to say is that the "third outrage" shows the unresolved problematic nature of sexual desire: the issue goes far beyond its presumable practical infeasibility; it rather comes up against a blatant theoretical deficiency, whose symptom is the reduction of desire to a mere inferior part of the soul—on which we have already reasoned.

Thus, only the philosopher is the true politician, able to realize a good, virtuous, and happy city. *And yet, who is the philosopher?* Here we have come to the heart of the matter.

Fifth Figure

The Invisible

Scene V: The Philosopher's Drama

125. To get to the philosopher, Socrates significantly begins with love. Whoever loves something does not love only a part of it but loves it entirely. For example, whoever loves the young always finds a reason to love every one of them, whether fair-haired or dark-haired.

Now, the philosopher is someone who loves wisdom as a whole—that is, who loves its entire manifestation. And so, we come to *aletheia*: true philosophers are *lovers of the vision of truth* (*tous tes aletheias philotheamonas*). They are the "desirers" of *aletheia*. They love to see the manifestation of the whole, so that the entire "reality" may become manifest (*alethes*) to them. In this sense they love the entire *phainomenon* of being.

We must emphasize the potency of the verb "to see" (*theorein, theoria*): the *invisible* truth must become *visible* for the philosophers, *phainomenon*, precisely.

In other words: the invisibility of the power of desire (of love) must become visible in truth, or through the vision of truth. And it is precisely this vision that legitimizes philosophers to hold political power.

126. Let us introduce a brief digression, through a comparison with the tale of Gyges. Gyges too wanted to see the invisible, which in his case was the forbidden, and in this sense invisible, nakedness of the queen.

In essence, Gyges wished to see his own naked, incestuous desire, by having it penetrate to its origin, that is, to the *chasma* of Mother

Earth, where man's desire finds acceptance and a salvific shelter, for it rejoins its beginning, its origin.

We know that, just for having seen the queen, Gyges acquires political power—a public and visible power that is precisely founded on the private power that Gyges must see the invisible. In particular, the power to see the naked, generative desire of the queen (of Mother Earth), thus winning its fruits, which are the earth's fruits.

However, to achieve his goal, Gyges must first make himself—that is, his own desire—invisible: a power of invisibility that allows him to appropriate all bodies, and thus all things.

It is the power of the ring: a transferable object like the girdle, or the phallus. In plain words: the power of speech and money; the invisible power of the *sign*, the carrier of *value*. We are now familiar enough with these passages, although we cannot exactly say we have fully understood them.

All this considered, we can observe that the sophists, and particularly the character of Thrasymachus, perform an up-to-date version of the ancestral anthropology embodied by Gyges. They simply desecrate it, as Gyges himself begins to do by presenting himself as a tyrant and introducing money.

Through their seductive speech and their extravagant rhetoric, the sophists confer power, whose invisible incarnation is money (which they themselves wish to collect as compensation for their teaching). Besides, money is the main instrument both for a politics of the world above (Cephalus) and for a politics of the world below (Glaucon).

Now, to this power entrusted to the "body" of *signs* Plato opposes the power of the "soul" that *desires* the truth; that desires, that is, the *meaning* of the sign, its sense and ultimate purpose: that by which everything "is" and is what it is.

The passage is delicate, as the truth is after all what is invisible in bodies (their true purpose, their raison d'être); and yet this truth cannot be attained by the desire for possession, through the possession of bodies. In fact, the opposite is true.

In short, the issue stands as follows: the philosophers' desire is not the desire to constitute themselves as desirable bodies, through that recognition *of* and *in* the body which arises from an unequal exchange based on sexual difference. All this is removed politically, that is, philosophically.

Since they have no desire to constitute themselves as desirable bodies, they also have no desire for desiring or desired bodies. The philosophers' *eros* is asexual, or rather, sexually indifferent. Their *eros* is transferred elsewhere: not in the seductive sign of the bodies, nor in the sign of money, or of the written speeches so dear to the sophists, but rather in the dazzling light of the signs of truth directly intuited.

In other words, instead of desiring to constitute themselves as desiring bodies in a dialectical relationship with a desired body, philosophers *desire to constitute themselves as "souls"*: not sensible vision of the invisible desire in or for the body, but suprasensible vision of the invisible truth that causes the body to be how it is.

Freud might say that this desire of the philosopher to see the truth is a sublimation of the original desire to see the queen, her *chasma*, that is, from the child's viewpoint, a desire to see the parents' *secret*, to watch the forbidden mystery of their bedroom, driven by the unasked question: Who *am* I? What is my *origin*? Instead of commenting, let us return to the scene.

127. True philosophers want to attain the truth, but to do so they must first of all distinguish between *episteme* (science or knowledge) and *doxa* (opinion). And it is soon noted that to each corresponds a specific form of desire (as you can see, we are on the right track with our backstages).

Knowledge's desire is the desire for what "is," that is, Being (*ousia*). Opinion's desire is the desire for what is and at the same time is not, insofar as it continuously becomes; it is, in other words, the desire for bodies, primarily sexual desire.

Those who stop at opinions, for instance, desire beautiful bodies or beautiful things, whereas those who achieve knowledge desire beauty-in-itself, the "being in itself" of beauty, that is, beauty's *idea*. We have thus arrived at the heart of philosophy: the vision of ideas or "things in themselves."

But allow me one brief observation: that sexual desire is merely a matter of desiring beautiful bodies is but one of Plato's *mise-en-scènes*, a clever retroflexion prompted by *his* desire to assert the idea. Plato himself knows well that sexual love is something else, and indeed has masterfully described it in several places—for instance as divine madness (*theia mania*), deploying in this all his art as a great playwright and author.

At any rate, let us now listen to Socrates.

SOCRATES: Then those who see the many beautiful, and who yet neither see absolute beauty, nor can follow any guide who points the way thither; who see the many just, and not absolute justice, and the like,—such persons may be said to have opinion but not knowledge? . . . But those who see the absolute and eternal and immutable may be said to know, and not to have opinion only? . . . The one loves and embraces the subjects of knowledge, the other those of opinion? The latter are the same, as I dare say you will remember, who listened to sweet sounds and gazed upon fair colors, but would not tolerate the existence of absolute beauty. . . . Shall we then be guilty of any impropriety in calling them lovers of opinion (*doxophílists*) rather than lovers of wisdom (*philosophers*), and will they be very angry with us for thus describing them?

Thus, we have passed from the drama of men and women to the drama of the philosopher.

Scene VI: The Philosopher as Human Type

128. Plato stages two human types whose juxtaposition is already fully inherent in the character of Socrates—the figure that, in Plato's theater, represents, more than philosophy, "the philosopher." Philosophy is rather the fruit of Plato's opus, with that characteristic identification of science and politics that is completely missing in other recollections of the Socratic personality, such as can be found, for instance, in Xenophon or in the minor Socratics.

As for the rest, some features of Socrates' nature go back to the tradition of the absentminded philosopher, whose archetype lies in certain anecdotes related to Thales.

129. Let us review, in a nutshell, these two human types.

i. Those who are "able to grasp the eternal and immutable": these are the *philosophers*, and to them is reserved the government of the city.

ii. Those who wander in the region of the many and variable. They "have in their souls no clear pattern (*paradeigma*)": in fact, they are unable "as with a painter's eye to look

at the absolute truth." In sum, they do not differ in any
respect from the blind. They are the *non-philosophers*, unfit
to be the leaders of the city.

Note the opposition between the sighted and the blind. The exact
meaning of sight and blindness, however, is still far from established.

What is, then, the nature of philosophers?

They are lovers of a *science* "which reveals to them the immutable
eternal truth, which does not wander under the events of birth and
death." And they love all of it, without any preference, unlike those
who favor the passion of love or the passion for honors (the *philotimía*
Thucydides talked about).

This is enough for us to withdraw backstage and think.

130. We need not emphasize further the significant and certainly not
accidental choice of the examples that Plato offers. Rather, the crucial
point here concerns the eternal *reality*, which is the essence, the *ousia*:
that which always is. The passage is crucial because it establishes the birth
of the idea of a "reality in itself" altogether disconnected from desire.
Which goes hand in hand with the emergence of a truth of *theoretical
seeing* distinct from the *practice of desire*.

It is imperative that we grasp the unprecedented boldness and novelty of this gesture, of this Platonic *mise-en-scène*: something completely
unknown in his time. Thrasymachus, for one, knew nothing about it
and had not ever heard of it, and neither had anyone else.

But that was not all. Even when listening to it, Plato's contemporaries were not able in general to understand the meaning of what
was being said or claimed: blind and deaf, they could not reply to the
initiatory gesture of Platonic philosophy.

In reversed terms, this reflects on us as well. We, too, find it very
difficult to understand the unprecedented novelty of Plato's gesture,
because from time immemorial we have been entirely constituted and
conditioned by it—in a sense, "enchanted" by it.

Plato's gesture is the act of birth of public reality, that concept
of *reality* which is self-evident both to the common sense of us all and
to the scientific common sense, a notion consistent with the idea of
objective truth. This public reality arises through the Socratic-Platonic
dialectical and definitional discourses to beget the epistemic "object in

itself"—immutable and paradigmatic—of the new philosophical science. It is from these very definitional discourses that Aristotelian logic develops, along with an encyclopedic arrangement of knowledge which is, in its foundations, still widely canonical for us.

131. Now we must be clear about the fact that such a reality of an objective world *does not exist anywhere, except as an effect of the practices of objectification formulated by philosophy and Western science.* It is only within these practices that this concept of reality emerges; only in them does this concept take on a meaning of truth: of "objective" truth, precisely. A truth that is self-consistent yet also self-referential, which means, ultimately, *tautological.*

It is the event of a meaning of truth that embodies *a* figure of the world, with the characteristic and characterizing presumption of being universally valid for *the world.* Which is, again, tautologically true within the practices that constitute and exercise that figure of the world. The very phrase "the world in itself" is a typical example of this. It has its meaning within the practical outcomes it pursues; but outside of them, no one certainly ever meets or has met or will ever meet "the world in itself."

It is equally important to point out that this reality, public and in-itself, does not arise out of sheer theoretical love. This is what Aristotle, taking a cue from Plato's *Theaetetus,* would like us to believe. At the beginning of his *Metaphysics,* Aristotle will extol the "disinterested curiosity" of philosophers and scientists, praising it as the peak of human civilization, as what "by nature" is implicit in every man, and even, in some way, in "myth": amazement *before* the world, love for its "pure" contemplation and desire to *know* its principles and causes in themselves. This is philosophy's ideological tale, a perfectly self-justifying and self-celebratory tale whose (still enduring) rhetorical influence on our minds is nothing short of remarkable.

But this disinterest, as we have seen, has been primarily staged by Plato as a characteristic feature of philosophers: those who have no preferences, only a "virtuous disinterest" whereby they love *all* reality, without repudiations or passions.

It is the lesson that old Parmenides teaches young Socrates—yet another of Plato's characteristic inventions, one which, under the pretense of describing reality as it is in itself—in its *ousia,* concretely shows *what attitude* (*ethos*) is to be assumed in order to exert the *objectifying* practice of philosophy. It is this attitude and this practice that produce the supposed "realities in themselves."

Now, as I had begun to say, the idea of a public and objective reality of the world, a world which eternally is as it is, does not arise in the least out of sheer theoretical love. If we look carefully, as we have been, at the scene from the *Republic*, we can clearly see that this objective or in-itself idea *is the result of a political operation*, and is as such by no means disinterested.

Which means that at the core of the whole science lies a constitutively political intention, or rather, as we will see, a choice about the economy of life and of death. Forget about scientific neutrality! It is high time we did away with this fairytale, if only for the dignity and truth value inherent in the very scientific practices that we exercise.

132. *Political passion*, therefore, is the backstage of the theoretical scene: here is the great lesson we learn from our backstage practice. In this sense, as we have repeatedly maintained, the politician is one with the philosopher. Which is peculiarly in accordance with Plato's "letter": not, however, with his "spirit," which would have us believe he is founding the "true" politician on the "true" philosopher and not vice versa.

We can also put it this way: this apathetic scientific objectiveness, this reality that would be as it is regardless of our desires, is the result of a "representative practice" made possible by the philosophical *logos*. People educated accordingly, that is, educated to the exercise of the "logical mind," become able to see things and the world "objectively" (*sub specie objectivitatis*). In a way, they acquire an extra eye.

The repercussion, or reverse effect, of this operation is the establishment of psychological subjectivity—not public but private, that is, "pathetic" and "illogical." It follows that even love—expressly invoked by Plato as that which the science of reality must exclude—no longer a sacred pathology becomes, in the West, a *sentimental* pathology.

In the West, therefore, we psychological subjects—a residual consequence of having become "logical subjects"—*fall in love*, giving inspiration and work for our poets.

A lot more could be said about this eternal reality where birth and death have no place. Eternal life as the eternity of matter, where nothing is created and nothing is destroyed, as modern science will say. But the question is far more complex, and we are not yet ready to grasp it.

133. Meanwhile, the philosophers' nature is being analytically described. They are incapable of lying (because they love truth). They pursue the pure pleasures of the soul, renouncing bodily pleasure entirely. They do not have an intractable character and they are not unjust. They learn easily and have good memory, and they know no triviality or pettiness, as is only inevitable in men seeking to embrace the totality of things both human and divine.

Here Socrates' words are again worth listening to.

SOCRATES: Then how can he who has magnificence of mind and is the spectator of all time and all existence, think much of human life?

A sentence that wonderfully illustrates Plato's *philosophic passion*, his love for what he, first among men, had *seen*.

Scene VII: Adeimantus' Objection

134. Adeimantus, at this point, has his say. Socrates' reasoning makes sense, yet most people will remain unconvinced as they will argue that, leaving logic aside, philosophers are *in fact*, for the most part, rather extravagant, or even wicked, characters. Entrusting the government to such men is sheer folly.

Socrates, who had been expecting this objection, offers a long articulate reply, focused on two main points.

First, in corrupt cities, like the ones we live in, even philosophic natures are subject to corruption (Who would disagree with this statement? It continues to hold true today).

Secondly, the keenest and brightest minds, if they become corrupt, are precisely the ones who eventually will turn into the wickedest people. (Alcibiades might come to mind.)

Nevertheless, Socrates reiterates with great force: "Cities will never rest from their evils until philosophers are kings." The true ones, of course.

SOCRATES: And so the philosopher, holding converse with the divine order, becomes orderly and divine, as far as the nature of man allows.

It remains to be shown *how* all of this is possible. Socrates agrees; we must not repeat the previous mistake, when we talked about the common possession of women and the anonymous procreation of children; we should not postpone the issue, but we must immediately take responsibility for this *how* and show its feasibility in practice.

Socrates' myth of the education of philosophers begins.

Scene VIII: The *Chasma* of the Philosopher

135. Socrates says: the aspirant philosopher must not only be tested in those labors and dangers and pleasures which we mentioned before, but there is another kind of probation which we did not mention—he must be exercised also in many kinds of knowledge. Finally, and most importantly, we must observe whether he will be able to endure the greatest notions (*mathemata megista*). Only then will the aspirant philosopher be able to access the highest knowledge.

136. But then, his friends ask, as can be gleaned from what you say, there is a knowledge still higher than this—higher than justice and the other virtues we have listed as necessary to give a foundation to the city. Yes, Socrates replies, and that is "the idea of the Good." This is the highest knowledge.

In fact, only if we first attain the idea of the Good can the just and all other virtues really become useful and advantageous. As we have not yet discussed it, Socrates concedes, we know but little of it; even so, one can say from the start that, without having attained the idea of the Good, the possession of whatsoever virtue or thing will profit us nothing.

In other words: it is not enough for something to be beneficial, such as richness, beauty, health, and so on. To be truly beneficial, it must also be "good"; otherwise, and against appearances, it will not be. (We might venture to say: only the righteous desiring and the righteous being desired will produce the "good." But let us leave this aside.)

137. And yet, what is the Good? Here is the definitive question.

Most people, Socrates reminds the party, are positive that the Good is pleasure. But then we must admit that there are bad pleasures and good ones. The more refined say it is intelligence, but they cannot explain what they mean by intelligence and remain vague.

Now, the Good is a crucial issue, about which we cannot afford to stick to generalities or be satisfied with mere appearances: how to seem beautiful without quite being so, or even, in Glaucon's words, how to look just without being it at all.

In fact, when it comes to what is called good, no one can settle for appearances; it is completely unsatisfactory to us that a thing may only seem good without being so. What we want is to possess the good "entity" as such, its full *reality*.

And that is why we can temporarily conclude that a guardian who is ignorant of how the just and beautiful are good is not a politician of great worth.

138. Now we must come back to the point. What is, in sum, the Good? Leaving his friends speechless, Socrates, the champion of definitory questions, declines to define the Good. He claims, as is his wont, to be unable to do it, and he might well be hinting, ironically, at the fact that the Good, because it is beyond being and any being (beyond *ousia*, as he will in fact go on to say), cannot be defined nor is there any sense in trying; in *this* sense, it is undefinable.

Therefore, Socrates will not speak directly of the Good, but rather of what he thinks to be "the offspring of the Good"—*ekgonos*, that is, born, generated, product, fruit of the Good, just as we speak of the "fruits" of the earth. This offspring is indeed "most similar" to the Good.

Now we get to the bottom of the *chasma*, and Plato will directly stage *philosophy*. Every step he takes, every word he utters, will become hereafter precious and crucial.

139. That is how Socrates reasons: through our speech (*logos*) we say that there are many things that are good and beautiful, and so on; through our speech, in fact, we define them as beautiful, good, and so forth.

In so doing, we show that we consider all these things in a unified manner, that is, according to a single *idea* having a single essence. To be clear: *beauty in itself, the Good in itself,* and so on, under which we gather respectively all the things that we hold to be beautiful and all the things that we hold to be good.

140. But now, pay attention!

> SOCRATES: The old story, that there is a many beautiful
> and a many good, and so of other things which we describe
> and define; to all of them "many" is applied.

Now, precisely this passage, which establishes the difference between seeing and conceiving, is the crucial point: we are at the crossroads between "visible" and "invisible"—the Ariadne's thread that, as I promised you, will lead us to the bottom of the philosopher's *chasma*.

But we need to be clear about this. Plato is not just opposing things that are visible to things that are invisible—such as would be, for instance, mortals on one side and the Gods on the other. His point is deeper and more complex. He is showing that all visible things *contain an invisible*; they contain, in other words, something that our sight as such cannot see and that cannot be perceived in what is purely visible.

This something that mere sight cannot see is precisely the conceivable, the object of conceiving (*noein*), which is purely invisible.

141. Now, these two ways of being do not exclude each other, *but on the contrary, they imply each other.* A visible Gyges excludes an invisible Gyges. And yet, all visible things would remain "blind," that is, unseen, without the invisible which is in them, and which manifests itself in making conceivable what can be seen.

According to the well-known example, if I see a horse, I also see the essence of the horse; or, as Husserl had it, if I see a color, then I also see the essence "color."

Of course, we speak of this second "seeing" in a metaphorical or figurative manner. What we mean is that by seeing a horse, we "conceive" at the same time of the essence "horse"; or better, and this is the point, we *know* that we are seeing a horse.

Indeed, if I did not conceive of this essence, I could not say that I see in the actual sense a horse. I could not even say, strictly speaking, that I see. What would I see, in fact, if I could not *say* that I see *a horse?*

We could say—you might remark—that we see something brown, and so on. That is to say: the essence of "something in general," the essence of "brown"—and we're back where we started.

142. What is coming into the open, essentially, is that we are dealing with the relationship between vision and language. We will understand it better further on, but for the moment we should remember what Socrates said at the beginning: we describe and define many things within our speech (*logos*) . . . As you can see, language comes on the scene right away, nor could it be otherwise.

In other words, this is about the relationship between the fact *that* we see (pure vision without a particular notion) and *what* we see (the notion as the invisible side of vision, which, on the other hand, illumines it, enabling it to happen as an actual seeing, determined and concrete).

Thus, the invisible is the definition of the visible, what defines it in every sense of the word "define." Plato will fully develop this dialectic in the *Sophist*, but it is here where he shows its origin.

We see many things, but we do not conceive them for the mere fact that we are seeing them. We conceive, instead, the unitary idea of the many things, their essence, which, however, cannot be seen. Now, Socrates asks, how do we see all these different things? By sight, he answers. And by hearing we hear, and with the other senses we perceive the other objects of sense (*aistheta*). Yet, Socrates concludes, "Sight is by far the most costly and complex piece of workmanship which the artificer of the senses ever contrived."

143. I understand that this new digression will bother you more than usual, but at this juncture we cannot help but pause a little and have our say: we cannot, at this juncture, allow ourselves to be enchanted by Socrates' performance, by his matchless music, and least of all by the sublime tricks of his puppet master.

Indeed, I am sure, you are hearing "sight, hearing . . ." and everything seems plausible to you. You are already in full agreement with Socrates, only waiting impatiently to understand what he is leading up to and where he is going to take you. And yet, this is precisely what you must not concede.

That there are "sensible things" in relation to the five senses (sight, hearing, etc.) seems obvious to you. How could you possibly doubt that? And so, by ingrained habit, you overlook the extraordinary novelty of Plato's elaboration: he creates the *concept* of "sensible reality" by difference and in retroflected opposition to the concept of "intelligible reality." Having established intelligible reality (the domain of the conceivable with its ideal and "invisible"—that is, "not sensible"—essences), he extracts from it, by subtraction and opposition, this "sensible reality"—"pure" seeing without a concept.

But then I ask you: When have you ever experienced this supposed pure, *sensible* seeing? Moreover, isn't what you are referring to *also* a concept? *Seeing, the sensible, sight, hearing,* what else are they if not ideas and concepts?

It is the very staging of the definitory *logos* and its supersensible objects that produces, as a retroflected consequence, a supposed layer of merely sensible reality: a reality, in fact, which is "not intelligible," "not conceptual," although this statement, as we have seen, paradoxically undermines itself.

144. I realize very well that my remarks have produced in you a profound puzzlement, without offering a way out of it. These very remarks might even appear to you to prove the judiciousness of the platonic gesture. Isn't Plato saying, after all, that conceiving is always related to the idea? Therefore, it is only natural that in order to conceive the "seeing" we have to resort to the idea of "seeing in itself," which, however, is not *this* empirical seeing (although even the "this" is in turn an idea, a universal, a concept). There is, then, an empirical side, a sensible reality, which is not conceivable in itself.

And yet I daresay you have already conceived it, by defining it as you do; in other words, if it must be "not conceivable," you declare you do not conceive it . . . thereby conceiving it! Whatever do you mean, in short, when you speak of a "sensible reality"?

I invite you to be patient: we will unravel, I promise, all these puzzles. Meanwhile, however, think about this: *"The organ with which we see the visible things . . . is the sight. And with hearing . . . we hear, and with the other senses perceive the other objects of sense. But . . . the artificer of the senses . . ."* Here Socrates has recourse to a mythical phrase (*ton aistheseon demiurgon*) as if to disguise his operation by cloaking it into a fable. This is a characteristic gesture. The mythical image intends to mask and deflects us from the fact that the artificer of the senses is Socrates himself, inasmuch as he posits a distinction between conceivable and sensible, light and shadow (as we will see), that is, light's shadow.

Socrates, the "father of the concept," does not want to be identified with the author of the operation, which he ascribes to an imaginary artificer. And while he is at it, still in mythological mode, he proceeds with his explanation.

145. Now, let us return to the scene. "Sight is by far the most costly and complex piece of workmanship which the artificer of the senses ever contrived." (Here the exchange of looks between Gyges and the queen comes to mind.) Whence, then, comes this privilege that sight possesses?

It comes from the fact that, unlike voice and hearing, which communicate directly to the senses, sight and visible things require the intervention of that *noble* intermediate which is light (*phos*), that is, the sun. Who would dare deny the noble divinity of the sun and, in general, of the light that illuminates the universe?

You might well object that both hearing and voice, too, require the intervention of an intermediate—air. I don't know what to say to that. I can only remind you that the Greeks had been uncertain for a long time whether air was an element or not. Whereas it can hardly be denied that most everywhere we look the sun and light are the primeval or fundamental divinities.

In any case, Socrates is here most anxious to arrive at the reasoning that I am going to summarize for you.

The sun, Socrates says, is not sight, but the author both of sight and of being seen. In fact, neither sight (*opsis*) nor the eye (*omma*) is the sun; they see visible objects by derivation from, and because of, the sun and thereby they also see the sun itself.

It follows that the light of the sun is the *invisible* intermediate element that causes the eye *to see* and the *visible* to appear, including the sun.

146. Having established this, we finally come to the "Good," through a perfect relation of *analogy*. In fact, Socrates says that the Good begets an analogue of itself, namely the sun: here is the offspring! It is being said, in other words, that the Good performs, in the intellectual world,

the same function as the sun in the visible world, where the sun is the mediator between sight and the objects of sight.

The Good, then, is not the intellect but the cause of understanding and being understood. It is an intermediate intellectual (invisible) light that causes the intellect to understand. By the same token, the intellect (*nous*) is not the Good, but by derivation from the Good it understands the intellectual objects (the ideas, the essences) as well as the Good itself.

"Will you be a little more explicit?" Glaucon said. We should not miss this line from Plato's skillful script. It marks the complete novelty of what Plato is saying, which no human ears have ever heard before. An *analogy* that, on the contrary, appears to us quite simple and clear.

Once again, we must be able to deconstruct in ourselves the foundation of what seems obvious to us, that is, those images and relations that have become for us, over thousands of years, obvious and self-evident.

And Socrates, patiently, explains with an example. "Why, you know, I said, that the eyes, when a person directs them towards objects on which the light of day is no longer shining, but the moon and stars only, see dimly, and are nearly blind; they seem to have no clearness of vision in them? . . . And the soul is like the eye . . ."

But now we will listen directly to the words that follow, because they enunciate a discourse of vital importance, which is the origin and foundation of all our tradition and culture.

147.

> SOCRATES: And the soul is like the eye: when resting upon that on which truth and being shine, the soul perceives and understands and is radiant with intelligence; but when turned towards the twilight of becoming and perishing, then she has opinion only, and goes blinking about, and is first of one opinion and then of another, and seems to have no intelligence?
>
> Now, that which imparts truth (*aletheia*: unveiling) to the known (*gignoskomenois*) and the power of knowing to the knower is what I would have you term the idea of good, and this you will deem to be the cause (*aitia*) of science (*episteme*), and of truth in so far as the latter becomes the subject of knowledge; beautiful too, as are both truth and knowledge,

you will be right in esteeming this other nature as more beautiful than either; and, as in the previous instance, light and sight may be truly said to be like the sun, and yet not to be the sun, so in this other sphere, science and truth may be deemed to be like the good, but not the good; the good has a place of honor yet higher.

You would say, would you not, that the sun is only the author of visibility in all visible things, but of generation and nourishment and growth, though he himself is not generation?

In like manner the good may be said to be not only the author of knowledge to all things known, but of their being and essence (*to einai kai ten ousian*), and yet the good is not essence, but far exceeds essence in dignity and power.

148. The Good, therefore, is "beyond essence" (*epekeina tes ousias*). As such, it is also beyond knowledge and truth, and thus the so-called "science of the Good," established by Socrates as the culmination of the philosopher's formation, is rather the supersensible intuition of the purpose (*telos*) for which all things that are, are. A purpose that causes the universe to be and, within it, organizes paradigmatically all beings and their functions.

"Political virtue," founder of the "good" city, is thus inscribed into an ontological and cosmic framework that the *Timaeus* (which, by no accident, Plato intended as a prosecution of the *Republic*) will portray in full, solving its last puzzles: a "divine" picture surmounting the ruins of the "sacred" world of the false and untruthful Gods.

An impressive picture, before which we cannot but experience amazement and veneration. And yet, once again, we cannot give up our hateful and cruel *desire* not to be "enchanted" by the old serpent, by his marvelous and sublime scene, so as to be able to freely observe, in the meantime, what goes on behind the scenes.

Indeed, let us not forget that it is precisely the political necessity to educate the ruler-guardians that leads to this psychic cosmo-anthropology, to this cosmo-ontology of the mind and soul, of the essence and the Good.

Sixth Figure

The Analogy of the Written Word

Scene IX: The *Chasma* of Words

149. Now it is time to draw some conclusions. Plato has established two utmost principles: one rules over the intellectual world and the other over the visible. It is revealing, for what we have just noted, that here Plato puts into Socrates' mouth the question: "May I suppose that you have this distinction of the visible and intelligible fixed in your mind?" This is the unprecedented novelty of the threshold we are about to cross.

There follows the famous image of the "line," both the torment and delight of many an interpreter. It shows the two realms or worlds subdivided into two further sections, so that we have four corresponding places of the soul: two representing the visible or sensible and two the intelligible:

The realm of shadows which corresponds to the sensible image (*eikasia*).

The realm of sensible objects which corresponds to empirical belief (*pistis*).

The realm of geometrical figures which corresponds to reasoning (*dianoia*).

The realm of ideas which corresponds to intellectual intuition (*nous*).

It is the origin of Plato's theory of the image, which will be developed in the *Theaetetus* and later perfected in the *Sophist*. The "topic" of the soul will then achieve completion, and with it what we are here calling the "strategy of the soul."

This topic is the fundamental appearance of the "psychization" of (Western) man and of the correlative ontologization of the world. A foundation that has henceforth been canonical. Descartes, in modern times and under the impetus of scientific writing, will herald its scholastic version, to which, too, we remain to this day beholden.

150. On the basis of the aforementioned four places, Socrates will elaborate the celebrated myth of the cave, that is, the real description of the *chasma* of the philosopher and of his drama: how the philosopher, having broken the shackles that bind him to the world of shades, gradually rises toward the truth and the light, until he can behold directly the light of the sun, metaphor of the idea of the Good—science's journey toward enlightenment and the mystical-ascetic intuition of good purpose.

Moved by pity for his fellow brothers shackled in the cave, the philosopher descends again among them to help them, by way of his political and philosophical knowledge, to free themselves from the shadow of "titanic" passions and from the illusory images of desire: an arduous and dangerous task in pursuit of which the philosopher is fully aware he is risking his life.

There is no need to go into this now. The myth of the cave is undoubtedly the founding myth of the West, of the West of knowledge, but its precondition is the very connection between *seeing* and *conceiving* that Plato has staged. This is the fundamental and decisive threshold where all our forms of knowledge converge: both the ones we depicted at the beginning in the circulation of the "cross" marking the places and components of political virtue, and, in general, all forms of knowledge constituting the scientific encyclopedia of the West.

Herein is rooted the crucial theoretical question, and unless we clarify it thoroughly (indeed an arduous and complicated task), we will not be able to understand the full range of our questions and genealogical efforts regarding the backstage of the Platonic scene: indeed, the "primal scene" for any subsequent staging of the knowledge that characterizes us.

151. We have already recognized that language is what is chiefly at stake in the seeing/conceiving nexus: and thus begins *our* descent into the *chasma* of words.

We finally confront the center of our cross, where we can write a "S" to signify "Speech" (*Parola*),[1] and also the politico-philosophical pedagogy that is the Platonic *mise-en-scène* of the philosophical *logos*, as a protagonist of the theater of philosophy's political rhetoric. (Listen carefully to every word I say.) Of this *mise-en-scène* we have been carrying out our backstage reading, which is, however, far from concluded.

But our descent into the *chasma* of speech is also the beginning of our "auto-bio-graphy," because at stake is also *our* word, *our* theater and its *desire*, which rules over us implicitly.

Evidently, now the proscenium turns out to be our entire scene, inhabited nevertheless by a question (or, if you prefer, "suspicion") behind the scenes.

152. After these introductory considerations we get to the heart of the matter, with some remarks of a very general nature.

What is *the visible*? A simple, legitimate question, yet one that leads to paradoxical conclusions. What could the answer be, in fact? For every answer must inevitably transcend *what* the question is asking, to show *something other* than the visible: words, definitions, concepts, scientific theories, and so forth.

The question itself, for that matter, already deals in *words*, asks for *words*. What else could it possibly ask for?

It would be more appropriate, then, to ask instead: "How can we talk *sensibly* about the visible?" Indeed, this is what we will set out to do, though "at first sight," the matter does not look at all easy to resolve. If we resort, for instance, to "descriptions" such as "the visible is bright," or "the visible is colored," we find ourselves again dealing in *words*.

Notwithstanding, these first remarks do lead to at least one positive result, if only because now we clearly realize that "the visible" is not really a "thing" but rather a concept. A *noeton*, Plato would say. But then, we may retort, insofar as it is a concept, it must be *invisible*. The visible is invisible! This is what we are saying, even by virtue of merely mentioning "the" *visible*, as we are doing, and we cannot help but do.

In Plato, the concept is but the reflection, or the consequence, of the supersensible vision of the idea: something we can only catch "with

---

1. *Parola* (word) has been translated primarily as "speech," except when it was necessary to preserve the original meaning of the singular or plural form (*parole*)—Trans.

our mind's eye." In other words, something that we cannot see at all, that we can only "think" or "conceive."

This is precisely what Hegel reiterates when he sarcastically affirms: the concept cannot be grasped with our hands.

153. Very well. But then the issue must—of necessity—be put as follows: the occurrence of the visible, specifically, of the visible world or of the world such as it is seen, *is an invisible event.*

We must think of this event as a threshold phenomenon: it is on the invisible threshold of its occurring that the world shows itself in its visibility, that is, in the figure of a visible world and thus concretely seen. An invisible threshold, of course, because if it were itself visible then it would be an occurrence belonging *to the* visible world, a phenomenon internal to the world, rather than the event *of the* visible world; or of the world *such as it is* visible (a figure of the world).

154. Indeed, modern science frequents precisely this constitutive invisibility—constitutive of the visible: the events it talks about, including the ones that originate vision, are not in principle, and even less in fact, visible.

It is nonetheless true that scientific practice cannot help but frequent the visible world and use it—as Husserl had it. It must presuppose that very "having the world" in its pre-categorial visible mode which we all experience by living. On the other hand, scientific practice does not concern itself with this presupposition, nor does it question it. In a pinch, it merely justifies it ideologically by way of the classical distinction between primary and secondary qualities of experience—which is plain and simple nonsense.

Of course, this does not happen because scientists are absentminded or shallow people. It happens by necessity, insofar as modern science has inherited its foundation from Plato, from that nexus of seeing and thinking with which we have been dealing here. Science has long lost any sense of this foundation: today it simply implements it, taking it for granted yet ignoring it completely as such, since the training of scientists to scientific practice is predicated essentially on the oblivion of the metaphysical roots from which that practice originated. In fact, science, in its pragmatic certainties, dreams precisely of having emancipated itself, once and for all, from metaphysics.

However, even having recourse to the pre-categorial is far from conclusive. It does not do justice to the scientific operation because it does not understand the crucial and peculiar fact of its "writing," the fact that modern scientific practice unwittingly frequents a threshold that effectively revolutionizes, and in some way subverts, the writing of metaphysics. But we cannot deal with this now.

Let us draw instead a first temporary conclusion from what we have said. This can be formulated as follows: we cannot see where the visible comes from; if it were seen, the visible would have already happened.

A paradoxical conclusion, indeed, which nonetheless opens the way to an important breakthrough.

155. What we are essentially saying is that the visible is as such *ineffable*.

Not because the visible cannot be said: by saying "the visible," as *you can see*, we are precisely mentioning it; but what we say, as it were, *hails it*, signals it, heralds it, translates it, in other words, substitutes for it. And this saying is certainly not the same as the effectuality of the visible as such; it is precisely in this sense that the visible is, as such, ineffable.

Plato would put it as follows: the Good, which is beyond essence, and which brings about the intellectual visibility of the soul through its *analogon*, the sun, which brings about the sensible visibility of the eyes, cannot be seen. But it can be *said*.

The discourse of the Good (*logos tou agathou*) is precisely the *mise-en-scène* itself of philosophy and philosophers; the ability, in fact, to tell the "truth" in the light of the Good.

So, as we pointed out, "saying the visible" amounts to *transcribing it* into words. Or better, it amounts to providing a *sign* for it: a replacement which, as such, inevitably *fails the original*, the thing itself (*pragma auto*), which vision *is*.

But the thing itself is also the "thing" of philosophy (and thus of politics): the object of its science. For instance, that very thing Plato talks about in the *Seventh Letter*, where he denies that speech can adequately express the philosophical *vision* of truth and the Good. And much less the "written" word.

156. On the other hand, speech is precisely what tells us that the visible exists, retroflecting the rift, or threshold, within its practice. It is in the

light of words' universe of meaning, a universe retroflected to indicate vision, that speech itself asserts the existence of the visible.

And so, speech, by translating the visible into the mentionable, by making it in fact mentionable, that is making it, in a sense, visible, *incarnates the invisible.*

It incarnates the invisible in the sense that speech makes the visible perceivable in the voice and indeed even literally visible in the writing of the voice. That is actually how the voice incarnates the meaning of speech which is precisely invisible: we conceive it, but we do not see it.

Writing makes meaning visible: this seems evident. And by the same token, writing makes the voice visible, which is by itself invisible.

Slow down! Things are not so simple. As Plato already knew, the matter of invisibility runs deeper and is also of a different kind. We really get off cheaply if we say that writing makes words visible, as we often do, without being able truly to confront the enigma of meaning—and therefore, only producing, despite it all, empty talk.

Indeed, what is visible in writing is not the meaning that writing embodies, and which makes it "writing"—this meaning remains nonetheless invisible, just as it remains inaudible in the very sounds of the voice. Therefore *the* visible withholds itself as such from the overt visibility of writing.

Which means we must rethink the whole matter.

Scene X: The Analogy of Writing

157. Ineffable is the visible; invisible is speech. Or: unsayable is the visible; invisible is the sayable.

Here is the crisscrossed connection that we can infer from this first confrontation with the problem. It will take us some time to really understand this connection, to be able to talk about it properly. Let us start by getting rid of the so-called visibility of writing.

What elements of words does writing—alphabetic writing—make visible? To answer this, we must first refer to the concrete "practice" of speech. And we also must acknowledge the fact that there are no "pure" practices: every practice is a tangle of many practices constantly in motion.

It is precisely through the motion of their constant integrations and differences that objects come to emerge, objects internal to these tangles of practices (there aren't any others), which go on constantly to shift and change their meaning with the constant changing of the tangles of practices.

In the practice of words, therefore, we apply ourselves to the intentions of saying; we are caught up in practices of expression that are each time peculiar. It is this very intention that articulates and qualifies itself through words; or better, through the practice of *saying*.

In so doing, we *use* the "meaningfulness" of words, without making them the object of explicit attention. We do not think about words and to a certain extent we do not even know they exist, not unlike children starting to talk, or illiterates.

In practice, we do not have *words* at all, nor are we dealing with words: these objects do not exist, they have not yet emerged as objects of our experience and in our experience.

And keep in mind: even when we say, "I can't think of words right now," we are not really thinking of words in general—speech as an object in itself—but only of *that* particular word, the word we need to express what we intend to say, except that a sudden amnesia has now erased it from our memory.

158. Now, in the practice of writing we ideally transcribe all the complex experience that inheres in the aforementioned practices of expression yet focusing our attention exclusively on the vocal and verbal gestures: we assign visible signs to aural signals, thus constructing an analogical repetition.

The matter is not that simple (it appears so to us only *after* we have learned to read and write). In its analogy, in fact, alphabetic writing does not limit itself to "transcribing." How could it? What would it really transcribe? What is visible in a vocal sound so that it can be *transcribed*? What is elementary or literal in a vocal gesture that unfolds, modulating continuously in its expressive flow?

Writing does something completely different. And it does it through a long process of intertwined practices that progressively change its meaning and modes of operation, constantly changing its *supposed* objects (writing itself, the voice, words, etc.).

Here let us just say, in a general and even generic way, that writing analyzes and splits the acoustic experience, establishing an analogical parallel with visible signs. Establishing this analogue scale goes hand in hand with analyzing and splitting: the two procedures coconstitute themselves through the same gesture.

And so alphabetic writing classifies the past acoustic experiences, thus retroactively assigning them to a phonetics. It is this written phonetics that marks, by difference, the "acoustic" (which never existed before), or rather, that makes the acoustic appear as such. This is also when we start knowing that speech is made up of *sounds*. The fact that speech is made up of sounds becomes true and experienceable only now, thanks to, and by difference from, its "being made visible" crystallized in writing.

159. It is through this very process that all meanings—which were initially not known as such insofar as they were directly acted and lived *in each given situation*, within the various practices of life and expression—become accessible to knowledge. Thanks to alphabetic writing, these meanings become, or more precisely *can* become, known.

We are talking about that scientific, *logical* knowledge which is triggered at some point by the practice of alphabetic writing and reading—synergistically connected to many other practices—and which culminates in the very *philosophical* vision of reality and of the soul with which we have here been concerning ourselves.

Now consider the following. Alphabetic *transliteration* allows us to read any word, thus transcribed, of any language, even without understanding at all its meaning. The alphabet, in fact, can be applied to any spoken language, which is precisely one of its strengths.

But now consider how meaningful is the fact that it took so many centuries before this virtue of the alphabet was, as it were, discovered. For a long time, medieval writers and amanuenses thought alphabetic writing to be intimately linked to the Latin language, to which it had been indeed exclusively applied.

The discovery of universal transliteration was the primary cause for the rise of modern literary languages, namely, Provençal, Italian, French literature, among others—with all its consequences for the forming of the modern European *soul*.

We are thus able to read even without understanding the meaning transcribed and crystallized in the alphabetic signs. Rather than a reading, we here have a performance (in some respects analogous to a musical performance) that applies a phonic body to the letters.

I perform for the ear and the outcome of this is understandable if the sounds are related to the living experience of an *oral* language that I know. Which shows that the graphic signs, in themselves, do not carry at all an invisible meaning, which they would make visible, as sometimes people mistakenly say or think.

160. Another example. I can recognize the internal value of a coin thanks to the classificatory system, or the ordering system of arithmetical signs. I can understand that five old shillings are worth half of ten, and fifty half of one hundred, and five hundred half of one thousand, and so on. But in this manner, I still do not understand its economic value. I do not know, for instance, whether five shillings will buy me a sandwich, or a full meal.

A comparison with the geographical map can also be useful. A map shows conventional signs on a two-dimensional sheet. These signs demand to be translated to the three-dimensional experiences of finding our bearings and of walking in a specific situation.

Only by referring to these already known and frequented experiences can we understand that two long parallel lines mean the presence of a road, that a triangle signals the presence of a mountain, the green spells countryside, the blue stands for the sea, and so on.

In a way, there is an analogy with iconic writings. For example, a face in profile with an arrow indicating it might mean "I"; two open bare hands might mean "to lack"; another face with an open mouth from which issue ever wider semicircles might mean "words." *I lack words.*

161. Well then, alphabetic writing does quite a different thing. It does not reproduce meanings such as "face," "word," and so on. It presupposes them to be known in the practice of oral linguistic expression—just as the geographical map presupposes our pre-categorial (pre-geo-*graphical*) experience of the territory, of our ambulant "getting our bearings" in the world.

The alphabet limits itself to *dressing* the orally acted word with its analogical clothing (clearly metaphorical and sham); in so doing, it conserves and crystallizes all its meanings, that is, all the morphological shades of meaning. These nuances are somewhat frozen in the letters, waiting, as they unfreeze in the voice, to recover the taste, that is, the meaning that belongs to them.

And so, the alphabet can write "lack, lacked, will lack, would lack," docilely modeling itself on the spoken language. It does not limit itself to the general "to lack" of iconic writing.

It is nonetheless true that, by focusing on pure meaning, that is, by making meaning emerge and by confining it in the written words—we have already said that words really appear only insofar as they are written—the alphabet overlooks or relinquishes many components and nuances of experience: for instance, those nuances that are hopelessly phonic *and therefore cannot be transcribed into a visible body.*

For instance, if I see the written expression "go down," I can certainly give voice to these signs, but while I can grasp their meaning, I do not necessarily grasp their sense. What is *meant* by that? The sense of the phrase is very different if the two words are uttered in a threatening way, in a beseeching tone, or as a simple invitation.

I must know the context, the emotion, the aim, and so on, that is, all the experiences that writing cannot reproduce immediately, but only in oblique ways. Consider, for example, a theatrical script with notes on the margin. Or, even more aptly, the analogy with musical writing.

The map, we could say, by presupposing our visual (and not only visual) experience of the territory suggests, with its visible conventional signs, a muscular translation: it schematizes routes. In turn, alphabetic writing demands muscular translations through the voice, although with the aim of reviving meanings, as well as a certain route of the sense, which cannot be signified but in oblique ways.

162. With a free analogy, we can then consider the different scenic and dramatic positions of Thrasymachus and Socrates.

Both are engaged in discussion to express the essence of the Good. Yet Thrasymachus enacts this expression in contexts of sense such as: the appropriate or effective course of action for those who act according to certain ends, thanks to which they may be well, that is, feel good, pleased, satisfied, proud of themselves, so that they can feel fulfilled and happy in their nature.

Whereas Socrates enacts the expression in quite a different sense and manner. He asks how the Good can be defined, what real thing the Good is and how we can discover it and get to know it, hence, what is good for us *to know*, because only this knowledge makes us happy—of course very differently from how Thrasymachus envisions happiness.

In both, the analogy of words brings forth figurative images of happiness and goodness: images that prescribe itineraries of sense for action, which also mean political images, closely connected to the fundamental economy of life. And yet, only Socrates turns the performance into an itinerary in meaning, that is to say, a path for that doing which is knowing. Philosophy becomes therefore, for him, that place of universal writing that translates, and promotes, the analogy of the Good into the unheard-of and invisible figure of "truth."

Scene XI: The Retroflex Vision

163. Back to the matter at hand. When reading a text, we incorporate back the meanings that writing has disembodied from the experience of direct expression enacted in situation. But mind you: *This action does not happen between "equivalences,"* that is, between presupposed equivalent "things."

It is not that there is an aural body that subsequently translates itself into a visual body, which would make us *see* (an outcome nothing short of remarkable) the aural body that was there before its visual "transcription." *This is not it at all.*

Not realizing this gives rise to the many paradoxes, absurdities, improper questions and matters that torment, consciously or unconsciously, the linguistic sciences and the philosophy of language.

The situation is very different, and we could try to describe it this way.

There is a joining of words with practices of expression: these practices are lived and enacted within practices of life that are each time determined and defined. Then there is a practice of alphabetic transcription that exhibits visual signs, which are the result of the classification and imposition of a code functional to the common practice of reading.

It is a matter of giving voice again to the written signs, in the different ways in which this happens and still happens.

One thing, in fact, is the inscription on the stone, and quite another is the donative to the God, or the text of a law for the public square, the *agorá*, and so on, according to deeply mutating modalities: mutations that in turn modify the situation and sense of writer and reader, of sight and voice, of meaning and sense, of subject and object, of text and message, among other things.

It is in this motley and fickle area that real visual bodies of writing gradually take shape.

164. Now, as we have incidentally remarked, it is these "visual bodies"—through the retroflexion of their sense and by difference from it—that eventually allow us to speak of an "aural body" and to think of it as something we assume to have existed before the effects produced on our mind by the practice of writing (that is to say, by the production of a writing and reading mind that the alphabet nurtures).

And yet this universal truth of the aural bodies occurs and makes sense only now: now that we have analogically reproduced them into written bodies.

In other words (please understand me well): the existence "in itself" of linguistic aural bodies is a retroactive effect of the cleavage that has reduced the practice of living oral expression (whereby we can say "oral" only *now*, by difference from writing) to words-objects-artifacts.

It is these objects that show—because of the way they are made—a twofold body. As we say today, the signifier and the signified; the former ideally audible and visible, the latter invisible and inaudible: the body and soul of the sign.

In fact, it is the visible that has produced retroactively an invisible aurality. A crucial remark, as we will see, for us to fully understand the sense we proposed at the beginning: Ineffable is the visible; invisible is speech.

165. Meanwhile it has become clearer in what sense we can say that writing makes visible speech. There is in fact nothing visible in speech. As a vehicle of meaning, for instance, the spoken or written word is and remains *invisible*. It remains invisible even in writing, in the "written body."

The observation that meaning is invisible is therefore in its turn improper and derivative (from the visible)—as we have now begun to understand.

As a matter of fact, Plato says "intelligible," entrusting the meaning (intended as a reflection of the ideas, as a concept) to the practice of understanding. But that this practice of the supersensible vision should in the end reflect the light of Goodness is, however, a *mythos*, a tale, a rhetoric, theatrical *mise-en-scène* of philosophy; not a comprehension that really "understands."

Which makes Aristotle's accusation of mythologizing (*mythologein*) leveled at the Master entirely justified. Nonetheless, Aristotle blissfully goes on in the same direction as Plato, assuming as obvious his ontological presuppositions and taking their staging as the *theoretical logos* of philosophy.

Aristotle's operation does not consist in problematizing such foundations but, on the contrary, in according to them a new scientific sense, thus *psychologically conceptualizing* the Platonic tale. Hence the psychologization of the concept and the reduction of the soul to a psychical faculty endowed with intuition and abstraction. Philosophy has thus become a *science*, a foundation of objective, specialized forms of knowledge, of which, for instance, *politics* is merely a practical-applicative branch.

166. For us, however, intuition (that is to say, thinking in its philosophical sense) is the result of a certain practice of writing, of its model of visibility, and it is through this avenue that meaning assumes its traditional canon of invisibility.

Now everything comes full circle, and, having seen its backstage, we will no longer be enchanted by its metaphysical, and then scientific, *mise-en-scène*: for instance, by the various psychologies, cognitive sciences, neurological sciences of language, theories of the mind, and the like, which are all the rage in our time.

From our point of view, instead, it is now possible to witness, with vigilant attention, a dual staging of *desire*. First, the primary desire for *expression*, taken in the contexts of definite and concrete practices of life. *Go down. Come up. Will you go down? How long does it take you to come up?* And so on.

Secondly, the completely different desire that rules the practices of alphabetic writing, in peculiar contexts of life and sense.

These practices of writing at some point of their implementation generate, by retroflexion, the notion of the difference between sound and vision, as well as the conviction that there exist "words" in themselves as entities containing a meaning, which would be the invisible "symbolic" component of the linguistic sign. A sign divided into vocal and graphic, where the latter would be nothing but the transcription of the former.

And so on and so forth, with that very set of ideas and theories that represent the effect of the metaphysical enchantment produced by the *mise-en-scène* of philosophy. The enchantment that still silently rules our common sense and the scientific common sense, with its characteristic ideological fancies—that is to say, with its characteristic *mythologein*.

Scene XII: The Three "Invisibles" of Speech

167. As a matter of fact, words are neither visible nor not visible: these qualifications do not fit them and do not concern them. They become so, in fact, because of the practice of writing that *specializes* a way of seeing in context; or better, a modality characterized by that definite, complex, and constantly transforming practice that is the practice of alphabetic writing and reading.

Yet the same must also be said of the practice of speech: this practice, too, goes through a complicated and mobile synergy of practices in situation in order to reach its peculiar specializations.

In fact, the vocal gesture in its own way *summarizes, recapitulates, and signals with vocal inflections* the complex globality of an experience lived in context.

168. Let us imagine, for instance, a man sitting on the ground holding his head in his hands and muttering, "Alas!" Anyone looking at him accidentally may think: "He is ill, for sure, but what's the matter with him?" Now, the cry or interjection is an integral part of the situation, that is, of the man's emotional experience. The gestural practice of the voice infers the experience in its step back and retroflexes it to translate the whole.

That is how the stereotyped articulation of the cry represents the complex starting situation: the utterance infers it, shows it, and exhibits it in its acoustic translation.

We thus have a *generic sign*. The voice emerges as the "figurative" depiction of a *nonvocal* complex situation.

Mind you, however: it is the retroflex voice that says this "non" (nonvocal) and ascribes it to the experience of the situation, which, in itself, is neither vocal nor nonvocal.

In the starting situation, then, the voice was an act constituting the overall gestural expressiveness as it is globally lived: body posture, facial expression, pose of the mouth, and so on. This overall gesticulation is potentially communicative and meaningful, in the sense that it can inspire and produce answers—for instance in a conversation of gestures, as G. H. Mead had it.

But let us take a closer look at the situation.

169. At the beginning, we say, there is a "synthetic," global whole. But, once again, we should not deceive ourselves. What does "synthetic" mean? It is not, evidently, the sum of separate elements: body gesture + facial expressions + vocal gesture and the like. These elements so differentiated are the result of an *analytical* practice: a result which is *later* retroflected to make up the global sum.

It would be like saying to the man in the aforementioned example: "Earlier on, while you were complaining and saying *Alas*, you were performing a beckoning vocal gesture." But in fact, he was simply complaining. He was, indeed, in a plaintive situation, yet by no means was he thinking, "I am complaining." He was even less involved in vocal gestures, which are objects arising on the threshold of our theoretical and analytical practices.

And even if we said: *at the beginning there was a synthesis, or better, a generic and undetermined globality*, it is still analysis that talks and retroflexes. Though analysis may now restrain itself from projecting back its analytical elements (posture, voice, etc.), that does not mean it can catch prior experience in any *positive* way. *That is exactly why* the latter appears to analysis to be generic and undetermined, which simply means: devoid of the elements recognized by analysis and therefore in no other way recognizable. Hence, "undetermined" with respect to such elements as were revealed by analysis.

And yet the starting experience was as it was, there was what there was, nor was it in any way a confused, undetermined, or generic situation.

Our reluctance to retroflect, for the sake of "objectivity," does not free us of the threshold on which we operate with our practices. Subject as we are to these practices, we can think of the starting situation only according to the objects of our practices *and it is what we still do even when we say that they were not there before*. And why on earth should they, or should they not, have been there? What is the point of saying that they were or were not there? What is there is solely decided by the practices in situation and by their living necessities; in addition to their being derived from an origin fallen into neglect and oblivion.

And so, negation in itself says little. A man can say of a woman that she is not a man, and a woman of a man that he is not a woman. Which says nothing else but the complementary difference of their respective threshold.

Yet the same must be said, in an auto-bio-graphical sense, in relation to our genealogical proceeding. Even our saying, that is, this practice of *mise-en-scène* of our *logos* and of its writing, cannot escape itself.

For instance, here we practice the warning not to retroflect the objects of the threshold defining the practice in which we find ourselves caught. It is undoubtedly a useful and virtuous warning, which, however, is not able to say "truer things" than those who retroflect their starting situation in a carefree way.

Our way to practice genealogy simply shows its interest in the backstage; it shows the *desire* to "reveal it," which must be obviously applied to this interest itself: the interest toward the backstage, in turn, must by nature show its own backstage. It must *also* practice this interest if it really wants to be "virtuous." And then it must clarify to itself what sense and figure of truth lie in this "virtue."

170. After this methodological interlude, we go back to the topic we are concerned with here. We are talking about the "step back" of the voice, on the threshold of which, aside from the simple beckoning gestures, conversation takes place. It is a peculiarity potentially inscribed in the vocal gesture.

In fact, the gestural expressiveness of the eyes or the hands does not reflect on the agent the way the vocal gesture does. The hands reflect themselves only partially, thanks to the synergy with sight. Hence the possibility of communication among the deaf, and the creation of a manual and visual alphabet. But the Word could never have risen from the hands alone. Words are, in fact and in principle, presupposed for any further gestural expressiveness that imitates them or substitutes for them, as in the aforementioned case.

The voice turns the transmitter into an object of its gesture, it affects the transmitter just as it affects the interlocutor. For the transmitter, in fact, the voice comes "from outside"—it bounces off the transmitter and at the same time off the receiver, making them such.

In this manner, the voice duplicates the transmitter, providing the first seed for the formation of self-conscious subjects, that is, subjects able to communicate with themselves and to themselves.

I am clearly summing up, very succinctly, the results of long and complex genealogical analyses that we need not repeat here. Let us just add that, right on the threshold of the signifying voice (*phoné semantiké*, vox significativa), there occurs a "step back" that uncouples the voice from the situation of its exercise in a much more radical way than in the case of a simple nonsignifying vocal gesture.

As we have seen, the interjection "Alas" emanates from a global and comprehensive situation, but at the same time, because of its nature of vocal gesture, it projects itself beyond, somehow representing this situation, summing it up, in this sense, implicitly uncoupling itself from it. But with speech, the uncoupling nature of the outcome is far more pronounced.

171. The essential lies in this: that speech disregards its being originally inscribed in bodies in situation and in action. Words say something about bodies and situations in general—not here but elsewhere, neither here nor elsewhere, to the point of having no longer any necessary reference to the situation at hand: which is why I can recall a rose in the dead of winter or speak of freedom while I am locked up in jail.

In this sense, speech is autonomous. By exploiting its vocation for duplication, speech is highly self-referential. People talk just to talk, for the sake of having a conversation or making small talk. It is nothing superficial or trivial; on the contrary, it is a fundamental structure for forming human social interaction and "psychicity."

172. All this quick foray into the gesture of speech has here the purpose of making us understand how it is precisely through the frequentation of the evidence and growing imposingness of words that we are initiated into the experience of invisibility—the same invisibility we commonly ascribe to oral language.

The voice cannot be seen, but I perceive it even in the dark or if I am blind. We should remember that Socrates himself made a reference to the darkness of night to differentiate between the blindness of the eyes and the spiritual visibility of the soul. The voice can*not* be seen; and we now know that this *not* is obviously a retroflexion.

But then: words speak also of what we no longer see, for instance when they tell of things that are not present, or that we have never seen; when they narrate and describe imaginary things.

Now, with the Platonic construction of the concept (of the definitional *logos*) a third invisibility finally emerges: the invisibility of the *object* of speech, specifically, of the "signified." That which by essence is invisible, or the invisible essence.

Of course, we must guard against retroflecting this invisible meaning as if the signified were the universal essence of language (which does not exist anywhere and is in turn a signified).

There is no *language*, *signified*, or *signifier* outside of the analytical, abstractive, and universalizing practices of the linguist. We must not allow ourselves to be dazzled by the results of the practices which "have become." Rather, we should always keep in mind their "becoming," their genealogical nexus, as well as the process of their synergies.

Scene XIII: How Words Became Signs

173. Now we are finally able to take an important step. We have seen the emergence of three "invisible" aspects of speech: its resonance, or its audibility, independent of the eyes; its referring to the not-here nor elsewhere; its capability to carry supersensible meanings.

Now the point is that this invisibility, which happens in retroflexion by difference from the word's relatively autonomous audibility, is not the same invisibility pertaining to the practices of vision (or connected to vision).

In the practices of vision, "invisible" means only that there is something I cannot see. For instance, in the pair, "now I see it / now I do not see it," with the meaning of "it is hidden from me." "Adam, where are you?" asks (inexplicably) God—incidentally, a borderline and ambiguous case on which, if we had time, we should dwell, for God knows perfectly well where to find the man who hid himself, unless, perhaps, He means that Adam, entrusted from now on to his mortal eyes, will no longer know.

Or consider the pair "I could see it / but I do not see it," for example, because the fog keeps me from spotting the mountains.

In the practices of vision, visibility and invisibility belong to the dynamics of vision pertaining to the original and always renewed experience that happens to us when we encounter the world, taken in the figure of its visible event.

What Husserl called "adumbrations" (*Abschattungen*) are structural and typical features of these practices: I see / I do not see. Not even God can see at the same time the six sides of the die—if His can be called a "seeing," that is. We cannot see, except by profiles and horizons, backgrounds and foregrounds, just as we cannot speak unless we place one word after the other. Not even God can "say" in one go "Adam" or "Adamwhereareyou."

174. Of course, the real dynamics are far more complex than we are summing them up here. Within the mobile tangle of practices stand out autonomous dimensions which, by difference, precisely make a difference. A difference between seeing and touching, between touching and smelling, between smelling and tasting, between hearing and seeing, and so on. These areas are constantly delimiting each other, not so much in the abstract, but rather within definite practices of life, and thus based on very specific meanings. Here we are simplifying things for the sake of clarity.

But you may recall Plato's words: "Do you not say that we see with the eyes and hear with the ears . . . ?"

"Do you not say . . ." Indeed, this is exactly the point. It is within the common denominator of words that differences are formed (seeing is not hearing, and so on) and become visible as generalities (*the* seeing, *the* hearing) determined by comparison, generalities that speech enacts even before they are "known."

It is the *vox significativa* that sets out the meanings (*the seeing, the sight, the hearing*, etc.), although it does not really *see* them or *know* them yet as such. It will get to see and know them eventually, because of the practice of alphabetic writing and from the philosophical exercise made possible by writing.

175. Alphabetic writing, therefore, does not make us *see* the invisible: And how could it? Instead, it educates us to the concept, to conceptual knowing, which it constructs precisely through its analytical and classificatory practice; it constructs, that is, *this* invisible object in its vision.

It follows that the logical mind—formulated by Plato in the *Republic*—is the staging and setting up of a practice of discourse whose object is logical definition.

And of course, Plato had to "write" if he wanted to outline the complex articulations of his dialogues and definitions (consider, for instance, the definitions in the *Sophist*); he was to be, above all, a subject that is subject *to* alphabetic writing and to its operational, implicit logic.

And so, the invisible "as such" emerges in full evidence as a product of the alphabetic practice. That is to say, the invisible "by essence," which is no other than the invisible *objectified* into an invisible *thing*: a supersensible or "hyperuranic" thing, where we should note this odd metaphysical and theological metaphorization.

This figurativeness reveals in an eloquent way that invisibility per se is not at all an object belonging to the domain of visibility, it is not an invisibility *of* vision; it is on the contrary the result of the "transcribed" *logos*.

176. To put it differently, it is the practice of alphabetic writing—in synergy with other defined practices—that translates into *signs proper* the universal meanings already enacted in the oral practice of words.

In fact, the world of signs emerges in its proper sense only because of the establishment of the logical writing of the alphabet; therefore, the notion that identifies the entire logic with semiotics is entirely appropriate.

Consider this: the oral word is always in situation and fades away with it. As it is said, *verba volant*. Writing, on the contrary, performs properly, *or literally*, a sign reduplication: it circumscribes parts or pieces of the visible world—such as rock areas, clay tablets, papyrus sheets, among others—and so it extracts them and abstracts them from their being lived parts of the surrounding world as it is encountered in situation in the practices of life. These circumscribed parts, taken as mediums for engraving, incising, and so forth, become places of representation, that is, copies or simulacra of the oral word enacted in the world. In this sense they become miniaturized figures of the world.

This is where the Platonic theme of the "copy" has its roots and condition of possibility.

Now, it is these *visible signs* that, once retroflected, make the meanings invisible. I encourage you to pay close attention to this retroflexion effect, because of its far-reaching implications.

It is precisely these visible signs that create the notion of super-sensible objects which we can grasp only with our "intellect," that is, with a mind correspondingly supersensible and invisible (indeed, nobody has ever seen it).

177. And now note this further consequence. It is this threshold of the supersensible mind, known through the writing of philosophy, that, by retroflecting itself by difference onto the body, makes the body sensible (*aistheton*), thus establishing it as a "body" (*soma*, connected, as is well known, with *sema*, sign), that is, as the place of sensations and the senses (sight, hearing, etc.).

Places which, as we said, are properly and literally "signified"—"mental" objects, that is. Such result does not appear and need not appear in the practices of writing related to corresponding practices of communication and expression whose object is not orally enacted speech.

Meanings (signifieds) appear only when *we write words* in the way of the alphabet, the moment this practice is taken in synergy with the practices of knowledge that culminated into philosophy, that is, with the staging of the definitional *logos*, as it gradually specialized into the discipline of *logic*, already as early as Plato and, above all, Aristotle.

Thus, the concept becomes visible only through alphabetic writing, suggesting the idea of objects ideal in themselves and in themselves correspondingly invisible, just as "invisible" is conceptual *intuition.*

That is why words become properly "signs" only when they begin to be translated into alphabetic writing. Prior to this threshold, words are signs enacted but not known as signs. It would be even more appropriate to say that, prior to this threshold, words and writing are not signs but "names of Gods."

Words become signs through the "incarnation" of the voice into written alphabetic signs (where *the voice*, too, appears as object). By retroflecting itself, the written sign creates the idea that words, in themselves, are signs; hence, our entire logic and our science, and particularly our linguistic science. Where does all our science come from?—Nietzsche asked. Now, apparently, we know.

178. We know in a very general way because a real genealogy of philosophy and the logical mind would require far more accurate and resolute

analyses, far more complex elaborations. The practical operation of staging philosophy and its objects—to which corresponding figures of subjects conform over time—has implied capillary tangles of practices in synergy, and a jagged *continuum* of thresholds and events whose genealogical transcription may well appear to be a sort of endless task, if only because of its auto-bio-graphical nature.

And yet there is one more thing we can now understand. As words came to be translated into signs, the "cage of language" rose before us, which would go on to motivate skepticism as an internal figure of philosophy, and which today inspires the ideological misfortunes of hermeneutics in its various declinations.

If words are signs, then everything is a sign and there is no cure for this situation. At most we can expose it or deconstruct it, even as we remain trapped inside it.

Is it not evident that, if I say "thing," or "world," or "reality," or if I say *man, God, soul,* or *matter,* these are signs and not *what* they purport to say? Hence our condemnation, our exile from the lost paradise of true reality and "things in themselves." We have been tracing out all along improbable routes in the desert, on a hopeless quest for the Promised Land.

This is, however, an ideological lamentation, which fails to notice that, in saying "sign," it is thinking of "meanings"; those meanings are what we would like to "see," in a supposed reality independent of the sign. But genealogical understanding has shown that meanings are but the inner object of the sign and that the sign is an effect of writing: of a certain kind of writing and of its determined practice. Which means that there is nothing to *see* beyond the sign, if not the practices of its genealogical formation.

The imaginary cages disappear; their supposedly closed doors reopen and the bird-thoughts can fly again. "There is yet another world to be discovered—and more than one. Embark, philosophers!"[2]

Scene XIV: The Invisible Knowledge of the Visible, or Plato's Secret

179. It took us a long and roundabout journey, and a lot of patience, to prepare ourselves for tackling the nexus of visible and invisible. Now

---

2. Friedrich Nietzsche, *The Gay Science: With a Prelude in Rhymes and an Appendix of Songs,* par. 289, translated by Walter Kaufmann (Vintage, 1974), 232—Ed.

we are finally able to bring it into focus with a legitimate hope to get to the bottom of it.

We have said: *the invisible is ineffable; the effable* (that is, speech) *is invisible.* Let me explain this better, considering what we have thus far ascertained.

We cannot "say" the practice of vision, that is, the revelation of world that dwells in the world in the form of the visible qua revealing encounter. I cannot say the world in its original, visible figure; I can only dwell in it and promote it in the various practices of vision. In short, seeing cannot be said.

Similarly, I cannot translate the practice of words into a visible thing without betraying[3] the word's constitutive invisibility, its vocal "signifying." Saying cannot be seen.

It follows that speech *displays* (*apophainesthai*), or better, puts on display, the visible: it circum-*scribes* it and translates it into the voice.

Words, the act of saying, make the visible appear into the object of words, the *meaning*, which is by its nature invisible and supersensible, that is, intelligible (*noeton*).

We said that the visible does not show itself as such—as *the* visible—in vision, which rather visits the visible and develops it within the concreteness of its practices. In fact, "visible" is a word, a vocal sign which, retroflected, leads us to believe that there is an object or a real thing that would precisely be "the visible." The one thing, in short, that the concrete practice of vision never encounters, is not acquainted with, does not know: an entirely verbal reality, as is also the word "reality."

180. In the practice of vision, mere differences of vision are *enacted*, not known or objectified: I see / I do not see; I see well / I see badly / I move to have a better look / I shade my eyes with my hand / and so on.

It is words that attribute the *belonging* of these enacted differences to sight and vision, building invisible meanings and thus laying the groundwork for the nexus, henceforth taken for granted, of visible and invisible. Which is after all what writing *visibly* displays or puts on display: here is a passage meriting careful reflection. It summarizes our whole journey so far and anticipates its future.

---

3. In the sense of the Italian byword *traduttore traditore*, "The translator is a betrayer"—Trans.

So: the visible, once it is constituted into speech, performs its own retroflexion and displays the word's ineffability. Or better, it displays what is ineffable in words. In a nutshell: "language" cannot be *said*.

This requires an aside reflection.

181. Plato's metaphysics, and then Aristotle's, considers individuals to be ineffable because it *ontologizes* meanings. We can only say the universal, or the idea, "man," not *this* man; and that would precisely prove that only the universal is *fully real*.

In fact, language translates everything into concept, as Hegel had it—just as Midas turns everything he touches into gold, until he dies of starvation.

Philosophical empiricism reacts to this conclusion by reversing it: only the individual is real. An illusory reversal, for it takes as its basis the very terms of metaphysics and their opposition. By claiming to overtake Platonism, it shares its strategy of visible and invisible, sayable and unsayable, real and unreal, in their reciprocal steps back and retroflexions, and that is why for centuries it has been getting nowhere fast, wasting time on prephilosophical chatter. Indeed, empiricism is nothing but an internal consequence of Platonism, mediated by Aristotle, without even realizing it and, in this sense, dwelling in a substantial philosophical unawareness.

The fact that it was, in the modern world, particularly popular in the Anglo-Saxon culture countries is not a fortuitous consequence, as we are now going to see.

By proclaiming the reality of individuals, empiricism does not even know what it is saying or from what source—what thresholds, what practices—it derives the lexicon it uses. So that it is appropriate to say, as it has been said, that empiricism is not even a philosophy.

Modern empiricism is an ideological stance in favor of social individuals. It is an expression of needs whose ultimate motive is, not by chance, political (though without having any inkling that politics—political science—is a consequence of Platonic metaphysics): the establishment of liberalism and of the bourgeois democracy centered on the individual free economic enterprise and on the ideology—myth—of the market. In fact, the defense of a community that has its foundation on money (timocracy), as Plato will say in the *Republic*.

We instead assert that the ineffable is not individual, but the event of every practice, or tangle of practices. The opposition is between event and meaning, rather than between the individual and the universal, which are internal objects of the practice of alphabetic writing and its logic.

The point for us is the event of the threshold, always embodied in a medium marked by its practices. Thus, it is the event of this medium that the practices inscribed in it cannot "say." Besides, they have no reason to, except in the auto-bio-graphical reconstruction which is genealogy.

182. Back to the point.

i.   The event of speech is invisible. Writing, too, is in turn invisible in what makes it precisely a "written sign"; it exhibits *visibly* the invisibility of the meaning.

ii.   The event of the visible is in turn ineffable.

Now we must think hard about these two assertions.

183. *The event of speech is invisible.* What we are claiming is this: that the "sayability" of the visible, *the transit from the visible to the sayable*, is invisible.

In fact, it is exactly the saying that translates the visible into the invisible, or rather, that makes it invisible by transferring it into the meaning.

The visible, in its original event of threshold, is that which is and does not even *have* meaning (rather, it is that which *is practiced* in *its own* way). Nor is it the visible, for this is just something the word says.

And yet the effect of this being said (the visible) makes the original visible invisible in its being visible, that is, in its being *said* as visible.

It is by virtue of this retroflexion that the visible becomes invisible. Not in the sense that now we no longer see it; on the contrary: we only now see the visible as visible, because we only now *know* that there is "the visible," that the visible is "visible."

It is this knowing of the visible which is invisible.

184. The knowledge of speech produces the visible. Or rather: it produces the knowledge easily frequented by a common sense educated by words. What is visible? Common sense readily answers: for example, individuals.

Peter and Paul are visible, and so are facts, or certain facts. The fact that it rained is visible, or that there was a fire, and so on.

This very knowledge of speech, however, reverberates with its meanings (what is properly said and known, and in this sense *seen*: that there was a fire and the like). The knowledge of speech is reflected into the invisible, that is, into the invisibility of concepts and ideas.

185. With this genealogical reconstruction we are putting on display the threshold of the Platonic operation; that is, we are revealing its *backstage*, which Plato turns into myth in the hyperuranic world of ideas. As if we needed the existence of "objects in themselves invisible" to explain the invisible character of the meaning of words (that is, of intuition and of the "soul"). The very character that becomes as such only after words have been transcribed into the alphabet.

By making references to the dynamics of the practices, to their steps back and retroflexions, we are staging the backstage of the scene of metaphysics, that is, precisely Plato's establishment of the philosophical vision: the supersensible vision.

And, of course, we should not elude the question about *our own* backstage, about what politics of words and what desire for truth motivate it.

We said that knowledge of the visible is invisible. It is *the invisible of the known visible.* Which is no other than the invisible of speech, of the word that has said: "the visible." The same is to be repeated for the word that has said "the audible" (that is, the unheard-of), "the tangible" (that is, the intact), and so on.

The concept cannot be grasped with hands.

The first assertion has thus been adequately clarified. Let's move on to the second.

186. *The event of the visible is ineffable.* That is: the visibility of what we call visible is ineffable. I cannot say what I see, just as I cannot see what I say.

What I can do (what I constantly do) is translate the visible, the entire visible, into words, showing it precisely as that visible which is known to be such, that is, which is said as such.

A translation that by itself shows speech to be incongruous with the event, with the enchantment that characterizes the encounter with the visible, with the experience of the world in the figure of its being visible.

In this sense, in fact, precisely *insofar as it is said*, translated into saying, the visible is ineffable.

Before being said, it is neither effable nor ineffable. That is *not* how the child encounters the visible world and sees it. Nor is that "the visible," that visible about which, precisely, "people talk about."

187. As a corollary, we may observe, "How exciting it is *to see you now*"—an excitement impossible to express. It is also essential, however, that you hear me say, "How exciting it is to see you now." It is not enough for you to see it enacted in my excited looks.

And so it is that lovers never tire of looking at each other lovingly *and* of saying this to each other.

At this point we can conclude that visible and sayable are hemmed in by their *opposite complementary*. The ineffable hems in the visible, the invisible hems in the sayable. Now, this play of "complementaries" discloses a field of observation of the utmost importance.

Scene XV: The "Complementaries"

188. The first, crucial, observation is the following: visible and invisible, sayable and unsayable, *are not on the same level but are distinguished through their complementariness*. Which is to say: the visible is distinguished from the invisible by the mediation of the ineffable; the sayable is distinguished from the unsayable by the mediation of the invisible.

It is the sayability of the visible that generates the invisible; it is the visibility of the unsayable that generates the sayable. Common sense, therefore, misunderstands by believing that there are "invisible" things and unsayable "things." Angels, for instance, who exist but cannot be seen; or divine intelligence, which could not be said or understood with human thoughts or human words (for instance with words that are discursive rather than intuitive, as divine thoughts were supposed to be, according to Kant).

Yet it is the voice that brings out and generates the invisible of the visible, by way of its retroflected difference. And the ineffable of saying is in turn a consequence, by difference, from the writing that puts it onstage. Since everything translates into the *sign* of saying, saying itself cannot be said, because it would be again part of itself.

189. Common sense is Platonic. In a more general sense, it is misled by the objectifying function of words: if I say "invisible," then there must be a corresponding thing, an "object," which is there, but is *invisible*.

Plato adds to this the ontological consolidation of the ideas, which is ultimately made possible by the *mise-en-scène* that the practice of alphabetic writing quietly executes.

This is the step that allows for the *birth of theory*, or of a "humanity of theory," as Husserl would call it, thinking of the Greeks: Euclid, Socrates, Plato, and Aristotle. A step that allows for the differentiation we saw earlier as it was, literally, staged. The differentiation, that is, between sensible vision (*theoria, theorein*)—a vision that sees but does not understand what it sees—and intelligible or supersensible vision, which understands but does not see sensibly or properly.

It is important to realize that this partition is correct since it establishes precisely the theoretical knowledge and the truth of its internal objects. Truth of the meanings, taken in the *absolute* sense, that is, independently of the truth of their events.

Understanding is not properly seeing but, as we have noted, "making see," "knowing" *what* we see, that is.

190. What, on the contrary, Plato does not see and cannot see is the *chasma* constituted by the complementarity of speech and writing, a complementarity set in motion by the threshold of alphabetic writing. Plato's nonvision eventually generates the blindness of his posterity.

As a matter of fact, Plato cannot see his blindness because his gesture is the inaugural gesture of philosophy, of the philosophic *episteme*, which generates by itself its shadow or its unthought. Plato is caught up in his *passion*, beholden to it.

Now, how it is that we can distance ourselves from that passion is a matter we cannot take up here, although we might well suspect that it happened through a gradual modification of the tangles of those very practices of writing that generated that passion.

The intelligible or supersensible vision is of course no other than the *concept*, which is the foundation of philosophical-scientific knowledge.

But we know (we have *seen*) that the *mise-en-scène* of the concept issues from a political operation: it will not fail, eventually, to turn into a theology, as the *chasma* of Er will help us explain.

191. For the moment we can only remark here, as a corollary, that modern age, by founding its science on mathematical writing, brings forth, consistently, a secular and antitheological politics, although this opposition does not exhaust the whole of its truth, as we will see further on.

And today? we might ask. Is not the supersensible *quantum* of energy, or the *bit* of information, the foundation of the so-called politics of economic and financial globalization? In other words, are they not precisely the foundation of the theater, the staging of the two invisible supersensibles: market globalization and financial economy (in a nutshell, *money*)?

The latter would then amount to a global represented reality, where the abstract—as it has been rightly said—functions as (and acts as if it had always been) concrete, insofar as all *subjects* are subject to it, in their operating, imagining, saying, and hearing.

192. We will now close this digression and return to consider the phrases "intelligible vision" or "supersensible vision"; these expressions are blatant countersense, as they hint at a seeing which is not a seeing and which does not see anything at all. They should then be deemed metaphorical expressions, not literal but figurative.

And yet to confine ourselves to this would also be a mistake and rather the sign of a problem, the indication of an unthought (Plato's unthought, which still blinds us).

We need to understand the aforementioned game of complementarity, the threshold that establishes both philosophical practice and the philosopher, in other words, the backstage of the theoretical practice.

And so it is that the *mise-en-scène* of an apparent paradox (the metaphorical vision which sees nothing and the sensible vision which is blind) hides, in the backstage of the tangle of its practices, the unraveling of its meaning, as well as the reason for its lasting effectiveness and unchallenged success.

193. The turning point of our understanding lies in this: now we can understand that *no expression is literal.* There are no absolutely literal expressions distinguishable from the metaphorical ones, as is naïvely believed by the whole contemporary metaphorology, completely beholden to Aristotle and to the founding gesture of metaphysics.

Saying *is* intrinsically metaphorical, because it transposes (*metapherein*), that is, translates (everything that is said) into the logical meaning which is implicit in the voice and which is rendered explicit by the practice of alphabetic writing.

This transposition into the alphabet is literal, and not *what* would be said "in its proper sense."

194. Common sense imagines things differently. If a man says, "My heart!" to his beloved, the heart he is talking about is not that of the cardiologist, and therefore this is the expression of a metaphorical heart rather than a literal heart. Consequently, passion fever is not measured with a thermometer, and so it is only a metaphorical fever. Literal would then only be the *prima intentio*, as medieval people said, specifically, the expression that refers directly to an object, which is mostly able to be exhibited: the heart that can be pointed at on the anatomist's table, or the lines on the thermometer.

This way of thinking has its truth and evidence on the level of already high and specialized practices of speech, with differentiated fields of objects.

But it makes no sense if this way is retroflected to mean *the threshold of speech*, its *event*. That is when it gives rise to empirical naïvetés without any philosophical awareness. Specifically, it gives rise to that empiricist philosophizing based on the evidence of common sense that is indeed so widespread and does not see, or care to see, its paradoxes.

But common sense does not come from heaven and its evidence is precisely the "having-become," about which philosophy has never stopped wondering.

195. Beyond the threshold of speech, and its entire universe of sense, lie *not things*, but rather *practices that are still anonymous* (called anonymous by speech, which on those practices retroflexes its naming, taken in a defective sense: without name, without words).

Because speech does not have "things" beyond itself, it cannot be proper (appropriate to the thing) or metaphorical (said figuratively, associated symbolically, etc.). It is what it is, appropriate to the sense of its determined practice; it operates by "objectifying" according to the fields of practices with which it acts in synergy.

It follows that the expression "sensible vision" is not at all more *literal* than the expression "intelligible vision." Or rather, it is, yet not in itself, but in a relative way. For instance, insofar as it refers to practices involving corporeal perception. In this context, the expression "Now I see a possibility for a happier future" is metaphorical only in that it does not hint, evidently, at a perceptive seeing with the eyes, but rather at an imagining, and so on.

And yet the fact that the vision with the eyes is, generally or absolutely, *literal*—for it has referents that can be perceived with sense and can be shown—is merely the effect of the (theoretical) retroflected intellective vision. Which is precisely Plato's (and philosophy's) great discovery.

196. Such vision has objects in that it sees conceptually: it knows the *thing* it sees, or it knows how to *say* what it sees. Otherwise, it is blind, as Plato says.

And yet Plato is in turn blind to the fact that what makes the eyes sighted is not a special "seeing of the soul." The eyes see just as they see, in synergy with other practices, and they are not at all blind if they lack the word or the concept.

What makes it possible for people to *know* what they see, and say it, is the practice of speech which, once nurtured by alphabetic writing, generates in people the experience of conceptual seeing—the very experience that Plato stages to make us *see* all this.

It is precisely at this point that the sensible and the intelligible constitute themselves and separate complementarily: this is when a sensible body comes to light for (conceptual) knowledge and when we are consequently able to distinguish literal seeing (limited to the "body") from metaphoric seeing (relative to the "soul"), and consequently the literal and metaphoric saying that incarnates them.

197. Now that we have made visible, by bringing it onstage, the enigmatic tangle between seeing and saying, between seeing and knowing,

everything becomes clear to us, as the genealogy of philosophy and of philosophers, at least in its basic outline, has come to light.

But please allow me a further corollary.

As others have noted, philosophers tend to exclude the senses of touch, smell, and taste (although the last was reassessed by Nietzsche for its pre-Socratic wisdom) from conceptual knowledge.

Here we can read an important difference between philosophy and the "aesthesiology" of the arts, whose signs are more widely manifested, though also dominated, in various ways, by the concept and pseudo-scientific abstractions of aesthetics. A matter, however, too profoundly complex to allow here for anything more than this brief observation.

Scene XVI: The Tale of Er

198. Let us go back, for the last time, to Plato's scene.

We had left off at the representation of the philosopher's *chasma*, as told in the myth of the cave. An image of its formation whose aim is the conversion of the gaze to the idea of the Good and the rational pleasures of knowledge. The philosopher will then be *forced* to rule for the salvation of his brothers and sisters chained in the cave and fooled by the deceptive shadows of their sensual passions.

Next, Plato will stage the four forms of government and the corresponding human types: timocratic, oligarchic, democratic, and tyrannical. In particular, the timocratic government arises as a degeneration of the perfect state, when its governing class miscalculates the mysterious "wedding number" that should regulate marriages to give birth to perfect offspring.

This is to say that natural generation takes vengeance for its rational reduction by turning into the transferal object of money: generation becomes thus degeneration. But we may well wonder whether this might not already be in place in the reduction to rational objectivity operated by political science.

199. Back to Plato. We come to a reckoning with the tyrannical man, which is essentially a final reckoning with Thrasymachus. We are shown the unhappiness of the tyrant's life, reduced to the lonely, desperate, beastlike existence of a man who cannot have friends but only enemies

and mortal rivals. In shining contrast to this stands out the life of the philosopher, who does not care for the pleasures of the body but prefers the pleasures of the rational part of the soul.

The human soul, in fact, is made up of three parts: a many-headed monster, a lion, and a man (corresponding respectively to the concupiscent, irascible, and rational faculties). Vice and injustice turn men into the slaves of the many-headed monster within them. Wise men, instead, realize the ideal city in themselves, harmonizing the three parts of the soul.

Therefore, as we can see, political virtue comprises anthropology, psychology, and philosophy, which has rational pedagogy at its heart. And so, our initial figure is confirmed and accomplished, with the four forms of knowledge in a circle: philosophy, politics, economics, anthropology at the vertices and language in the middle; anthropology is also psychology: the establishment of the soul in humankind (strategy of the soul); and philosophy is also pedagogy.

The philosophic discourse, the *mise-en-scène* of its typical rhetoric and writing, employs rational dialectics pedagogically; and so, it generates a new type of human being, endowed with a rational soul. Philosophical pedagogy replaces the ancient pedagogy of the poets. In fact, poetry and the arts relate to the lower parts of the souls and so they must largely be banned from the city: there is an ancient quarrel, Plato says, between philosophy and poetry, and he recalls the comic authors' mockery of philosophers—an evident hint at Socrates' misfortune.

The new man, born of philosophical pedagogy, has the skill to dominate *desire*, by sublimating it into the pleasures of knowledge—which culminate in the supersensible vision of the ideas. Conceptual delight replaces sensual delight.

The new man (the philosopher) pursues in this way an individual's politics of life whose ultimate end is happiness. At the same time, this is the model or paradigm of political virtue: the (large) writing of the just and happy state conforms itself to the (small) writing of the just and happy soul.

200. In our backstage, however, the situation is reversed, and Plato's concealed stage direction is revealed. Political need is the true and concrete motive for the birth of the philosopher: he who turns the need for happiness into a science (*episteme*) of happiness, both for the individual and for the social community.

Hence philosophy has its motive and its heart in the politics of life interpreted in the large writing (the state) to arrive at the small writing (the individual).

It is in the play of references between these two writings that philosophy emerges. Plato stages the first to achieve the second, but the backstage is that his political need (large writing) makes him invent the small writing of the strategy of the soul and of philosophy. Philosophy is the pedagogical, rhetorical answer to the primary need of politics, reinvented as science and virtue.

In short, the birth of philosophy and of the philosopher is the fruit of a political operation, which in turn inaugurates a science (essentially, political science).

201. This science, however, does not reach its ultimate accomplishment without a further step, the lack of which would render Thrasymachus' confutation incomplete and purely hypothetical. It remains to be demonstrated that, whatever happens on this earth, virtue will be rewarded, and vice will be punished in the afterlife. Which also entails demonstrating the immortality of the soul.

To think of these steps as lying outside the scope of political virtue and its problem (as if political science could do without them) is simply a mistake. In this sense modern political science, which takes precisely the view that it can do without them, is naïve and superficial. We'll talk more about this.

202. And so, we get to the fourth and last *chasma* of the *Republic*: the tale and myth of Er, son of Armenius, a Pamphylian by birth.

Er in fact seems to be an oriental name. Clement of Alexandria saw in it a reference to Zarathustra. Besides, the Academy's orientalism is well known, reprised also by Aristotle in his *De interpretatione* (*Peri hermeneias*).

Let us go back to the scene and listen to the tale of Er.

203. Er is slain in battle, but his body is impervious to decay. As he is lying on the funeral pile to be burned, he is suddenly revived. He then proceeds to narrate the judgment of the souls which he has witnessed during his temporary death.

There follows the description of a double *chasma*, that is, one chasm in the earth and one in heaven, which the souls of the dead fall through in a circle, on their way up or down. The judges of the afterlife assess the deeds each soul accomplished in life. The unjust souls will descend under the earth through the chasm on the left, bearing their sentence written on their chest. The just ones will ascend into heaven through the chasm on the right, bearing their sentence on their back.

The unjust will receive punishments ten times over, with additional harshness reserved for tyrants. The just will reap their rewards in the same proportion.

After a thousand years, the two ranks of souls present themselves again. Only the ones who have served their punishment can be reunited with the rewarded ones that descend from heaven. Now all of them must choose a new life, human or animal (according to the Pythagorean theory of metempsychosis, or rather, of *metemsomatosis*, to which Plato appears here to subscribe).

The souls have many types of life before them and the choosing order is determined by drawing lots. Each choice is guaranteed by a demon (*daimon*), or genius, who will accompany the soul throughout its new life and inspire its actions.

Ananke spins the great golden spindle of destiny, helped by her daughters or maidens: Lachesis, who spins the past; Clotho, who spins the present; Atropos, who spins the future. They sing accompanied by the sirens placed on the upper surface of the eight circles made by the spindle: eight circles corresponding to the double tetrachord of the Greek musical scale.

In this magnificent and tragic scene (let us pause to admire it with the amazement it deserves) the *soul of the world* makes its appearance, followed by an outline of cosmology. The whole thing will be taken up again in the *Timaeus*. Here we are looking deep into Plato's eyes.

Once the souls have made their choices, they are led thread after thread from Lachesis, who assigns the *daimon*, to Clotho, who confirms the choice with a revolution of her spindle, and finally to Atropos, who completes the weave established by fate for the future life of each soul. Then the souls pass under the throne of Necessity (*Ananke*) and head for the plain of Forgetfulness (Lethe), where they drink from the river Ameles and lose all memory of their choice as well as of their past life.

At midnight an earthquake and a bolt of lightning awaken the souls who had fallen asleep. The souls are then carried back to earth where they will be reborn in their new body, streaking through the sky like shooting stars.

Er, who has witnessed these occurrences, is prevented from drinking the water of the Ameles. Er's task is to report back two things: the first is that he who in life philosophizes righteously is not only likely to be happy on earth but will also surely find smooth and pleasing his trip to and from the other world; the second is that the tyrant's fate is indeed the unhappiest and most terrible. This takes care of Thrasymachus.

204. At this point comes Socrates' comment we already recalled above: "Wherefore my counsel is that we hold fast ever to the heavenly way and follow after justice and virtue always, considering that the soul is immortal and able to endure every sort of good and every sort of evil."

Here is the *anabasis* and circular completion of the *Republic*. It brings to an end the *katabasis* begun with Socrates' descent into the *chasma* of the Piraeus. And here our scene also ends.

(End of Act II)

Act Three

Seventh Figure

The Encounter with Death

Scene I: The Supersensible of Morals and Science

205. The myth of Er is the fulfillment of political science and of its *areté*: it is, as it were, the last piece of Socrates' answer to Thrasymachus and Glaucon. However, how can we fail to notice that this answer is problematic? It means that, in the end, only a myth, no matter how grandiose or wonderful, can save the consistency and attainability of the ideal state.

In other words, only through the *ideology*, or dream, of the Beyond—with its rewards and punishments—can political philosophy *rhetorically* save itself.

Thus, politics becomes a "having-to-be" rather than a being, insofar as it takes as its foundation the hypothesis—or, in Kant's parlance, the postulate—of the immortality of the soul and of the infinite eternity of time, thereby securing for itself the gratification of the highest good in the Beyond. This move, however, does nothing but fashion an imaginary happiness as consolation for the city's permanent—and by no means imaginary—unhappiness, as Plato himself concedes.

206. Yet these preliminary, all-too-obvious considerations are not intended as a superficial belittlement of the last *chasma* of the *Republic*. The latter remains crucial to understand the structure and destiny of Western political philosophy.

Indeed, Plato's last move reveals that *theology* is the fulfillment of *philosophy*. And since philosophy and politics are one and the same, it follows that theology is also the accomplishment of political science.

What takes the stage here is precisely the *morality/science* pair that Nietzsche will expose and so sharply denounce—morality (Socratism) as an ideological screen for the political—a philosophical move which founds and motivates our faith in progress, and which is marked by the emblematic figures of Christianism, Liberalism, Socialism, and, today, of global democracy.

In reality, the Political continues to operate in the backstage of rhetoric, science, theology, and morality according to the pure and simple economy of forces—power, money, and the Reason of State. Precisely as claimed by Glaucon.

207. Thus, if we consider things from the point of view of our back-stage, we are bound to reach this perplexing conclusion: Thrasymachus and Socrates, in the end, become surprisingly reconciled, insofar as, in essence, Socrates replaces Thrasymachus' individualistic and tyrannical violence with public, or state, tyranny.

A tyranny that is scientific, as dialectics is with respect to the sophists' rhetoric. Dialectics, in fact, brings to completion the logical strategy of discourses qua the inspirers of political consent.

Besides, this conclusion is even obvious for us who have been reading the *Republic* as theater. Thrasymachus, Glaucon, Polemarchus, Cephalus, and everyone else are nothing but stock characters that Plato invents and puts onstage as foils for the character of Socrates, to make plausible the establishment of a philosophical-rational dictatorship.

208. By making these observations, of course, we are by no means trying to oppose some sort of *good* irrationality to *bad* reason. Rather, we wish to point out how *this reason*—founded on the distinctive feature of writing and alphabetical logic, and ultimately justified by mythical ideologies and hyperuranic hopes—*is itself irrational*, as well as the direct source of the Western universalistic superstition.

Who will dare come and tell us to our faces that this has not been the substance of all the Western political realities that have taken place through the centuries? Who will dare deny that this "holy" alliance between theo-logical rationality and faith in the Beyond has been the substance of all earthly dominations, at least in the era of the European spirit?

And we should add that all of this finds a significant manifestation in today's politics of digital-economic globalization. Which is obviously not to be ascribed to Plato's intentions, but rather to the centuries-long (or even millennia-long) consequences of the rationalizing practices initiated in Ancient Greece—practices that, over time, have in turn mixed with the countless customs, events, and circumstances of several other societies.

Of course, we are not seeking here to condemn or demonize anything, including the system that today, with no small amount of vagueness, we call globalization. What is important is, rather, that we understand (and understand ourselves in) the peculiar practices of writing the supersensible that characterize and permeate our way of thinking.

209. This persistent connection with the supersensible also explains why the moral and the scientific attitude (which at times consider themselves antipodal to each other) are, deep down, one and the same—as Nietzsche maintained. We are dealing, in the end, with a will to truth which, by instituting the supersensible of the soul and of modern science, reveals itself to be, in fact, a will to power. A *desire* to dominate over the souls, over nature, and even over the Christian God, whose death (and nihilistic transfiguration) Nietzsche prophetically announced: the technologically programming human would replace Him in an infinite—and at last ahistorical—journey of approximation to the world's objective truth.

What in general characterizes the habit of science is, indeed, *both the rhetorical domination over the souls*, submitted to persuasion and consent (essentially, Gorgias' triumph over philosophers), *and the technological domination over the bodies*, artificially manipulable: man as master of life and death. And for himself . . . nothing. In the end, what can possibly remain but the vagueness of progressive and humanitarian ideologies, once man has become the very terrain of the game of programmatic forces—their object, product, and tautological end?

Thus, from Galilean science (projectile science, the science of warfare and intelligent weaponry) we arrive at ethology (the universal science of the technologically induced behaviors of the human animal), to end up, finally, in the semiotic, educational psychology of communication science: an *in-formation* place of the subjects, which somewhat achieves precisely the "production of the soul" that Plato first attempted to imagine under the name of political science and philosophy.

But we are all moving too fast, with vague and far too generic statements, without the necessary articulation of argument.

Scene II: The *Chasma* of the Theater

210. The real issue we must take as a sign is not the generalities but the specifics of the representation we are pursuing here: the specifics of its scene and backstage. And the issue is, precisely, the sign. Or rather: the supersensible of the sign qua the ultimate secret of our backstages, and specific ground of our auto-bio-graphy.

Yet we have already seen that the genealogy of the sign has led us to "writing" as a *genuine sign*, because only writing is the threshold on which a genuine *replica* of the world—or analogic world—takes place.

A piece of the world already means "the world and the things of the world"; writing puts them onstage as a redoubled world or a world that redoubles the world.

From this perspective, then, we must affirm that theater—in its essential or primary constitution—is essentially a sign, or *the* sign. It is a microcosm: the replica of the world it represents, insofar as it puts it onstage.

Thus, it is fair to say that, from this perspective, theater is the *original writing*.

211. We cannot fail to conclude, then, that theater, as a constitutive representation, is therefore intimately bound up with philosophy. Representation is, indeed, one of philosophy's essential metaphysical themes. We could also say that the representation of the idea—both the sign and copy of truth—is the inaugural gesture of philosophy, which necessarily creates significant intrinsic connections between theater and metaphysics.

It is clearly no coincidence, then, that philosophy, too, just as theater, has an inaugural relation to writing, as a place where the world is revealed in the redoubling of its *mise-en-scène*: a represented world.

However, the theater's *place* must not be misconstrued. In its primordial origin, the theater's place is not that of its later aestheticization and literalization. Its writing is older than the writing of scenes, of costumes, of the literary text, though not older, perhaps, than the threshold of concealment and masking.

The place of the original representation is not the scene (*skené*), but rather the threshold of the *complementarity* between actor and spectator. The original representation is therefore an embodied figure of the complementary analogy of writing.

212. In ancient times, this threshold, this *in-between space* connecting *theatrical action* and *vision* (*theoria*, the spectaculum enacted by the spectator who "sees," as theater is precisely theory, vision) was occupied by the *orchestra*—the place where the chorus acts, by dancing and singing.

In ancient times, as is well known, the chorus faced the stage: it marked the distance between the audience and the dramatic action, by participating in—and thus connecting—both.

In sum, the chorus embodies the original dramatic vision and its transformative action. That is why the chorus plays a game of masks: the chorists represent, and stage, the "double," wearing a mask to look like half-men and half-goats. They are the very threshold of the human, whose nature is to be a "bridge."

Now, the complementarity—that is, the complicity—between actor and spectator is established precisely in this in-between space. It is an erotic complicity (as is all complicity), one in which the tragic desire is expressed.

Such desire must already be there at the very beginning. Why else would we stage a *fiction*? Why do humans stage fiction? In what way is fiction useful to life? And could humans ever refrain from doing so?

213. Consequently, the philosophical problem of representation must itself be tracked down to an original complementarity and complicity, and in this sense, to an erotic game of fiction. That is why whoever addresses the problem of representation by opposing an already constituted subject to an already constituted object, rather than pondering the genealogical issue of their complementary, has understood nothing about philosophy.

Subject and object mutually constitute each other as actor and spectator. In a sense, philosophical representation is a replica of that first cell, as Plato's *theater* shows emblematically by staging the problem of representation in its "textual" action—that is, in its writing.

Theater, we have said, is a place in the world that exhibits the world. To a seeing *in* the world, theater adds a seeing *of* the world. Of course, the exhibited world is not something presupposed and already existing. The world is never a "thing," however we may understand it: it is, rather, the threshold of whatsoever thing.

Threshold in the sense of immeasurable and unobjectifiable limit: the space where Achilles and the tortoise endlessly approach each other without ever being able to meet.

In this sense, the world is an event: the event of the world *in image*. For example, in the image of a visible world, of a manipulable, penetrable, speakable world, and so on. And an event is always the event of a "signified" image: the event of meaning.

In sum, "world" *means* no other than the original redoubling that the world, qua event, is.

214. Because the redoubling is the origin, it does not have an origin before itself. Which means that the represented world does not have a world before itself as its origin: that is, it does not have a world "in the original" of which it would be the image. The origin harbors its condition—that is, its image, its double—within itself.

Which is to say: every original is a redoubling. The world staged, depicted, imagined, or represented by theater does not have a *real* world before itself, because theater is a threshold event: the happening of the world in the representative figure of theater. Of course, we should think the same of philosophy, as well as of every threshold phenomenon, in fact, of every event—which (as we have observed) is always an event of meaning, that is, of an image of the world. An event of *its* truth.

This seeing of the world represented in the theater is in turn a seeing *in* the world: a *fact* of the world. In this sense, the theatrical representation is made of replicas: it is always a replica, thus showing its intimacy with the sign. Every day, theater inaugurates itself and *celebrates*, or commemorates, its opening night: the first of many nights.

What we have here is the *mise-en-scène* of an event which is simultaneously the event of a *mise-en-scène*, in a perfect and indissoluble weave of event and meaning: the sign of their constitutive dual unity, which—as we are about to see—relates theater to an even more primordial phenomenon.

215. As an actual sign of the Real, theater displays the world in its own body. But just what, exactly, is theater's body? Where can we find its being a medium of writing?

We have said that theater is the original writing. We must now add, then, that its body is precisely *the body*: the original body, that is, the body in action—in signifying action (indeed, all actions are signifying actions, including the unsignifying ones, which are the former's defective inverse).

If theater is the original body, then it follows that its body is but the continuance of a "natural" act (as we would call it based on our intellectualistic categories): for instance, the threatening act of showing one's fist to signify anger; or the act of tenderly opening the hand to signify desire and the intention of a caress.

Thus, theater exhibits first itself, its threshold, or its event, in a conversation of gestures that holds within itself the complementarity of the response, because every gesture is, implicitly, a relationship—or, at the very least, it carries the *possibility* for communication.

The response, of course, can be more or less internalized. It can be a direct reaction: if I show my fist, you will most likely draw back; if I hint at a caress, you might offer your cheek. Or it can be a reflected reaction through the mediating work of language: an internalized mediation that makes me *aware* of the fact that, by showing the fist, I express to you the threat of my anger.

216. At the same time, the advent of the representative threshold discloses the possibility of pretense. I pretend to assault you to make you run away, anticipating your reaction. My intention was not to carry out the assault, but only to simulate it. This is also a new threshold of appearance for the "double," a threshold which connects the gestural conversation of animals and human beings under the sign of a certain continuity.

We are always dealing with the double, insofar as every gesture, even a simple real-time representation (e.g., when I make as if to punch someone), reveals the void of *distance* and *absence*. A relation of unequal complementarity arises, one wherein desire is always awaiting fulfillment.

And in this sense, every gesture is erotic in its own way, as it pertains to the erogenous zones mentioned by Cephalus. This eroticism is patent in the animals and children—whereas adults suppress, and sublimate intellectually, its primitive sense. Indeed, every gesture aims at *fulfilling* and *accomplishing*. It is potentially fecund.

Thus, the gesture (which should always be thought within definite practices of life) evokes the world's complementary responding complicity, wherein all living beings have their first condition of existence.

Here is where the economic need of life is grounded, a need whose foundation lies in the corresponding of the world (with all its parts and figures) to the invocation of the gesture. The mother cat's nipples for the kitten, the mother's smile and voice for the infant, the earth's air and water for birds and fish, and so on. Such economic need is indeed inscribed, portrayed in the gesture's *desire*.

217. This matter of desire is the focus on which both the stage and backstage of all reckonings with Plato have ultimately converged, insofar as political science is established through the removal of the disturbing feature of the complementarity of desire—of its precarious constitutive nature—from the two cities designed by Socrates.

In the first city—the "natural" city (which is, in fact, altogether unnatural, and therefore unreal)—desire is effaced by translating the need for unequitable complementarity into a socioeconomic need ideologically invented and retroflexed. In the second city—the "opulent" city—desire is obliterated by the philosophic *paideia* of its guardians, who have virtuously freed themselves from it.

What happens with the gesture, then, is the representation of the origin in its duality, in its redoubling. The relational place of the gesture grounds and connects the two implicit ends of the *pro-posal* and the *res-ponse*.

In this connection lies the first origin of rhythm: *arsis/thesis, solve et coagula*, and so on. Similarly, we can think of the rhythm of breathing as the focus of Eastern meditation techniques, as primary osmosis of the world in itself: the living being, that is, the threshold of life, inhales the same world that they exhale, separating it in the unity of breathing.

By the same token, we should also look at rhythm to understand the duality of the original: a Two that does not have a One before itself, since duality is the oscillation of the threshold that retroflexes a One in order to recognize it in a Three; a Three which is in turn a replica of the event of the Two, and an indefinite reopening of the rhythmic phase.

What concerns us here, however, is the constitutively complementary character of every occurrence: the *proposal* of a world that prefigures the world, that is, that represents it in the figure of a *response*. This is precisely how the world occurs as a double: *proposal/response*.

218. The origin, we said, is always split in two: an event of the double qua event of the representation, because the origin has its condition in the figure and every event of the figure is the same as the original.

A symbolic original, in the sense of the *symbolon*: a fragment that refers to a totality which is only imaginary (just as imaginary is the *One* alluded to by the event of the *Two*). The *symbolon* would therefore hark back to the nothingness (of totality), to the void surrounding its "cleft" threshold. A finite thought of the finite, which is all *there is*, fragment and partialness "lacking nothing."

This is how we could put it; although, considering the original complementarity of desire, we might actually wish to tweak that statement: because what concretely is there is but a complementary fragment prefiguring the complementary fragment that corresponds to it—both figures, of course, which do not exist in themselves, but rather occur in their mutual complicity.

This means that there is no void outside the *symbolon*. The only void there is, is the event qua event of the fissure that holds and separates the two corresponding and complementary "symbolic" parts: the occurrence of their "birth." The world, therefore, is all full—as Parmenides would have it. There is no void in the world; rather, the void is the world, in the sense of its event.

A remark which, far from exhausting the depth of these issues, is at least sufficient for our analysis of the place of theater, that is, of its *chasma*.

Scene III: The Truth of the Theater

219. The world corresponds to the gesture in the figure of its "occasions." It bounces off the proposing gesture, modifying it with its response. When the response has been internalized, the rhythm reopens, giving rise to a new re-proposition, as a further figure of the double and of its occasions.

Children bawl because they are hungry; then, once they are looked after and the helping gesture corresponding to the cry is internalized, they bawl to be picked up.

It is well known how the internalization of the vocal proposal/response generates—gradually and for reasons associated with the peculiarity of the vocal gesture—the internalization of our self-conscious habits of speech. The latter eventually unties us from the situation of the gesture (knowing "how"), putting us on the path to the supersensible itself of knowing (knowing "what").

It is a *critical* threshold that translates fiction into the possibility of falsehood qua the ability to speak falsely. Which is inseparable from a new threshold of truth, considered now within the corresponding duplicity of *speaking truly / speaking falsely*—precisely what infants and very young children do not know (but eventually learn) how to do.

220. On the other hand, a *complicity* constitutive of speech is needed so that we may correspond to its essential lie: the lie whereby speech, as we have already noted, *is on the road to meaning*, which at first it enacts unknowingly; meaning will be eventually attained through writing, through the birth of the actual sign.

We are talking about a shared lie made legitimate and canonical by the social function of language. It is the reason why we say, "Pass me the salt," though I will never be able to "pass" to you this Platonic idea, this structural "concept," since you can't grab salt with your hands.

In this sense, speech has a corresponding object only insofar as it is a designated object, whose existence we contrive so that we can interact in dialogue—including the inner dialogue we entertain with ourselves.

There is a *constitutive misunderstanding agreement* in language, which is most likely sparked by the desire for complementarity produced by common action.

221. This series of genealogical considerations allows us to better understand the nature of theater and of its peculiar representation. For example: we understand, by difference, the lie of theater.

Such a lie does not consist in speaking or not speaking the truth: theater embodies a more original fiction than that threshold—which, as we have seen, materializes later.

Rather, as the economy of represented life in action, theater reveals the *drama* of correspondence, insofar as it always also entails a noncorrespondence.

It may indeed happen that the response to a gesture—the gesture's fulfillment—fails to occur. And even if it does occur, a difference or fissure remains so that the accomplishment is always partial, temporary, precarious, eccentric with respect to the desire expressed by the gesture, extraneous to its place.

Fulfillment is not identification, which would amount to the cancellation of desire and therefore of every relational event. In other words, it would amount to absolute nothingness. Fulfillment needs the void of distance, if only for practice; and it constantly risks falling into the void of desire's demand, which is constitutive of its distance and *provocation*.

This is how theater mimics—by replicating it in its own double—the original double, its desire for complicity.

Please note: desire *and* complicity, where desire *is* complicity.

222. Now we can finally understand how the body of theater, its medium, *is entirely inscribed in the actor's body*.

It is the body's figuration—its figuring or posturing—that first opens a scene, a *place of representation*. Hence, a space-time situation that stands for, *supponit pro*: a situation in which the story of the world is represented.

Theater, the space of vision, the spectaculum, the place of representation: all of that *emanates* originally from the actor. And not merely from the actor, but also and in conjunction with the spectator's complicity. Theater *happens* precisely in the complicit and mirrored desire of representation.

Thus, the scene emanates from the complicit gesture of both actor and spectator, creating the *sacred space* of theater (we'll see shortly why "sacred").

223. In a nutshell, we might say that the truth of theater consists in the representation of the "double," so that theater could be defined as the "double of the double."

Being a *representation* of the double, however, the complementarity and complicity theater aims for are not of fruitive, but rather of contemplative (*theoretical*) nature: the request and implementation of an *ethos*, of a contemplative behavior. Indeed, the very implementation of speech carries within itself the seed of contemplativeness: Doesn't speech sometimes ask to represent something in saying, suspending the doing? Isn't that precisely one of its virtues? And even the philosophical suspension of desire has here an origin that ties it once more to theater.

For example: the actor may arouse an erotic involvement, without it resulting, however, in an actual sexual performance, which, on the contrary, must be suspended—or merely simulated—in its theatrical unfolding. Hence the important perception that deems the Dionysian rite a performance aimed not at the celebration of the vital and titanic impulse, but rather at the latter's sapiential transformation and sublimation.

Which means that the origin of philosophy, too, is double: it has in Dionysus the double of Apollo and of its truth.

Every representation is double: but theater is the representation of representation's double—that is, as we have suggested, the representation of the drama of a correspondence which is always also a noncorrespondence. Hence, life's tragic nature—and it goes without saying that the tragic entails the comic as well, by reflected difference.

Theater represents the original double, being itself double: the *proposal* and desire for a *response*, the complicity and complementarity between actor and spectator, and *eros* portrayed in its constitutive—unusable and unbridgeable—distance.

224. Because of these features (very briefly examined here) theater reveals itself to be a sapiential form *originally akin to the sacred rite*, to the celebration of the "festival" qua repetition of the origin which *is* the origin. In fact, theater is largely the same as a sacred rite: a masked invocation of God, a learning of his manifestation—of his *aletheia*, the truth of his revealing and prophetic word.

We already noted that Plato invented his philosophical theater by borrowing its form from the dramatic text of tragedy (and comedy), which was its stylistic precedent.

Philosophy, therefore, has its antecedent in Dionysus. Yet philosophy is not tragedy, insofar as it conceals Dionysus in the mask of his complementary twin: Apollo.

We can appreciate here the depth of Nietzsche's intuition, who saw in Socrates the man who killed the tragic spirit. On the other hand, we decry the inconsistency of the theories advanced by those who read tragedy—and poetry—as if they were an expression of philosophy. Such theories fail to understand the genealogy of the philosophical practice—its actual politics—and do no justice to either tragedy or poetry (say, to either Aeschylus or Leopardi).[1]

---

1. An implicit critique of Emanuele Severino's works in which Aeschylus and Leopardi are entirely subsumed by the philosophical gaze. See Emanuele Severino, *Il giogo. Alle origini della ragione: Eschilo* (Adelphi, 1989), *Il nulla e la poesia. Alla fine dell'età della tecnica: Leopardi* (Rizzoli, 1990), *Cosa arcana e stupenda. L'Occidente e Leopardi* (Rizzoli, 1997)—Ed.

As the original writing of the body, theater is the oldest form of knowledge. It has been at work ever since human beings started using their bodies to portray life—that is, desire—representing it simultaneously to themselves and others, man and woman both assimilated and split within the original complementarity of a complicit *theoria*.

Scene IV: The Way Back

225. We began this third and last act by calling onstage the masks of the supersensible and then by evoking theater itself as the mask and figure of all masks.

The subject of the mask is far too extensive and wide-ranging to be dealt with in this venue. What we can say here is that our evocation inaugurates the return (the repetition, the Two) that will unveil the backstage of the backstage. (The Two had already been heralded by the exhibition of the supersensible.)

Let us first remember how it all began: by conjuring up onstage the ghost of Aristotle and heeding his ancient yet still relevant voice.

226. "Man is a political animal, the animal who has speech," said the voice. "The two things are one." This is how both anthropology and the ethology of speech defined the desire-power of speech as desire-power of the political as such.

Indeed, Aristotle's ghost uttered amazing things, worthy of their centuries-old influence. I will now quickly recall them for you.

227. The political habit is necessary for beings who cannot exist without each other, such as male and female—beings, we would say, which are united and first constituted through complementarity and complicity.

What essentially unites these beings is *desire*—above all, the sexual desire for reproduction, "the natural desire to leave behind them an image of themselves," said the shadow. The only way for mortal beings to attain eternal life is by imitating—if nothing else as a species—the immortal life of the blessed Gods.

228. This is, we might say, the mystery of the sexual drive, the enigma of eros as the economy of life, always willing to risk death to affirm

itself. An unsolvable contradiction, which famously tormented Freud, and which is certainly one of the powerful root causes of humans' unextinguishable bellicosity.

Please excuse my digression, but if I do not make these brief remarks now, later I might not get another chance to do so.

Both Aristotle and Freud agree that sexual desire is the most powerful desire. Would you like to solve its mystery, unravel its puzzle? Don't even bother to try, as every argument you might make, every judgment you might arrive at in this regard would inevitably come too late.

How so? It is easy to figure out: because everything we call mind, word, judgment, and so on, is born and developed precisely within the drive it would wish to explain. The original words, which by mirroring and reflection *educate* our awareness, are "genital" and "parental" ("genitorial") words: if we had the time, I would show it to you with a multitude of concrete examples.

229. Thus, every *individual* is already assigned since birth to this *dividual*, to this original complementary separation between male and female.

We cannot talk about it *in general*, as if nothing ever happened. We cannot *speak* in general of difference, or sexual desire.

Or rather: we can if we assume the universalistic perspective of the *concept*. Be mindful of the word I just uttered: "concept" means "conceived." Indeed, the genealogy of the concept clearly shows its male and patriarchal origin: it is no coincidence that we witnessed its birth in Plato's cave and in the agonistic game of the erotic-political speeches he assigns to competing male characters.

Which does not mean that this male origin, too, does not carry a trait of the complementarity with the feminine which is constitutive of every sexed being.

Complementarity and complicity with the other side who shares the drive and turns it into a mirror for the word "male."

230. It is Eve herself, you might recall, who offers Adam the apple of knowledge—tempted, we might add, by the serpent qua metaphoric phallus of the "good" (?) Lord. No wonder, then, that the cycle must eventually end with the immaculate conception through an angelic serpent: a figure exactly antipodal to Lucifer, who is punished and cast

into hell for falling into error; hence the inversion—as they said in the Middle Ages—of EVA into AVE: *Ave Maria.*

But never mind that, this is too complicated and premature. Forget what I said and let us return to Eve offering Adam the apple of knowledge (a gesture, we note, which will result in death for both). What did Eve *mean* by this gesture?

We should be prepared to answer that she was offering him *regality* and power: you will become like God. In fact, woman is supposed to be the mirror of man's procreative power, that is, of man's ability to promote eternal life, the privilege of the Gods.

We learned all this from Gyges' *chasma,* that is, precisely from Plato. A recognition worthy of a minute of silence as a sign of our gratitude and conscious admiration. A symbolic celebration of the divine Plato and divine philosophy. Let us show then how the whole theater can rise, silently and unanimously, and share in a moment of dignified and peaceful awareness.

231. Very well, Adam receives the apple. Now I ask you: How must he return the gift and reciprocate Eve's gesture according to justice? Isn't this very justice, after all, the central and essential issue of the entire *Republic*? Isn't this the reason why, in the state of philosophers, women are associated to power and to men's wisdom?

Ancient man sacrificed to the ancestral female deity, to the figure of Mother Earth, in exchange for power over nature: the power to control the production of cattle as he saw fit, and the power to penetrate the mother's *chasma* with a plow to obtain its fruits.

Ancient man paid for the wound of human *hybris* with sacrifice; until a man from the recent, sacrilegious age dared ask: "What do you know about the Gods and their desires? Are you sure that the Gods really desire your sacrifices, that the smoke of your victims is dear to them?"

We still dwell in the shadow of those questions, which find their solid continuation, but essentially no answer, in the political science established by Plato. That is precisely why, I wish to remind you, we are trying hard to penetrate the *chasma* of its backstage.

Scene V: By Hook or by Crook

232. Let's return to the scene and conjure up the words of Aristotle's double.

He says: the lord and master of the family community—that is, of the original sexual association—is he who can foresee by the exercise of intelligence. And who could that be, if not man? Only man has full ownership of the *vox significativa*. Exactly why it should be so, is left unsaid; we are given no reason for this proposition, as if its truth were rationally self-evident.

Let us recall the essential passages, which we will read now in their true order, that is, reversed from the order they follow in the ideological play staged by Plato's disciple—who not by chance has been deeply educated in the theater of the Master.

233. Man is the only animal endowed with a voice, the *phoné semantiké*, thereby, beyond pleasure and pain, fear and desire, he can also express what is beneficial and what is detrimental—good and evil (the fruits of Eve's tree), just and unjust, as well as all other values.

On the strength of this ability, man (literally *man*, as originator and archetype of all human beings—it is no accident that we still say "man" to mean human beings on the whole) does not merely feed and reproduce himself by accident, as the other animals do, but also provides all means for a safer survival, keeping the family united and then uniting families into villages, until he arrives at the state, where, having fulfilled all his needs, he also finds happiness, the happy life. The latter culminates in *politiké areté*, a condition having its roots in "nature," that is, in the need of all beings—who cannot exist without each other—to attain eternal life through reproduction.

In this sense, man can foresee; and he foresees all the more, and all the better, insofar as he is able to *see* the essence of things, their principles and their causes—insofar as man, in other words, becomes a philosopher and scientist.

234. It follows that the signifying voice of reason (*vox significativa rationalis*) is the real goal and fulfillment of *politiké areté*. And precisely in this sense we placed ethology and the genealogy of speech at the center of our initial cross of the forms of knowledge.

As far as Aristotle is concerned, the die is cast; man, he states, is indeed the legitimate lord and master. Yet, specifically, he means the Greek man, or rather, the philosopher, whose theoretical life (as shown in the *Nicomachean Ethics*) is the happiest because it is closest to God's life and to the eternal, imperturbable light of his *nous*, of his intellect.

Barbarians, women, girls, and boys can only stutter: it is in their political interest, then, to be ruled by those who see and know (how to speak).

235. Take a good look, then, backstage at this "luminous" discourse, which has been blinding us for twenty-five hundred years.

Common to all men is the "natural" desire to reach the condition of citizens of the state, structured by justice and the rule of law. Which properly means that everyone is "by nature" potentially a Greek as well as a philosopher, as this is the ultimate goal, the perfectly realized stage of the human.

Men must be made to reach this stage politically. By hook or by crook, and for their own good, they must be brought to reason: it is the highly universalistic nature of the politics of the concept that the pedagogue Aristotle tried to hammer into Alexander's head—to only partial success.

Since then, the West has reasoned along the same lines. Kant spoke of human reason or reason *überhaupt*; Hume, who was more of an empiricist, spoke of human nature; and Descartes, with a touch of Jesuitical slyness, wrote: "Good sense is the most evenly distributed thing in the world . . . nor is it likely that everyone is wrong about this; rather, what this shows is that the power of judging correctly and of distinguishing the true from the false (which is what is properly called good sense or reason) is naturally equal in all men"[2] (as if he were implying: get busy backing this up, or else woe to you!)

Nowadays, the Catholic Church, with its encyclical *Mater et Magistra*, claims *apertis verbis* that all men are philosophers by nature, which consequently means: potentially Christian and Catholic, if only they learned to reason as they should, that is, as was taught by the Scholastic Doctors, followers of Aristotle.

The same goes for the universal democracy that the "hawks" in the White House in Washington would like to force imperialistically upon all

---

2. René Descartes, *A Discourse on the Method of Correctly Conducting One's Reason and Seeking Truth in the Sciences*, translated with an introduction and notes by Ian Maclean (Oxford University Press, 2006), 5—Ed.

the inhabitants of the earth: men, women, and even animals, if possible, which is but the final incarnation—although a far more crude, naïve, and irresponsible one—of our entire Western tradition.[3]

236. But we should also not forget Aristotle's remark that, outside *politiké areté*, man becomes the worst of all living creatures. Indeed, armed injustice is supremely dangerous.

One cannot refrain from admiring Aristotle's greatness, which always shines brightly, even when there may be reasons to part company with him.

Scene VI: The Backstage of the Backstage and the Two Questions

237. We begin to understand Aristotle's *mise-en-scène* of the genesis of the state as the one backstage that is still powerfully impacting our own backstage.

Mise-en-scène of the threshold, of the gaze, of the theoretical voice, caught in the nexus of visible and sayable, invisible and ineffable.

It is the retroflexion of this threshold that creates, in retrospect, the following notions: nature, animals, needs and natural desires, the prehistoric and mythical antecedents of the state (the history of prehistory), savages, barbarians, women, and so on.

The action of the theoretical voice has been intertwining for centuries with numberless practices of life and knowledge, even to the point of becoming subsumed into theoretical stances antagonistic to Aristotle or Plato; but these stances (religious, philosophical, scientific, or political as they may be) have not yet been able to acknowledge, with the necessary genealogical clarity, their substantial dependence on the very epistemic threshold heralded by the two Greek masters.

238. That is why this backstage of ours cannot stop at its mere genealogical action, but it must insist on what is hidden in its own threshold, in the backstage of the backstage, precisely.

---

3. The immediate reference here is the Iraq War, which started in 2003—Ed.

Thus, I will begin with two questions.

The first sounds like this: Why is it apparently necessary for the human being to descend into a *chasma*? What kind of *chasma*, what kind of abyss, hollow, or depth is that, exactly?

239. Second question: What is this *demand for knowledge* which does not have a voice in animals—so that, we may add, just by retroflecting this demand and will to knowledge, man *sees* animals as "animals" and differentiates himself from them?

240. What we do know, having seen its operation on our stage, is that the will to knowledge, the demand for truth (*aletheia*), is used as the foundation and establishment of the political and its justice—the pedagogical establishment, that is, of a political virtue that authorizes the use of force by "he who sees and knows."

241. This pedagogical threshold of the political (the political as political science) tends progressively to replace the ritual and primordial threshold characterized by the penetration into the queen's *chasma*, by her *subjection to a secret (segregated) possession*, and by *sacrifice* qua ritual killing: for instance, the killing of the old king, who once must also have faced the very same *chasma* of eros and death in order to acquire sovereignty.

In this ritual threshold, the political necessarily entails a ritual war: the exhibition of the political *areté* of the leader and his children, who extend their ownership over other men's women. (Rape, a symbolic phenomenon as well as the "obvious" compensation for the risk of death, is constitutive of this figure of human bellicosity.)

242. The threshold of the political, founded on knowledge, rejects this precedent with horror, consigning it to an imaginary, prehistoric time of barbarity (while every epoch to this day continues to show us how barbarity has never really ceased to exist).

With the advent of knowledge, the political is established without "penetrations," but rather *by force* of persuasion, that is, through the virtue of speech, the place and possession of which becomes now the real place of politics.

Just how *real* this place is, or in what sense, is an obscure problem, for it gives substance to the imaginary shadows that have forever accompanied speech.

On the other hand, language's scrim of shadows and mirrors cannot prevent us from discerning—if you will train your eyes on the figures outlined behind me—what is hidden within it.

You will notice, for instance, how the original "penetration," which we thought had been supplanted, has in fact returned in the guise of as a "penetrating word" which—unsurprisingly—generates submission. Ever since the practice of alphabetic writing coalesced into early forms of knowledge, the Greeks have been absolutely clear about the nature of such penetration and submission. Plato, too, seems to allude to it when he assimilates knowledge to an erotic trade which is plied through a sort of "noble" and "spiritual" pederasty.

We modern people have completely forgotten about all this, or even believe the opposite is true. Today we see countless flocks of entertainment-dependent sheep who think of themselves as free and democratic citizens, without even noticing the ram sitting on their backs.

243. In any case, rhetorical persuasion legitimizes violence, translating it into political violence, that is, into the accepted and shared exercise of force.

From this perspective, Thrasymachus is no different from Socrates. We have seen them both worry and talk themselves hoarse. Why on earth would they do so, if in the final analysis things legitimized themselves, in their truth—as they both would have us believe? Force legitimizes itself because it "is," and insofar as it is, it cannot but prevail. Dialectics legitimizes itself insofar as it speaks the thing as it "is," and as it cannot otherwise be.

And yet things do not legitimize themselves. Thrasymachus *must* persuade us that there is no other legitimization of force than force itself; but what force? Evidently, that of his discourse. Only by accepting it, do we accord force the lasting legitimacy of its prevalence—namely, its political, institutional, and legal significance and value.

At the same time, Socrates *must* persuade us that the thing ought not to be thought this way; that there is a wild violence driven by a wild desire which we have to oppose with a legitimate violence that may act as a counterforce: a political violence which is good and holy because it is founded on the vision of the absolute Good and of its truth.

But what *truth*? Only by embracing Socrates' vision, as well as his retroflexed ghosts (the wild desire, the many-headed monsters, Ananke's spindle, the siren's song, and the Fates), can Plato's state impose itself, legitimate itself, and possibly, endure (unless it relapses into wild desires).

244. But now I wish to warn you. A sophisticated, though quite widespread, theory states: the establishment of political power and of its legitimization requires, *of necessity*, the exercise of force—a violence which is not and cannot be legitimate.

Think about it, says the theory: How can somebody arrogate for themselves the right to speak in the name of the law, if the law exists precisely insofar as they are the ones who established it? How can an assembly claim to speak in the name of the "sovereign people," if people's sovereignty is instituted precisely by such assembly?

We might add: How can someone speak "in the name of truth," establishing at the same time the legitimate (i.e., truth-bearing) ways of this word, its justness and justice (be it *ideological* or *dialectical*), even to the point of founding political justice on it as a universal ethics of communication? Is this procedure not (in addition to being naïve), evidently, a violent one?

Undoubtedly it is. Yet limiting ourselves to this argument is very *superficial*.

245. Pay attention. The theory says: because a politics institutionally constituted, with its justice, is not yet in existence (we are, indeed, pondering the event of this threshold), a regulated and legitimate exercise of violence cannot exist either: hence, the act which founds the political institution and provides the criteria for legitimate violence cannot but be illegitimate—the expression of a violent, *illegitimate* imposition.

That sounds logical, doesn't it? But this only means that logic, too ("our" logic—as Nietzsche would say—logic as we conceive it), has its own violence (admitting this would be at least consistent with the argument). As a matter of fact: Why illegitimate? Why violent? What are you talking about? Isn't it obvious that you are carrying out a pure and simple retroflexion here? The moment you ask this question, the whole logic of our sophisticated argument melts away like snow in the sun—or at the very least, it becomes completely irrelevant.

It is precisely because of the visibility/sayability of what is "legitimate" and "illegitimate," and therefore of what is "violent," that we interpret backward the preceding situation. Blinded by our threshold, and due to a sort of internal difference, all we can glimpse in that situation is, indeed, illegitimate violence.

246. What precedes, however, is neither legitimate nor illegitimate, neither violent nor not violent. What we have is rather a knot of practices taken in the peculiar dynamics of their constitutive complementarities, finding expression in configurations of meanings that are consonant with them.

There is, for example, the complementarity of the sexual act and its complicit desire, a complementarity manifested in the most varied figures: for example, the magical-sacred meaning accorded to procreation and life. There are the ways of the shared word, for example in its for-mulas—that is, practices of meaning that guarantee its authority. And, of course, there is also violence (whenever is there not?) but precisely in *its own way*.

247. In these cases we might say that the foundation of the communal threshold is symbolic, or better *symballic*: a logic of the broken fragment (*symbolon*) referring to a whole which is precisely symbolic, or ritual.

For example, the ritual repetition of symbolic intercourse with a God or Goddess qua the exemplary, paradigmatic doubles of man and woman.

Man and woman legitimize themselves in violence, that is, in the violation inherent in the sexual act as it is "felt," in the *name* of the God or Goddess (this is how the Virgin Mary, symbol of the Church, becomes the bride of her son Jesus, as portrayed in many ancient frescoes). The supersensible naming of the God or Goddess properly identifies human beings and properly establishes them as complementary individuals, by instituting the (con-secrated) legitimate whole of the community. In this way, the sexual act becomes a ritual and a sacrifice (in Christianity, it is still a sacrament).

248. And so our original question comes up again: What do we seek in, and draw from, the exercise of this hypothetical original abyss, the

penetration of this *chasma*? What unavoidable and inalienable human truth?

Scene VII: Speech and Death

249. Demand for knowledge and demand for truth: the first question is intertwined with the second one, as it calls speech into question, the center of our cross of the forms of knowledge.

In other words, the economic and political exchange is but the consequence of the original linguistic exchange. Adam Smith had warned us of this. And Nietzsche, who taught in Basel how the Greeks' agonistic spirit had given rise to the force of rhetoric as the royal tool of political virtue and, ultimately, of power.

Our present-day notion of a forthcoming planetary democracy is still marked by it. Such notion is merely the continuation of Aristotle's concept that sees in the rational state the final condition of civilization overcoming the mythical, barbarian state of Gyges—that is, all states that somehow still draw on it and whose establishment is ultimately entrusted to sexual penetration and ritual murder, in accordance with the archaic logic of sacrifice. Though these may indeed be things that we find it hard to endorse, we "rational men" cannot reject them merely on the account of a feeling, without first attempting to answer a question as to the "why."

250. This is where the aforementioned query comes into play: *What does speech want to know?* We know that, in a lot of senses, the virtue of speech—with its demand for recognition within the unequal exchange of desire—coincides with the establishment of political virtue. For example, as the establishment of the "name," and subsequently, of the "law." But in what consists, then, the justice of speech? What, and how, does speech say *justly*?

The query also patently includes the *mise-en-scène* of discourses we have been practicing here. It includes, in other words, the backstage of the question, that is, the backstage of our exercise of speech, which promotes an ethical upheaval of the gazes and interests: precisely the same upheaval, we might observe, which Plato asked of his philosophers. This should not surprise or worry us: as we have often stated, our very auto-bio-graphy is at stake in our backstage practice. Hence the exchange we are constantly witnessing between the scene and its backstage—an exchange which, in its play, exhibits the political virtue of speech and of its knowledge.

But what knowledge? The time has come for us to answer: *the communal knowledge of death.*

251. While we take a deep breath and unwind from the tension of all these queries (the answer has already been given, the—tremendous—word has been spoken; for the rest, we will wait and see), I should point out that we have already caught a glimpse of this knowledge, though it was still in inchoate form. Remember what was at the root of the myth of Venus' girdle, where, too, an unequal exchange was performed driven by desire for recognition.

In that context, we evoked the dark *chasma* of Hecate/Bendis, which attracts—with the complicity of a transferal object (the girdle, the name, money)—the desire of Paris-Socrates, consigning them to a destiny of death (not surprisingly, the *Republic* is a dialogue among the dead).

But also, to a fate of rebirth, because this is an initiatory descent, meant to achieve an *anabasis*, a transfigured rebirth.

Herein also lies the clue to understanding the relation between the *chasma* of sexual desire—which is bound up, as Aristotle noted, with a desire for eternity—and the *chasma* of death.

But we'll leave this matter aside for now, and come to focus on the essential question: How do death, speech, and knowledge become entwined?

252. I also have an initiatory revelation of mine to offer, hoping it will become yours, too. I put it like this: speech carries its knowledge; this knowledge translates action—the performance of practices—into an expressed meaning; it is, as we know, a knowledge that designates the "what"—a knowledge we encounter from time to time in the living experience. And this is also how speech carries *the knowledge of death.*

This is the very knowledge that, originally, constitutes "mortals." Anthropological par excellence, this knowledge says "what everyone knows," the knowing of which is precisely what turns them into men, as opposed to animals: all men know, specifically, that they must die. Animals, on the other hand, are entrusted to, and inscribed in, the eternal and ineffable instant of the unavoidable and unavoided life.

253. You understand that a lot could be said about this; here, however, I will limit myself to what is essential for our journey.

The knowledge of speech identifies the presence in the name. The impending presence is that *continuum* of the Event which we have already defined as unique and unavoidable, that is, coinciding with eternal life or with eternal living (the animal life that is ignorant of speech).

Knowledge of speech—that is, knowledge of the name—is therefore the establishment of the meaning that stops the *continuum* of the event: it stops it precisely at the threshold—imperceptible insofar as it is supersensible—of meaning. The threshold where, as we already know, the relation/difference between event and meaning occurs.

254. I can see your puzzlement: you are right; precisely in what I said, an important difference has occurred, which we should not leave unsaid. A difference and indeed, more properly, a substantial, and in many ways, crucial correction. Listen, then, and pay attention as much as you can.

So far, we have referred to the Event as the occurrence of the break which delimits the threshold, thereby determining the retroflexion and anteflexion of its figure. By putting it this way, I was suggesting (for example in my backstage) that I meant things as follows: the event of a practice occurs (for example, the practice I am now exercising with you), and this practice cuts a threshold, producing a break, a void, from which we go on to establish a provenance, origin, and destination. The figure of the occurring practice fills the transit of the present with meaning, deducing from itself also the existence of a past and a future.

This way of thinking, however, raises several problems and ultimately will not hold up to keen criticism. First, it suggests that the Event is a string of events and thresholds, that is, of empirical occurrences according to our common (and untenable) view of time: a sheer physical series of instants, of moments, each of which would correspond to the occurring of a threshold with its break. Yet this way of saying or seeing is in turn a threshold and a break, as it is precisely the threshold practiced in this manner that assigns and measures the string of the instants, by carrying out an empirical time-ography (*tempografia*) that starts with itself. And this is something absurd and indefensible.

Moreover, this way of reasoning—unwittingly—substantializes the Event: the *event* occurs and, by occurring, performs a break; the event, then, creates the void that *actualizes* the *continuum* of time in the instant of the threshold. But the Event itself, we might observe, is also void, insofar as it is always an event *of* meaning and not a "thing," no matter how we intend it; the Event itself is nothing, nor does it *have* a meaning. It is, precisely, devoid *of* meaning, as it rather limits itself to letting meaning occur—that is, to being the threshold of meaning.

And yet, by speaking the way we speak, we are giving the impression that the Event is nonetheless "something," albeit something special, mysterious, not empirical, and thus ineffable: we call this the negative theology of the Event, which is thereby assumed as the *not* of meaning. We try in vain to remove these difficulties, pointing out that, after all, the threshold is one, and so is the Event. The threshold, we say, is the being-always-here, the end moment of every practice that accords to itself an origin and a destination. And this is why, we emphasize, the threshold plunges continually into its void, that is, precisely into the *vacuum* of the Event. But what do all these objections really amount to? Just in what sense would the Event have created the void in the *continuum*? Starting from what sort of *fullness*? By causing, perhaps, a tear in it? But the Event is itself void, and as such it cannot cause any tears, nor, in fact, do anything at all.

255. In light of our recent considerations, however, the situation appears completely reversed: because *the void is introduced by meaning, not by the event.* Or rather: the void is generated from the occurrence of the constitutive distance that is inherent in the practice of words. It is speech that creates the void, plunging everything else into its *chasma*, that is, the *chasma* of meaning.

Think about it: seeing events, occurrences, the banality of the fact that at every instant we are experiencing something (what is more ordinary than the fact that different things keep happening: Tom talks, Dick turns his head, bells ring, rain begins to fall . . . ?); this registering of occurrences *is only possible to an educated sight, a sight that has been transcribed in the exercise of words.*

Before enacting the event of the threshold of words, we *enact* events. Of course, I am saying it wrong, because it is constitutive of every act of speech to come out "wrongly"—though, for the purpose of speech, it gets the job done—precisely insofar as it is an act of speech. So please try to understand me. I shouldn't have said "before" or "events," or even "we enact," and so forth. What I am suggesting, instead, is the undivided unity of direct living (undivided, of course, with respect to speech, in that the word, precisely, divides), a unity which is not even a unity (as it is not set against a multiplicity), and which we call here "eternal life."

Since the direct living experience is translated into the distance of language and its expressed meanings, eternal life distances itself from itself, entering at the same time the realm of knowledge as knowing how to say and knowing how to name.

256. The culmination of this process is reached precisely with philosophy (in the essential places of the philosopher's *chasma* that we have seen staged in the *Republic*): philosophy, in its supersensible practice, stages this "trained seeing," which is conceptual seeing.

Modern science inherits it and translates it, insofar as it can, into a mathematical writing of sheer events altogether decontextualized from whatsoever meaning.

In this manner, the success of actions that were originally directly acted becomes now a "known and wished" success, whose objectiveness and universality is all the greater the more it is decontextualized. These are "truths" that apply ideally and generally *to everyone, in every time and place*; in other words, they apply where each individual is reduced to "everyone"—a process that begins, in fact, with the very first resonance of the voice that names.

257. In conclusion, the void is introduced by the dynamics of meaning (because meaning *translates* into the distance of a supersensible "else-where")—meaning being precisely the threshold which we cross to penetrate the *chasma* of words and names.

It is the event, instead, that is the fullness and the *continuum*, as we said before: an Event that is one and eternal in the sense of the unavoidable omnipresence of the world, the event of the world or cos-mos, substance which is always-already there.

In the figure of the event of speech and of its knowledge, however, the *continuum* stops. It stops at the identifying sign of the name, that is, at its empty meaning, at the supersensible void.

Thus, it is meaning—that is, the name—that causes the tear in the compact and unanalyzable continuity of the event of the world:

an a-chronic and a-topic event. It is meaning that makes judgment occur—judgment as the original separation (*Ur-teil* in German): A (the indistinct) is B (the name).

The whole is prior to the part, said Aristotle. But in the whole there are no parts, nor is there a whole; so that in the living body, taken as a whole, there are no organs: no hands, no eyes, no feet, and no ears: it is a body without organs, to use Artaud's phrase. And if the body is the support of every transit, as I have argued before, then the ultimate support is the body of the world, that is, the *continuum* of the event that supports meaning.

258. After this long albeit necessary digression, let us return to our topic: the relation between speech and death. Speech emerges as a process of identification through the event of the name. And the name requires, implies—carries within itself—recognition, the quintessential relational phenomenon: *You are Peter!*

Recognition requires in turn a *complementary complicity*. We already touched on this when, with respect to words in general, we observed that both the transmitter and the receiver (just as the actor and the spectator) are accomplices in the *mise-en-scène* of language's constitutive "illusion." I tell you, "Pass the salt," and through this impossible reference, you understand what I am asking and what I need, and "miraculously" you pass it to me. Accomplices in "lying"—that is, in feigning an existent that is not there—we paired off and agreed on what to do.

Thus, we can conclude that speech is characterized by two complementary features:

1. Speech makes the absent present.

2. Speech makes the present absent.

Scene VIII: The Absent Presents Itself

259. The word says the meaning. It says, for instance, "the rose." But "the rose" is never present, even when "a" rose is. The supersensible of the concept, we might say, is that which by its nature is absent, and which the word somehow makes present. The word makes it present, mind

you, *while at the same time leaving it absent*, because the word contains implicitly the nature of the *sign*—that is, the presence of an indication *for* something that is not there.

The word is vicarious of the "thing," making it happen as a thing; as a thing that is not there and can never be there from the moment in which it is introduced by the name.

260. This in general terms. But now, in more concrete terms, we must point out that speech makes *the complementary character of the response* present. It makes such character present within a practice of recognition of the partner.

"Those who cannot exist without each other," said Aristotle, thinking of male and female. But the same happens to speakers, once they have entered the experience of speech and the name: they, too, cannot exist without each other, because singular words do not exist, and neither do noncommunal, nonpublic names.

Thus, if I say, "Give me the rose" and you hand it to me, you show you are sharing in the dynamics of the name, consisting in the actualization of meaning—that is, precisely the act of "making the absent present" that we have been discussing and trying to represent.

261. There is a constitutive complicity, then, which is *the secret of speech*. In this complicity, we have switched roles—in fact, we have *become roles*; roles in a common project of which speech is sign, pledge, and result; a project where, in turn, we play the roles of the proposal and those of the response.

We confirm once again how essential—in its primordial and founding character—is our constant resorting to "practices." There are no objects outside the practices, we say; but objects are indeed meanings, meanings/objects set by the word and in the word: *rose, salt, man, woman,* and so on. In this sense, we must bring the objects back to the practice that sets them to work, that is, to that complementary relation that implies complicity and desire. Complicity in desire, in the *project's* desire.

262. Thus, now we can say that what is really absent in the word, and for this reason making itself present, is the institutive threshold *that assigns*

the roles: it is this complicit complementarity that is always presupposed whenever the word is spoken (you can see we are taking giant steps forward, each of them marking the world's fate in an essential way).

So, in general terms, we are talking about the threshold that marks and separates preverbal action from verbal knowledge: then again, of course, it is speech's knowledge that talks this way—that says "threshold" and "preverbal action."

But in so saying, we can see what presents itself by naming and how, even as that very thing absents itself in the name.

Scene IX: The Present Absents Itself

263. Now we must see the complementary side to what we have just shown. Speech makes present what is absent by definition, that is, the supersensible of meaning. But in so doing, speech casts presence into absence. As soon as it is named, identified in a name and a meaning ("this is a *rose*"), the living presence—what we called *continuum*—evaporates, empties itself, absents itself, becomes pure name (flatus vocis). Discriminated by speech, the presence identifies itself and disappears: "Oh, it was the *rose* . . ."

Presentifying the absent in the name is the same as reflecting the presence into the mirror of a constitutive absence, that is, into a sign already dead to presence, and always deferred a little further away. *I? Who* am I? As an "I," I no longer *am*. My eternal living presence vanishes into the "I"; in other words, I am the nothing of the "I"; but then the "I" is the nothing of me, of my being a living presence before every "I" and every "me."

264. Now if you look closely, you can observe (and it's a refreshing and remarkable thing) how the so-called enigma of time has its roots precisely here. The enigma is expressed by saying: the past is no more, the future is not yet, the present never is (because it is always beyond itself, either already passed or yet to come). So, where does time stand? What sort of *thing* is it? Mystery! Time passes and goes, and for the rest, nobody knows.

Come on, don't worry now, and keep a cool head! I don't mean this in the (baffling) sense that the present is a mysterious moment always on the run as if it were suffering from an unthinkable St. Vitus' dance or absolute becoming—unthinkable, in fact, even as becoming, given the paradox of a being which always "is not," while at the same time being traditionally deemed the most profound substance of every event which is. This is a distorted reading of the matter, a reading that becomes bewitched by words precisely when it undertakes to describe "time as it is" in its "mystery."

Let us attempt, instead, to see and say this in the simplest and most direct way: *it is the named present—and precisely insofar as it is named—that never is.*

What enters time as living *continuum*, through the also living practice of words, is the constitutive absence inherent in the name or meaning. It is for *this* reason that past, present, and future are always absent, absent in speech, which at the same time differentiates them and presents them as such.

It is interesting to note that Augustine had come to precisely this conclusion, as he remarked: "If no one asks me, I know [what time is]; if I want to explain it to a questioner, I do not know." With that, he had said it all, and there would be nothing more to add, except that this is precisely what knowledge is. But he didn't listen to himself carefully, I think, driven as he was by the project—in the end also appropriate—of conceiving God's creation as an eternal event.

265. Speech invokes and calls: it e-vokes by pro-voking—provoking presence and into presence. Which is to say: by directing our reflected naming attention to what *we do*. In this sense, we are awakened into the *logos*, as Heraclitus said.

This gesture of reflection is the *vox significativa*. Its originally constitutive habit is the invocation, that is, *prayer*: My God, my God, why hast Thou forsaken me (*Eli, Eli, lama sabachthani*). Do not turn your attention from me, so that I, too, may pay attention, may be present to myself, and so be it. This is the indelible ground of every religiosity and every sanctity, of every *religio*. In the divine we celebrate and invoke the symbolic incarnation of the supersensible meaning.

By the same token, the fundamental and founding bond between child and mother—or between lovers—is originally a practice of invocation and naming.

266. In its invocation, speech makes the caller and the called simultaneous and contemporary: they *are* for each other—it is the *proposal* that calls you and makes you into the called; it is the *response* of the called that makes me a caller.

This way, the called *assign* a presence to themselves, or they assign themselves to presence, *in the name of the word*. The word is a living, present sign, the living threshold of meaning. It is a threshold that makes absent—by presenting it—the event of the complementary desire for complicity—the desire that underlies and supports the event of the name.

Put it differently: speech actualizes and identifies desire in the sign. It is primarily an *index* (but only an index, that is, an indication, a trace) of satisfied complementarity, of fulfilled complicity. "Ah, there we are. We've finally said, 'I love you' to each other."

267. Undoubtedly, the spoken complicity is then identified in knowledge, which increases both desire and gratification. It is significant, however, that gratification, in its enacted culmination, lowers—even erases—the threshold of the known individuality: in the effectually attained and fulfilled ecstasy, the "I" experiences a "little death" of its own. We forget ourselves in those moments; or rather, which is equally significant, the only voice we have left is the shout. Speech regresses to an ecstatic shout, just like at the peak of the Dionysian initiation. In fact, the two levels—that of speech present to itself and that of the ecstasy at the fulfillment of our most powerful desire—cannot be enacted simultaneously, they cannot coexist with the same intensity and the same degree of presence.

On the other hand, this shows well the nature of speech's desire—as I am going to show to you momentarily.

Here we reiterate the following point: what is eclipsed in meaning (qua constitutive element of the sign) is not "the thing"—say, the thing we call the signifier, the so-called empirical support of meaning. I do not generically hear sounds in speech, nor do I read traces of ink in the written text. What is eclipsed is rather the complementary desire for complicity that enacted us and made us precisely complementary up to the threshold of the name, sustaining us even beyond that.

Scene X: Chronic Knowledge

268. Just like speech, then, desire, too, shows a twofold threshold:

i) Desire for coincidence in the action; for example, complicity in the shout that, by crossing—thus *marking*—the distance, at the same time, and precisely for this reason, assigns it to us.

ii) Desire for recognition in the name (complicity of speech).

What is it about, exactly? Perhaps a desire for control of the already occurred distance, through the *vox significativa*? If this distance has not occurred, however, how could desire possibly arise? Indeed, we are speaking here of a desire that somehow precedes speech—but we are not saying it right. Before speech, desire cannot *properly* be there, so that we should rather postulate a kind of impetus, as it were, toward complementarity and complicity. Why, for example, should children in their mother's womb desire to talk? What could they possibly have to say? It has also been said that they dream—quite an exceptional thing to understand, one that would call for a separate discussion on dreams, which we cannot have here.

When Chauncey Wright said that life is an end in itself,[4] he meant to shoot down all metaphysical reveries claiming to offer reasons or justifications for life, or even sit in judgment of life as it is. He was right. However, we should add that, once life has inscribed itself on the threshold of speech, it *no longer* suffices unto itself. Its economy overflows into a new figure of desire, or simply into desire tout court.

This is after all the root of those fantasies that wish to justify life or reject it, without ever being able to succeed, because the pretension is unfounded and meaningless.

269. Now, you can easily see that it is indeed the response to speech, i.e., the mutual establishment of the habit of recognition, that makes the *known distance* appear, after and regardless of whether it has been *enacted* (for example in the shout).

The known distance is therefore the structural feature of speech.

As such, this distance is ineliminable in speech or by speech—that is, in our knowledge. No response from speech will ever silence my desire

---

4. "All the ends of life are, I am persuaded, within the sphere of life." Chauncey Wright, Letter to Miss Grace Norton, July 29, 1874, in *Letters of Chauncey Wright, with Some Account of His Life*, edited by James Bradley Thayer (Harvard University Press, 1878), 274. Also quoted in Philip P. Wiener, *Evolution and the Founders of Pragmatism* (Harvard University Press, 1949), 37–38—Ed.

or fear; at most, it will relieve, for a while, my desire or fear, precisely because they have been expressed, and thus they are known.

And yet this impossibility to eliminate the known distance must not be regressed and retroflexed into the enacted distance. In its own ways, the enacted distance can be overcome; it does not prevent satisfaction and fulfillment—quite the opposite! *This* distance is precisely what makes them possible.

There is certainly a distancing threshold that cannot be eliminated in the bodies and in their complementarity of desire—or better, in their complementary and complicit impetus. However, this is precisely what makes them attractive because the total abolition of distance, and total identification, would bring about not fulfillment but obliteration. Here we rather see a constitutive oscillation between satisfied and unsatisfied which rules the habit—the active practice—of possession/acceptance, and which fulfills—and therefore also happily (albeit temporarily) extinguishes—desire, or more precisely, the impetus.

270. Then we can easily see that, due to its structural distance, the knowledge of speech has a "chronic" character, in that it implies a "mortal disease." In this sense, *those who are born to speech assign themselves to the knowledge of death.* In a general sense, those who know they are born, shall die.

On its living threshold, speech shows that the speaker's living presence is already dying, and thus, that it will die ("Death is atoned for by living," says one of Ungaretti's lines).[5]

That is how the speaker can finally see the difference that the animal cannot see: *the difference between the corpse and the name,* the difference between the mortal coil and the spiritual meaning inscribed in the community's intersubjective response of words and names.

It is precisely in the complementarity of words that everyone becomes the other of the other, and thus both one and everyone, a participant in the public community; this happens because they are *evoked* and called to presence, that is, to the communal, supersensible public presence, and

---

5. "La morte si sconta vivendo." Giuseppe Ungaretti, *Sono una creatura* (*I Am a Creature*, 1916), in Giuseppe Ungaretti, *Vita d'un uomo. Tutte le poesie*, edited by Leone Piccioni (Mondadori, 1969), 41—Ed.

presence in the name. And so, man has, in addition, the name—and not only "casual unions," that is, anonymous sex in the great forest, as G. B. Vico said.[6]

By having, in addition, the name, human beings have in themselves the supersensible meaning which, as such, is eternal and cannot die; they have, in addition, the soul, as tradition has it. That is, precisely the absolute individuality of the name: the name that the ancients invoked and celebrated by shouting at the top of their lungs, all together, in front of the funeral pyre of their dead companions.

271. That is why men and women can see, by retroflexion, death in the sensible body: the body becomes mortal for them, mortal body, *caput mortuum*, in knowledge, by difference from the (retroflexed) name.

Of course, they cannot experience death—this "non-actuality," as Hegel said very well[7]—they cannot experience it because death is a knowledge, an effect and an object of speech.

And this is the reason why every lived "thing"—in that it is also known in speech—takes on a posthumous meaning and is in turn consigned, through our knowing experience, to death and temporal irreversibility ("The flowers I sent thee . . . were withered . . .").[8] The essentially posthumous and artificial character of speech, which we were discussing earlier, finds here further confirmation and clarification.

Scene XI: The *Pharmakon* of Speech

272. We can summarize all we have said as follows: in speech we are all accomplices in the death which is spoken (or alluded to) in it. It is this secret, this secret knowing that we evoke when we speak. From this, an

---

6. *The New Science of Giambattista Vico*, par. 410, translated from the third edition (1744) by Thomas Goddard Bergin and Max Harold Frisch (Cornell University Press, 1948), 118 ("incerti concubiti," *Principj di scienza nuova d'intorno alla comune natura delle nazioni*, 1744, Libro II, Della sapienza poetica. II. Logica poetica, 2.VI)—Ed.

7. G. W. F. Hegel, *Phenomenology of Spirit*, translated by A. V. Miller, foreword by J. N. Findlay (Oxford University Press, 1977), 19—Ed.

8. From T. S. Eliot, "Song," published first as "A Lyric" in *Smith Academy Record*, April 4, 1905; quoted here from T. S. Eliot, *Opere 1904–1939*, with facing English text, edited by Roberto Sanesi (Bompiani, 1992), 12—Ed.

ethology of speech could find reason for an extensive phenomenology of word practices.

For example, we could further underscore the long-noticed pleasure inherent in talking. Consider how incessantly men and women chat! The pleasure of telling, of being told, of hearing it said.

On this basis Gorgias showed the thaumaturgical power of speech—the place of desire, hope, fear—as well as the political value of rhetoric, captured in all its ambiguity. Words as consolation for the pain of living and desiring, for the ungovernable darkness of chance and fate, where the propitious moment (*kairos*) is always poised to surprise us, to turn us in an instant from winners into losers, from rich into poor, from triumphant monarchs into desperate beggars.

A word that is both consoling and deceiving, always out to fool us, always prompting us to pursue the most varied fantasies: it is what happened to ill-starred Helen of Troy who, completely overcome by the lure of Paris/Alexander's apparent beauty (he was the one wearing the girdle), doomed herself to a tragic destiny of exile, guilt, violence, and the vituperation of peoples. A word that is twofold, just like the Greek meaning of *pharmakon*.

But above all else is the need to drown out with words the agony of a silent world—a world that has become silent for those who have crossed the word's threshold and can no longer dwell upon the quiet gathering of the flock, and of animals in general, as both Leopardi and Nietzsche observed.

It is the need for everyday chitchat—for its inauthentic sound, as Heidegger would put it; yet a sound which is essential to all "mortals" insofar as it diverts them from the thought of death, always present in the mind of those who talk, especially to themselves.

273. And also: the economy of language in its sexed difference, where man (at least "historical" man, as we know him) talks less, not out of distrust for words, but rather out of too much trust in the rationality of the *logos*, that is, in the rationality of the life-world practices, in the governable rationality of the world and of its events; for many centuries, in fact, men have been brought up to write reality alphabetically and to elaborate its—mainly political—consequences. Women, on the other hand, are said to talk much more, and to abandon themselves to a squan-

dering of words. If that were indeed true, it would not be because they really trust those words, but rather as a means to return to the directly lived and shared experience of "moods"—the only thing women really trust, and the enduring advantage of having been excluded for so long from alphabetical, rational pedagogy.

Herein lies the origin of two comic masks that theater—and later Greek philosophical theater—have created: that of the chatty Xanthippe and that of the patient and silent Socrates: the man who on every occasion claims (to men . . .) that he does not know, yet before Xanthippe keeps quiet, slyly, because he "knows" . . .

274.The secret of words, then, would lie in the desire to exorcize death precisely in speech and through speech; to exorcize, that is, the very death we give ourselves by speaking and thus assigning ourselves to a name, to a soul.

Lastly, there is the desire for a theory and a theology. It is no longer enough to meet God in the sacredness of experience, of its constitutive desire (sex, birth, death, the moon, the sun, the seasons, and so on—all occasions for the *Parousia*, the manifestation of the divine); now one also needs to demonstrate the existence God, to make it logical and scientific.

On the other hand, if "I" *am* my supersensible meaning, my name and my soul (which is what word practices educate me to think), then "I" *am* eternal life, I cannot die. Hence, the sense of absolute absurdity that sometimes seizes every one of us when, like a revenant Ivan Ilyich, we are faced with the thought of dying: an inconceivable event! How come the world is still there and I no longer am? Where on earth did I end up? How can time end once and for all, and then nothing happens, nothing ever again? What does it mean, how can we conceive of this future eternity in which "I" *am* not, "I" am not there, the "I" is no longer there?

275. Speech's desire could be phrased as follows: since speech has posited evil (the knowledge of death), it must also answer to it so as to free us from it (i.e., guarantee our rebirth in eternal life). Besides, speech has always been required to provide impossible explanations: "At least tell me the *reason* why . . . you don't love me anymore!"

This complicity of knowledge that inscribes us in speech and sums up all that which we call civilization ("weddings, courthouses, and altars")[9] is ultimately the political foundation of *science*. This is where Western man's theoretical desire is rooted, as well as his political science and, in general, his science.

If I may be allowed a brief digression, I could put it like this: science (*all our science*, as Nietzsche would have it) does nothing but take to extreme consequences the supersensible of words and above all their alphabetical transcriptions—the supersensible which has always been the capital threshold of the human, the place of anthropology. This taking to the extreme is shown in our hope and drive to transplant and transfer ourselves at will into container bodies, saving our soul in the process: a technologically concrete version of the latter's immortality, which Socrates (or Plato) stipulated "rationally" long ago.

In this regard, it is very significant that the Catholic Church, hostile to many a biotechnological practice (such as stem cell production), does not object to organ transplants—at least so far: the possibility of a brain transplant might well cause some uneasiness in the future.

After all, Christian theory (or philosophy), long associated with Greek and Aristotelian philosophy, has itself been completely captured by the nihilism of technics as well by the superstitious vision of the world of science—a world which, after the unhappy Galileo affair, it has indeed learned to treat with more caution and substantial agreement.

276. In speech we are accomplices toward the death spoken or alluded within it, and *at the same time we are complementary in the desire for recognition through the response.* Now we must focus on this second point.

You *must* acknowledge me as immortal, that is, as an *end* in myself and not as a means to an end—Kant stated as he was founding his moral theory.

Hence the public prohibition to inflict death: a timeless sovereign law, in no way *relativizable, controvertible,* or *breakable* but, rather, the foundation of every other law, which means, the substance of every politics, of every *politiké areté* (as Glaucon had already somewhat intuited).

---

9. "Nozze, tribunali ed are," the first institutions of mankind. Line 91 of Ugo Foscolo's poem, *Dei sepolcri* ("On Sepulchers," 1807), inspired by Giambattista Vico's *New Science*—Ed.

Public subjects, equalized in the name—that is, supersensibly spiritualized in the manner of Plato—cannot, and must not, inflict death on each other. And yet the matter, here and elsewhere, is extremely ambiguous.

277. Philosophical politics translates our ancestral horror for death and murder into soul truth (the voice of conscience whispering in Socrates' ear), thereby repressing such horror without really understanding it.

By canceling its provenance and ignoring its categorial retroflexion back on that provenance, the civilization of the soul harbors illusions about itself and then finds itself to be powerless against the inevitable return of the repressed.

The ancestral horror for death, in fact, goes hand in hand with the contemporary ability to inflict death and frequent its violence in many ways, including ritual ones, even deriving from it a specific pleasure. Which is precisely why the Greeks considered man to be the most terrible of animals.

At the same time, by carrying violence and death within itself (which the law of the soul has by no means eliminated), Western civilization shows in the clearest way that where violence and injustice avail themselves of the most powerful weapons, the human animal becomes the greatest threat to the life of the entire planet.

Eighth Figure

The Occasion of the Sign

Scene XII: The Sign of "Nobody"

278. In speech we are complementary in the desire for recognition through a response. And yet, we know all too well that this recognition is never pure: rather, it is an *unequal recognition*.

The assimilation of recognition to *equality* is but the result of a conceptual, merely semiotic operation. Its underlying criterion is essentially quantitative-segnic (*segnico*), and as such it is always already *commodified, reduced* to the sign of the money-commodity—the quintessential transferal object.

Herein is rooted the illusion of democratic equality, as well as the latter's involuntary yet incurable degenerative relapses: for example, the structural linkage between politics and criminality. On the other hand, as Nietzsche had guessed, *science*—modern science in particular—cannot but be democratic: hence, its strength and weakness, its infinite ability to expand but also its internal limit, a boundary threatened by dogmatism and superstition, as well as by speculation and profiteering. Which of course is even more true of political science and its justice.

279. As I said, recognition is never pure, insofar as it entails the complementary, unequal reciprocity of desire that binds men to women, parents to their children, and so on.

Desire is by nature dual and thus unequal. We saw it clearly represented in the myth of Venus' girdle—an economic exchange wherein two desires mirror each other from an unequal standing, demand, or discrepancy:

i) The desire to become an object of desire, a transferal object for the other, a body marked by the girdle—which is to say, the desire to be idolized and envied.

ii) The desire to possess the object of desire, whereby the dazzlement of the girdle validates the body (i.e., the desire to possess it) and constitutes it as a transferal object; in other words, the desire to control the transferal object itself, greed, and avarice.

280. Constitutively caught up in this primordial economic exchange of desire, everyone *is*, or *becomes*, someone *for* the other, which means—keep in mind (though you should already know this)—that everyone is essentially a *relation* and not a substance, whether material or spiritual. In ourselves, we are "nobody," as Odysseus introduces himself to Polyphemus. In this deceitful wordplay thought up by the shrewd and ingenious Odysseus—but words are, indeed, constitutively deceitful—we could read many surprising truths, truths which, on this shared journey of ours, are becoming familiar to us, but which "nobody" generally likes and about which the "nobodies" that you are, that I am, that we all are, do not like to concur.

Don't hold it against me, but please listen to what I'm saying; if such is the original situation of the subject, then the center of the subject is *elsewhere*—a notion I already touched upon in the past, but which perhaps didn't strike you then as much as it does now. Because now it is clear to us that this center is displaced (that is, originally situated) in the event of the name.

Twice elsewhere, we might say, insofar as the name implies being identified through and by the other within the universal public community of speakers; and because the name is the ultrasensible, "hyperuranic" essence articulated in the practice of speaking and writing: it first echoes and emerges from the outside, creating the inside as an aftereffect. The center of the sub-ject is actually a super-ject: not an origin, but an outcome.

For this reason, we might observe, any attempt to establish at what level of development the fetus should be considered a subject—a human subject—is not only futile but also completely absurd. Expecting an answer from science is a glaring case of second-degree superstition: even scientists are embarrassed by the issue, and in chatty bioethics conferences they remain noncommittal about it—"you decide," they tell the jurist, who was hoping they could shed some light.

281. Caught in the name game, *we all live out our "segnic" death in the other* (in the other's desire). Specifically:

i) Those *who are recognized*, because in the name that identifies them, they meet the void of the supersensible meaning that plunges their present-eternal preverbal life into an unbridgeable chasm. "You are Peter," all right. But Peter's life is unaware of this, and he will deny his identity three times before resigning himself to accept the meaning of his name, and with it, the inevitability of his death. Of course, he does so on the strength of his acquired faith and hope for eternal life, and above all, out of the charity of his love for the Master, because this is ultimately how things work.

ii) *Those who recognize*, because they must in turn be recognized as the ones who recognize and speak *in the name of the Father*, that is, in the name of the supersensible meaning (don't forget what we said about the e-vocative character of the name and its constitutive demand for attention).

282. When people speak with the intention of naming, they always speak "in the name of the father." In the name of God the Father (The Eternal Father) and of His law, or in the name of Adam, father of all mankind. Hence, the naïve inadequacy of any attempt to remedy this situation (at least in the languages where the grammar allows it) by enforcing the use of professional feminine nouns.

We should rather ask ourselves why the supersensible meaning—the concept—seems to be masculine by default, which might lead us to believe that the origin of language is masculine—a truly nonsensical notion, insofar as speech is grounded in the desire for unequal recognition.

We could, at most, put forward two anthropological conjectures—for what they're worth! We could imagine that words had their first "segnic" roots in the collaborative action of the human group facing death in the savannah, that is, the fight to the death—a fight in which, at least among primates, the male prevails physically over the female (as Plato, too—as you might recall—pointed out).

283. The second conjecture is more ingenious and draws inspiration from Alfred Kallir's segnic and alphabetical theories. A man's sexual role in the act responsible for reproduction is—or is mainly felt to be—"active": it is the man who, by impregnating the woman, causes reproduction to move from potency to act (as Aristotle would have it). That he is the one responsible—what we call the First cause—is shown by his bustling about, that is, by the various stages of his behavior which, after he has chased down and subjugated the woman, culminates in the act of penetration. Thus, a man undertakes to violate—not without pain—the woman's threshold (the biological mystery of the woman's virginity as well as of her "metaphorical" hymen), which makes him the "active" and "creative" being par excellence: from man comes the "conceiving" as well as its figurative effect in language.

However, this (as is all too evident) describes the situation from the man's point of view without regard to the woman's reaction; without considering, that is, their "passive activity," which, according to Kallir, we find expressed in the root and meaning of deponent verbs.

And finally, we should remember Desmond Morris, who tried to prove scientifically that it was the woman who educated emotionally and sexually the man, persuading him to transform the coitus from a violent assault—mostly performed from the rear and merely suffered by the woman—into shared, frontal copulation.[1] Of course, Morris' theory is much more intricate than this brief mention, as it factors in the compound action of several other forces—biological, social, psychological, economic, pedagogical, among others.

284. Whatever you may think about this matter (and I would not wish to impose my views on you) it is possible to note that our considerations lead logically to the following conclusion: since speech generates death, retroflecting it ambiguously where death does not exist; since speech, by difference from itself (i.e., from the supersensible void of the name) *shows* death (i.e., shows the corpse of its difference from the name), it is only natural that speech might also wish to *know* death.

Which means that speech wishes to know *itself*, speech being indeed the place and threshold of every knowledge in a literal sense.

---

1. See Desmond Morris, *The Naked Ape: A Zoologist's Study of the Human Animal* (McGraw-Hill, 1967)—Ed.

Speech wishes to know *the* meaning of death, wondering what it means for us to die.

In this way speech manifests its desire to regain eternal life.

285. Freud came to think that this impulse to return to the bosom of the eternity of death ruled all animal life, because he considered (as everybody else) the anthropological knowledge of death to be an absolute and universal thing.

On the other hand, the fact that eternal life, in the sexed complementarity of life, is gained through sexual reproduction before and beyond the individual's identification with the name (as Aristotle maintained), assumes a more understandable sense. Or even a possible one, which is precisely what puzzled Freud: that the sexual impulse, fundamental and primary for the living being, might express (as Freud came to believe) the living being's desire to return to the eternity of nonlife, that is, of death.

To us, however, things look a little different. Before speech's knowledge there is neither death nor life, but the *continuum* of the event, which is in any case always already there, prior to any separation and judgment. I hope you can follow me.

I do understand your difficulty: it is mine, too. How can we not see death?

286. Hegel, of course, got it right: the animal does not die, the animal comes to an end; only man dies, only man has ahead of him death qua death and is under the custody of its shrine—as Heidegger confirmed. Nevertheless, it still seems to us that, somehow, animals also die—and, indeed, they do. They do die, and, not infrequently, we are to blame for that: they die to us, exactly as every man dies to the others—as Gentile had it.[2]

It is extremely difficult, if not impossible, for us to cancel ourselves in our difference, removing our evidence of life and death; it is enormously hard to try to condense, even by the intuition of a moment, all the multifarious unfolding of time and its occurrences, to dry it down into the only unlimited, untarnished obligation of the world's

---

2. "One who dies, dies to someone." Giovanni Gentile, *Genesis and Structure of Society*, translated by H. S. Harris (University of Illinois Press, 1966), 222—Ed.

eternity (which is neither alive nor dead): the obligation to simply be "nobody."

Scene XIII: The Dazzling Light

287. Thus, speech that brings death is *the accomplice of eternal life*: this is what, above all, I would like to bring to your attention. The knowledge of death that is the anthropological knowledge par excellence, in which everyone shares and from which all other forms of knowledge derive, at the same time seeks to become knowledge of eternal life.

This linkage constitutes the obscure ground of politics—its root and raison d'être—as I will try to show to you in detail, so that I may persuade you of it.

288. First of all, please note: the knowledge of death is sexless, just as the human skeleton appears to be, at least at first sight; it is, indeed, anthropological knowledge *in general.*

Indeed, as we already observed, the threshold of speech is egalitarian and equalizing, unlike the dual desire which establishes it and makes it evocatively happen. Such threshold progressively calls attention to the supersensible meaning of the sign; not only the fact that you have *this* name (and that you are a "you"), but also the very fact *of the* name: a universal and public intersubjective substance, the sign of a response that is common to everybody.

We understand more clearly, now, Plato's quandary as the name was rising to be conceptual *logos*, by virtue of its written semiotization. In the realm of the concept (which is the very realm of death, as Hegel realized) the difference of sexual desire cannot subsist, men and women are equal.

289. By imposing more and more of its relevance in its relation to the other practices of life, the universal truth of speech, and of its writing, culminates in the science/democracy pair responsible for the public and political equality between men and women—at least on paper and in intentions.

This development seems ineluctable today, and indeed, we can certainly believe, for several strong reasons, that it is appropriate and wise for us to welcome it and promote it actively, both for the sake of justice and for the positive consequences it unquestionably produces.

However, we must firmly reject the ideological illusion that public equality can ever cancel out the unequal complementarity and complicity of men and women, that is, the constitutive and ineliminable duality of the sexed human being and of its truth—at least if and as long as it remains a sexed being.[3]

It must be clear to us that erasing, or aiming at erasing, such complementarity and such complicity will lead to denying the very eternal life that speech wants and promotes (an eternal life that often dazzles us either theologically or technologically, which are but two aspects of the same presumption to know and appropriate the will and the law of God).

Pure equality between man and woman erases *life*, human life, along with its living experience; this may well be destined to happen, but for us it is a matter of *knowing it*—that's what *theater* is for.

290. Speech's desire, we said, is *to resurrect into eternal life*. This is what speakers obscurely desire when they reason and provide reasons (as Aristotle expressly stated: *logon didonai*—we must explain our reasons and not tell fables like in the time of Gyges).

Therefore, *politiké areté*, which is the ultimate consequence, for now at least, of the institution of the threshold of speech and anthropological knowledge, *is in turn an accomplice of eternal life and of its desire*. An accomplice, that is, of the fact that political virtue is most desirable by human animals, endowed as they are with *logos* and originally inscribed in it. And so now, if you take a closer look, you shall see all there is to be seen here.

In the first place, you can see the need for the descent into the *chasma*—that is, for an initiatory journey into the realm of death, which

---

3. *La virtù politica* was originally published in 2004. Sexual difference and gender theories have undergone seismic changes in the last twenty years. However, the author's point—contrary to the perfect Socratic city where differences are obliterated, and castes are reinforced—is that differences must not be flattened, and in fact all differences should be acknowledged. Sini's observations on sexual difference should be read alongside Adriana Cavarero et al., *Diotima. Il pensiero della differenza sessuale* (La Tartaruga Edizioni, 2003), and the various works of Adriana Cavarero, Luisa Muraro, Carla Lonzi, and other Italian feminist philosophers. See *Contemporary Italian Women Philosophers: Stretching the Art of Thinking*, edited by Silvia Benso and Elvira Roncalli (State University of New York Press, 2021)—Ed.

is the realm itself of speech and of its invisible, supersensible mark. *Politiké areté* is thus, essentially, an *ódos politiké*, a path to initiation.

Secondly, you can see the necessity to translate the fruit of the initiation into a skill (an *areté*) and a technique (a *téchne*): an art of representation, of the *mis-en-scène* of this transformative path.

Besides, it has been known forever that theater is political.

291. You can see, you can see . . . I am well aware that it is still difficult for you to see clearly all I have just explained in a quick summary: please have a little patience. First, you should at least note this: that even the *mis-en-scène* of speech that seeks to investigate the backstage of the theater (as we are doing here) is itself an eminently political act. The world-sheet (*foglio-mondo*) of this writing of mine, as I like to call it sometimes, is ultimately a political art—it cannot be otherwise.

A theater of words and writing, the world-sheet inherits the philosophical theater and, as it were, inhabits its stages. And yet its practice, like all practices, becomes entangled with the elaborate and invisible support of our present-day practices of life and knowledge, according to the way that words and writing operate on an economy of the bodies, which have become the mirrors of our reflected soul—a soul that is established from them by reflection.

Unsurprisingly, then, the quintessential political place emerges primarily in writing, that is, in the art of writing out the world-sheet: it could not be otherwise, and you will see this too, I hope, more and more clearly.

292. In its political gesture, our glance on Plato's backstage is now fully capable of showing its dazzle. Now we become aware, in other words, of how the scene of the *Republic*, by establishing the threshold of the Political qua political science, dazzles us with the white light of its knowledge.

First, with the knowledge, therein constructed, of philosophy, then with the set of knowledges which descend from it: political science, economics, anthropology, pedagogy, psychology—and which, not by chance, I have asked you to suspend, to hold in *epoché*.

The dazzle consists in this: Plato makes us believe that what is represented and dialectically founded in the *Republic* is *politics* captured in its eternal essence. Prior to its establishment, there are only "rough origins" (in the words of Vico, himself a great Platonist).[4] Aristotle, too, still thinks the same, as we have seen in his genetic reconstruction of the state.

Of course, looking at this notion from the institution of its threshold (as we cannot but do, influenced by it as we are), what Plato establishes is *tautologically* true. Before Plato and his times, there is no political science. Its institution becomes a criterion and a paradigm, a yardstick which cannot obviously find itself before and behind itself, and which must qualify what precedes it starting from itself.

293. The dazzle from this tautological retroflexed light, then, begets a structural *blindness*. Political science projects backward imaginary needs, imaginary natural disputes for supremacy (*pleonexia*), imaginary male and female identities, and so on, thereby inventing an imaginary anthropology and psychology, an eternal man that never existed.

Of course, the same is true of mythical thought—as it is usually called: it, too, cloaks the origin in retroflexed mythical figures. Yet mythical thought does not, nor could ever, lay claim to objective, universal, and critical truth—a claim that, on the contrary, is inherent in the threshold of our forms of knowledge. In fact, the "rational" light that dazzles these different knowledges is not altogether *rational*: and this is, indeed, the gist of our backstage denunciation. If you really want to be rational, you ought to learn to see through the dazzle of your prejudices and superstitions.

In reading its own past retroactively (that is, starting from itself), political science misconstrues its inheritance, thus failing to see the solid autonomy of meaning of the practices of life and knowledge that have made possible its very political threshold and scientific wisdom. It fails to recognize that its genealogy originates in a politics totally other than itself. It does not understand, in the words of Chauncey Wright, the continuity of functions in the difference of their new uses.

294. Political science, indeed, considers itself as a large transforming threshold of human knowledge in an evolutionary sense, but in so doing

---

4. *The New Science of Giambattista Vico*, par. 391, 110 ("rozze origini," *Principj di scienza nuova d'intorno alla comune natura delle nazioni*, 1744, "Libro II, Della sapienza poetica. Della metafisica poetica, Corollarj, III")—Ed.

it completely overlooks the specific weight of *its own* threshold. We might say that it ignores the economy of the threshold. Political science is unable to gauge what its threshold produces *ex novo* backward and forward, thereby changing the sense of both past and future.

Consequently, political science does not understand or see how the events made unrecognizable and unrecoverable by its way of representing *politiké areté* are already fully political. This is how the Western metaphysical narrative has come to shape our entire political science from Aristotle to Hegel, who, with the same mindset as Plato's disciple, evolutionarily lines up family, civil society, and state. Marx, too, will be deeply marked by that very same narrative.

295. Political science does not see in a genealogically correct way the political events that have contributed, with their tangle, to make its threshold possible—events which are, from its point of view, pre-political. And yet, it carries silently those events within itself, paying for their problems and paradoxes.

In fact, our political knowledge does not attain at all the solution, the peace, the justice Plato wished and pleaded for. Nor does it establish a pedagogical anthropology capable of enacting in humans the transformation that would be needed to reach the perfect state.

True, the arrival of the threshold of political science and philosophy—the affirmation of what Husserl called the "man of theory"—produces indeed a huge anthropological change, setting the Western world on paths which today take up planetary proportions and figures, yet with outcomes quite different from what had been ideologically envisioned.

Not necessarily good or bad outcomes: the matter is far more complex than the cheap little sociological-hermeneutical formulas in fashion today.

296. Outcomes that for a long time have evinced a political scene increasingly unintelligible and, above all, unmanageable. Outcomes that amount to the crisis of politics that we all feel we are experiencing. The institutions of political society show all too clearly and unmercifully their powerlessness and irrelevance. Hence the European citizens' growing disaffection and distrust in politics, although their political status continues to guarantee them enormous, uncalled-for advantages over

the world of the poor. Also, they share with the citizens of the United States the dubious distinction of causing the world's largest depredations and most shocking imbalances, under the guise of market freedom and other ideological lies.

States, parliaments, supranational assemblies, electoral events, social and economic representations are increasingly reduced to acting as mere shills for particular interests, always locked in irreducible, shameful conflict with each other.

On the other hand, the deep changes underway in our practices of life and knowledge—and the reflected figures of the individual and collective consciousness that derive from them—remain mostly cryptically incomprehensible and politically unrepresentable, to the extent that all these phenomena are now largely inconsistent with the categories of knowledge inherited from our metaphysical and scientific tradition.

There is, at bottom, a universal crisis of knowledge and of its manifestations, a crisis of their ideal and de facto encyclopedia. Thus, the first task of philosophy, which is the first origin of that encyclopedia, cannot but be to reflect critically and genealogically on its own history, exposing critically the limits of its traditional theoretical practice.

Scene XIV: The Secret of the Political

297. Now I would ask you to reconsider the entire matter with me in the light of our backstage glance.

The descent into the *chasma*, we have said, is the institutive act of *politiké areté*: a highly anthropological act, constitutive of the human, because it conforms with the fundamental anthropological knowledge, known and shared by everyone—the knowledge that belongs indistinctly to "everyone." It is the knowledge established by the advent of the threshold of speech that makes death visible, thereby giving rise to the community of mortals.

Man is a political animal insofar as he is a speaking animal: the great Aristotle had already guessed this essential fact.

The descent into the *chasma* is then a descent into the mystery of death.

Precisely this descent is the only path (*odos*) that allows man to achieve *rebirth*. The only method (*methodos*), the only vital art and technique.

298. What am I talking about? I could add many more details, but what I am saying is essentially this: the vision of death generates its double in an aware knowledge, which repeats this vision ritually, and by analogy, to escape from it. But isn't this paradox, after all, typical of every *initiation* ritual? The act of retrieving the origin by rejoining the end in a circle—alpha and omega, as we find inscribed on sarcophagi.

This circularity is, of course, the very image of eternal life. The image of the circle, the cosmic image hinting at astral perfection in which the eternal and intact *continuum* of life manifests itself.

And notice how this notion intertwines with the phenomenon of the name: the acquisition of a new name is typical of every initiation, insofar as every naming—as we have seen—is a proclamation. The new name is a sign of the acquisition of a new life, the guarantee of eternal life.

This might explain the widespread phenomenon of the nicknames that lovers give each other at the beginning of new love affairs: in these nicknames, we might say, they are reborn to love and in love (one that, as they invariably swear, will be eternal). The lovers descend into the *chasma* of the sexual little death where, in mutual ecstasy, their old social identity is transcended and lost, and then restored starting from a *private* name: first germ of the return of the couple—now a consecrated couple—within the public community. Isn't this, in a nutshell, the meaning of the tale of Gyges and the queen?

It remains nonetheless unclear why lovers choose nicknames related to animals so often: cats, mice, gazelles, fawns, swans, bulls, lions, bears, and so on. Could it be for an unconscious allusion to animal life, which is unaware of death?

299. Thus, the ritual—its *mis-en-scène*, its theater—is the political foundation of the human community. And theater itself, as we have seen, is in its roots nothing but ritual: a politics-economics of the body and its transfiguration into the representation of meaning.

The ritual assigns the parts or roles (as they are called in theater), shaping them on the concrete experience of the contingent practices of life and knowledge. An experience implying sexual complementarity and complicity, because the fundamental *parts*, in their irreducible duality, in their dyadic experience of human truth, are clearly man and woman. Complicity of the unequal desire—unequal because inscribed in *sexual difference*.

Such a difference, on the initiation threshold of the ritual, is transcribed back into the *name*, which thus becomes the common universal. Initiation to the human and to the divine, which is the human's complementary counterpart.

We have already recalled how this happens thanks to the eminently communal feature of the vocal gesture.

300. In the name, therefore, we have the ritual celebration of the linguistic community which above all man is: a celebration of his baptism, of his birth to spirit. Family names, such as Peter and Paul, and collective names, such as Athenian. Generally, the community identifies itself in the name of the eponymous divinity, a prototype and paradigm for human beings. For us moderns, the function of Athena for the Athenians is replaced by the names of saints: "You are Peter." Christian saints inherit many functions from the pagan Gods (which is why Protestants feel that the cult of saints smacks of pagan superstition).

The institution of political knowledge, of political science, necessarily frequents, too, a *transforming rituality*. Its first theater is represented by Plato's *Republic*: a philosophical dialogue which inherits the form of Athenian theater, and which is in turn a form of the pre-philosophical political rituality (consider, for instance, Aeschylus' *Persians*).

The transformative rituality of the *Republic* manifests itself in the *mis-en-scène* of the foundational discourses embodied in *characters*, in *masks*, with their parts wisely assigned.

301. The theater—double of the double, ritual form which, by embodying the figure of knowledge, is connected to the political character of speech—*plays with masks*. If I had more time, I would explain in detail how the mask performs a transformative action that puts the living in relationship with the dead and human culture in relationship with the eternity of the divine and wild nature.

Then I would show you that the animal, too, plays with masks in relation to the two crucial contingencies of fighting to the death for food and sex. The masking of predator and prey, of male and female, not to mention the masking of the play itself (just as the girdle, we might say, masked the face of Hecate the Dark).

These masking rituals remain somewhat constant. Even in the era of the secular and profane interpretation of politics, the sovereign people demand to be represented by the traditional masks of political force, as well as by traditional ceremonial pomp.

This ineradicable sacredness of power shows us, now, its peculiar *truth*, which we could phrase thus: the political, in its sacredness, is summed up in the *prohibition to kill*.

302. This, essentially, is the law: the law which is, also, the law of speech. What do I mean by "also"? I will show you right away. The law of speech is the obligation of common and communal speech, in a complicit complementarity inscribed in the secret of speech. The secret lies precisely in the constitution of the community of those who recognize each other and are, in turn, recognized in the *vox publica*. This voice that unites them is then also their salus publica: salvation of every individual life and its ideal eternalization in the name ("Committee of Public Safety," as the Jacobins in Paris would have it).

All of which boils down to the political prohibition to kill. Since speech establishes death, or better, the mortal condition, to the extent that it shows it, the speaking subject derives from it the *horror of knowing* and thus, precisely with speech, forbids and inhibits death.

Notice, then, the inherent *paradox of speech*: speech sees the *autophagy* of life—that is, from the speech's point of view, the desire of the living to assimilate the living. *And so, speech prohibits what, in a way, it also desires.*

As a matter of fact, as Freud noted, a prohibition does not make any sense if not to the extent that it spells a desire. A law would be completely superfluous if what it seeks to administer or forbid were able to spontaneously self-regulate.[5]

---

5. The author's emphasis on the prohibition to kill may seem counterintuitive, for politics has always justified killing. We may also think of Foucault's definition of sovereignty as "the right to *take* life or *let* live" (Michel Foucault, *The History of Sexuality Vol. I: An Introduction*, translated by Robert Hurley [Vintage, 1990], 136). Besides, as I said in my introduction, one can always kill in the name of the law that prohibits killing. Yet, with respect to ritual murder such as, for example, Gyges murdering the queen's husband as it is the only accepted way to gain access to power, the law of the city expounded by Socrates is precisely supposed to stop this archaic transition or, at least, to make it invisible. See par. 303–310 for further clarifications—Ed.

303. And here we come, also, *to the paradox of politics*, which Plato wonderfully inscribes in Thrasymachus and Glaucon's dialogues: a paradox born of the constitutive paradox of speech. It can be described this way: political virtue consists in pretending to abide by the law (which says not to kill) while doing exactly the opposite, using speech and its counterpart, money, as masks to cover violence. The logical and subtle Thrasymachus settles indignantly for the first, the rhetoric art of words; the more experienced Glaucon (more experienced in human nature) also embraces money, whose inherent intention he clarifies: money's goal is to give death, as it ultimately always does.

Herein, then, lies the *secretum*, the *arcanum* of the political, which explains the terrible complicity that binds powerful people together (including the complementarity binding together allies and enemies, both aware of their mutual complicity): their *arcanum* is death, which they must administer with personal indifference, under the guise of upholding the law and the eternal values while hypocritically and relentlessly doing the opposite.

All the time—they repeat to us and to themselves—they are choosing the lesser of two evils: eternal masks of Thrasymachus, Polemarchus, and Glaucon.

304. It is easy for Plato to marvelously stage all of this only so that he can condemn it by exposing its innermost inconsistency. On this basis, he concludes, there can be no true community, no true complicity, not even that of a community of thieves and murders, for they would end up killing each other.

No doubt a sinister consideration, should one wish to read nothing but this in the events of the politics of all times, as indeed many have suggested through history. The only possible political community would be a community of thieves and murderers, which would eventually dissolve into perennial *autophagy*. The monarch slaughters dissidents while enriching his ministers, who rob his subjects. The revolutionaries slaughter the king and his ministers. Then they divide up the loot as thieves. Finally, they slaughter each other. Then, one of them prevails and obtains power . . . and so on.

Not even a philosophically founded political science, however, is a solution because Plato is inscribed in the paradox of speech just like everybody else. In fact, more so than everybody else, insofar as he is a philosopher. It is Plato who brings to a climax, or to the limit, the domination of the concept, this extraordinary war machine that assimilates opponents to itself, making them disappear without need for violence or bloodshed, and leaving no room for future revenge. It is he who imposes the game of presence and absence, of surface and depth, the entire square of complementary knowledges: visible-unsayable/invisible-sayable. It is he who ratifies, with the birth of the theoretical gaze, the essential invisibility of the political, of the laws, of eternal life, and of the soul: transferal objects that open the way to all the paradoxes of the supersensible and its truth.

It is because of this revolution of theory and science that violence does not subside but, on the contrary, increases, reaching its climax precisely in the secular state, in modern science and democracy, however much the latter may claim to have curbed it. "Stunned and irrepressible dismay" in the face of the evil of men and in men, as Enzo Paci wrote shortly before he died.[6] He was talking about the horror into which the communist states of Eastern Europe had plunged in their attempt to fulfill Marx's ideal of the final liberation of mankind.

305. Precisely by exercising the law, the law that forbids killing, the art of politics *chooses its dead and its unborn*.

First, through the *writing* of power, by virtue of the quintessential sign that is *money*. The transferal object par excellence, money is the sign of value, that is, of the exchange value in which the fundamental economy of life is summed up.

And while in the ancient economy of power the chief transferal object was the phallus, which also grounded the right of the paterfamilias to administer life and death, in the modern economy this right is increasingly appropriated by financial capital, the ultimate judge of value—of the price based on which we determine what has the right to exist, what we can easily damn to hell, and what we are not even allowed to imagine that it can exist.

306. But notice how every prohibition opens the possibility of its opposite: I *must not* kill means that I *can* kill. Man, who makes death happen through speech, is obviously also he who can mete it out.

---

6. "Uno stupore incoercibile." Enzo Paci, "Sulla fenomenologia del negativo," *aut aut* 24, no. 140 (1974): 134–136. Also in Enzo Paci, *Il senso delle parole*, edited by Pier Aldo Rovatti (Bompiani, 1987)—Ed.

Here we can see one root of the complex universal phenomenon of war. War is something quite different from animal fights, nor is it exclusively motivated, as is sometimes believed, by purely economic causes, such as need, poverty, and the like. Rather, war is caused by evident and symbolic, sexed reasons, and as such it contributes a great deal to the formation of social roles—precisely on the basis of the sexual difference.

It is also said that war is nothing but an extreme tool of diplomacy—that is, of the art of politics, whose function is not to prevent wars but to utilize them. Of course, it is very diplomatic for politicians to insist on just the opposite; yet politicians know perfectly well they are lying, since the exercise of this lie is an integral part of their job, just as lying in general, as we have learned from Plato, is an integral part of politics. Thus, we should conclude: if there is an art of politics—if there is a politics in the sense thus far considered—you can rest assured that sooner or later there will also be a war.

But it is above all this desire—forbidden yet also permitted and even imposed by politics—that calls for an explanation, a desire that has been a constant source of amazement from the beautiful souls who, stopping at the shameless rhetoric of politicians (e.g., their repeated assurances that they *do not* want war, and that they are only making it for the sake of peace), find it totally unconceivable that men should be driven by a seemingly indestructible desire to inflict death, beyond any plausible reason or pragmatic interest.

It is true that, with the crisis of politics we mentioned above, the ways of war are also changing. War has become generalized terror: a noisy reply to the supersensible and constant noise of information, itself even more violent and terroristic. An invisible conflict that answers the supersensible of smart bombs. And a place of confrontation where the traditional distinction of sexual roles has disappeared: female soldiers, female cops and guerrilla fighters, teenagers and children of both sexes armed with submachine guns and grenades, walk the earth everywhere.

Scene XV: Sex and Politics

307. The prohibition to kill concerns at first the small group identified in the name: the Athenians will not kill each other. In fact, all that confirms and strengthens the supersensible identity of the name and its assimilation to it ("I"—which is already a name—am "Athenian") ensures at the same time the desired possession of eternal life.

A dialectic enters these dynamics according to which "your death is my life" (*mors tua, vita mea*), and it is beautiful to "die for the country" (*pro patria mori*). Hence the immortality of heroes, who are celebrated, deified, or sanctified in appropriate mausoleums, honored with laurel crowns symbolizing the immortality of fame.

308. Giving the lie to any economic explanation of human bellicosity, Freud famously maintained that giving death means, by psychological reflex, ensuring one's invulnerability (by making you die, I prove to myself that "I" am immortal). Only by exposing myself to extreme risk of death can I assure to myself that I am immune to precisely that extreme risk: an unconscious, superstitious thought which often seems to lead humans to engage in destructive and potentially self-destructive behaviors.

A problem of identity—or rather, of identification in the name—is most likely what fuels such behaviors, so that it is by no means strange, say, that teenagers, obsessed by their adult and sexual identity, should risk their lives so often for futile reasons. But the same drive is also seen in so-called adults, most notably in sport competitions, whose agonistic origin should be traced back, as G. H. Mead argued convincingly, to a sort of relatively pacific sublimation of war.

309. States find themselves constantly overriding the prohibition to kill through the state of war, whereby killing is imposed as a duty sanctioned by law. This way, the fundamental law that forbids murder can be easily evaded—the pleasure to kill can be pursued without guilt, giving free rein to identitarian self-exaltation. (Self-exaltation always involves the vaguely incestuous relationship with Mother—defending the Motherland is indeed a "sacred" duty.)

Mind you, however. We are not saying that states, by allowing themselves to make wars on each other through an internal law, remain in the state of nature, subject to "the war of all against all" (*bellum omnium erga omnes*). This commonplace is totally false, the fruit of a convenient political reading carried out by political science, which justifies the violence of states by explaining away rationally their criminal behaviors. Its argument sounds like this: if in the state of nature—where no political organization exists—everyone can (and therefore will) kill me, then I am legitimized to do the same. The implication is that in the state of nature what is established by the fundamental institutive law of every human existence (thou shall not kill) would no longer obtain nor have value.

In fact, in the state of nature there is no *bellum* of all against all. There is what there is, including violence and the risk of death; but a juridically organized state reads things backward, according to its own criteria. In the so-called state of nature, there are groups and human communities, therefore beings who recognize each other through the supersensible universality of the name, which sanctions their desire to be immortal and their mutual right not to be killed, because their human essence—sanctioned by the *vox significativa*—is a sign of the indestructible belonging of everyone to everyone. It is true that, in the state of nature, the identification in the name is generally enclosed in small clans and in small communities. Yet, while they undoubtedly make war on each other, they are also capable of acknowledging each other, of establishing behaviors of peaceful coexistence and active cooperation.

310. But now I want to underscore that the prohibition to kill as the fundamental and primary law of the human community is accompanied, as a parallel and equally founding law, by the *prohibition of incest*—a subject, as we know, of many an anthropological and psychoanalytic study.

Here, too, we need to consider that a living practice in the *animalitas* is inhibited on the threshold of the name: *in the name of the father*, precisely. That is why it is made both visible and desirable. As Freud observed: in *saying* that something is forbidden, we are saying that something is desired. In fact, it is precisely the *saying* that makes it desirable.

What is the reason for this desirability? Might it be the symbolic evidence that, in incest, a sort of joining with the origin would be accomplished—and thus a symbolic overcoming of death?

What matters most to us is that what was once impulse (in the *animalitas*), not desire (because desiring pertains only to the open dimension of words), now becomes desire.

311. All this helps clarify why the descent into the *chasma* of words is also a descent into the *chasma of sexual desire*.

The economy of life, once we come to know it, becomes a political economy, which is expressed in rituality and, finally, in the institutive communal law accompanied by specific sexual and ritual limitations in compliance with this law.

Regardless of the many reasons behind these limitations, we cannot fail to observe that there is always something forbidden in the exercise of sexuality (remember Antiphon?), just as there are always taboos of speech: you can do this and not that; in these, and no other, circumstances; with these, and no other, people; and so on. That is exactly why forbidden things become, at least in a hallucinatory way, something extremely desirable and enormously attractive or interesting.

It is also very significant that, unlike *animalitas*, the exercise of human sexuality cloaks itself in privacy: it is not a public act; in fact, in public it causes embarrassment and shame (as well as morbid, pornographic attraction). Thus, it is no accident that Diogenes the Cynic, in his radical antipolitical and antisocial critique, provocatively masturbated in the marketplace and publicly answered calls of nature. He was exposing his erogenous zones, which should be kept hidden (to become the object of a specific interest).

312. We must remember, of course, that sexuality is older than the law of speech. It is speech that sacralizes sexuality and turns it into the very foundation of the Political (as in the tale of Gyges) because it certifies the *generative power* of life, that is, the eternity of life. By retroflecting, speech makes sexuality into the antecedent of politics, which in turn becomes its origin and justifying foundation.

As we have by now understood, the exclusive and, as it were, private complicity of sexuality takes place before and outside the law.

In general, ideal terms, we might even say that sexuality is always somewhat incestuous, something forbidden with respect to the supersensible and sexless community established by the "name"—a community wherein, as Plato eloquently puts it, all citizens are, or appear to be, brothers and sisters, fathers and mothers, sons and daughters.

Concomitantly, we might also observe that women, historically less beholden or educated to the law of the *logos*, have always believed little in the laws and in political prohibitions: things established by men, Antigone would say.

313. So, we come to the traditional obligation, for a political man, to shield from the public his sexual entanglements, which, on the other

hand, the hidden exercise of power stimulates enormously; otherwise, what would be the point of desiring power?

And yet it is well known that even power, as such, can become the object of an exclusive, fetishistic desire. We stumble therefore across the most chaste and most upright Robespierres of all times, obviously very strict and moralistic, and also cruel, as always happens when sexuality is personally inhibited.

But, above all, we stumble upon recurring public and palace scandals, when we are made privy to the details and secrets of the sexual life of kings, ministers, pseudo-martyr princesses and phony rebels, and so on. These scandals are accompanied by enormous, prurient public interest, nourished and played up by the roguery of public information, which takes ruthless advantage of freedom of expression for venal and disreputable purposes.

314. Lately, however, things have been changing—which I think is a further indication of the ongoing crisis and decline of politics. We increasingly witness the public display, confession, not to say ostentation, of sexual preferences and exploits from senior officials, statesmen, politicians, and so on.

The public likes these frank admissions and behaviors far removed from any rituality and etiquette. Politicians must hide more and more the exceptional nature of their symbolic function and the real exercise of their power, showing themselves to be "like everyone else" and pretending to assimilate to the less sophisticated, more vulgarly widespread tastes and customs. And eventually, they truly become like everyone else, in the sense that we have never seen so many uncultivated bumpkins and ignorant hulks invade the political scene, although we cannot say that their more refined predecessors were any less cynical or violent.

In any case, the political man has learned his lesson, by showing, for instance, that—whether he likes it or not—for the sake of profit he is willing to honor the two-bit heroes elevated by the media and worshiped by "the people." Thus, presidents of austere states send touching sympathy telegrams for the death of popular sports, pop music, journalism, or showbiz idols, barely refraining from adding the most admired porn stars to the list.

These phenomena also entail, of course, a more serious aspect bearing on the issue of sexual difference, which today has become a truly political topic. It has to do with the general feminization (or emasculation) of public life, whereby we see with ever more frequency ministers and party leaders burst pathetically into tears in public because they have either lost or won the election, resigned their office, or just finished a heated speech on the floor of the Senate. The fateful tear that in times past, and quite exceptionally, used to wet the eyelash of very self-restrained sovereigns, generals, and prime ministers no longer has any currency.

315. Sexuality has always and everywhere been subject to laws, limitations, and prohibitions (starting with the wedding rules studied by anthropologists), which, on the other hand, encourage it as well. Eros is by its nature antisocial; it is, as we have pointed out, a life-drive older than the drive for a social community.

As soon as these prohibitions fade, the desire for eternal life begins to wane. For the first time in history, the human beings of the affluent societies devise strategies for not having children—after having devised the opposite for tens of thousands of years—doing anything they can to limit or avoid the "blessed event." This is truly an anthropological—and thus a political—revolution, one so extraordinary that its consequences still lie beyond our understanding.

Yet where the desire for eternal life wanes, another inevitably emerges, and that is a hidden desire for death: precisely at the heart of the society of economists and the technological assurance of life, life is worth less, it loses its sense and its goal. Without the risk of death and the pleasure of breaking the law, desire wanes. For example, the moment pornography becomes utterly legitimate and ready at hand—on the street, in the news, on every cinema, TV, and computer screen—it ceases to be desirable. It becomes merely boring, sleazy, and meaningless, just like the Girdle of Venus neglectfully tossed in a corner of Olympus under everyone's eyes.

Ninth Figure

The Truth of the Sign

Scene XVI: The *Arcanum* of Power

316. Let's get to the point. By being an accomplice of speech, *politiké areté*—I have said—is an accomplice of eternal life, which, by bringing about death, desires eternal life.

Thus, politics is a *shared desire*. It is the *art of inscribing bodies into rebirth and truth*. The truth that Plato has, in turn, inscribed into science. And please note that bodies are the retroflexed product of speech. It is speech that constitutes them as mere natural bodies with their natural needs because of their difference from the soul, that is, from the supersensible meaning of the name.

Politics, then, qua the *writing of active desire*. You will certainly recall that the old and pious Cephalus is excluded from it, insofar as he is deprived of desire, especially of sexual desire, which he has expressly rejected and renounced. Cephalus is therefore shut out of politics as well as of the "founding" dialogue of the *Republic*, although he significantly embodies its beginning. For him, religion takes on the trait of individual opium, while as opium for the people, religion becomes a political instrument for someone else's desire—the king's or the priest's, in Voltaire's eyes or Marx's.

317. In light of our foregoing discussion, then, it is easy to see how from all of the above the *political signs* descend—the signs and insignia

of power: *vexilla regis* (*inferni*).[1] Just as the verb "to re-veal" suggests the duplicity of veiling and unveiling, these signs are, at the same time, revelation and veiling of an underlying desire. Both a manifestation and a cloaking of what is manifested.

The sexual analogy is quite clear: clothes are both covering and revelation because *nakedness* is nothing but a retroflex effect of the veiling. You know that Adam and Eve discover they are naked after acquiring the knowledge of good and evil. Or, in other terms, and following Aristotle, after acquiring speech, the *vox significativa*, which makes them capable of death as well as of sexual transgression. The same function, you may recall, was carried out by the girdle between Venus and Paris/Alexander.

Indeed, sexual politics has always been a matter of dressing and masking—while, at the same time, revealing—the complementary nature of male and female desire, according to historically contingent modalities. The female breast is sometimes displayed, sometimes hidden, all the way to the current public and social frenzy over fashion shows, which, while clearly pursuing the logic of high-end brothels, are gratified with imaginary artistic and creative requirements, for the sake of economic interest and the general idiocy begotten by the so-called information culture.

All of this may seem ridiculous, futile, even ignoble to our intellect. Yet, due to the ways it manifests itself, any opposition to this or any fashion, too, is bound to remain caught up in the very same logic it seeks to dismantle.

The fact is that the way bodies offer themselves—their *proposal* and *response* as we have called them—to fashion is an effective sign of what, from time to time, is desirable in males and females (with all related masking and allusions to the contrary).

In short, fashion expresses, on the social level, the public reciprocation that masks the secret complicity of the privacy—in its way highly identifying and socially deidentifying—of the sexual act, an act that nowadays we are obligated to witness publicly in every self-respecting movie. The resulting political message is that, beyond the Political, there is nothing but sex—which, in fact, is ultimately the hidden truth of the Political. Thus, while the exhibition of sex contains indeed a reaction to hypocrisy, it nonetheless turns out to be a false one for the very fact that it must manifest itself in obligated signs.

---

1. *Vexilla regis prodeunt inferni* ("The banners of the King of Hell draw closer," in Allen Mandelbaum's translation) Dante Alighieri, *The Divine Comedy: Inferno* 34, 1—Ed.

318. To reassert nakedness—to unveil it—is to reassert the value of the sign as a transferal object bearing desire.

Gyges, who sees the naked queen, must *die*; we already wondered about the meaning of this ritual death. Undoubtedly, it expresses the violation of the law of the name (of the father)—which is essentially the same as sexual desire; a violation which the law itself must forbid and repress.

And yet repression is also the achievement of the repressed. In other words, Gyges is induced to do precisely as he wishes, which will not only free him from pain but also make him king—that is, the guarantor of the law he himself violated, and thus also the embodiment of the paternal guardianship that keeps women segregated, in that they are vehicles of the public sovereignty founded on sexual procreation.

All of this would probably sound absurd without the considerations we have hitherto been making, which, on the contrary, now make it all appear logical and necessary. Think, for example, of this traditional custom—once also widespread in Italy and the favorite topic of many a theater performance, comedy, opera, or operetta: A young man attempts to seduce a young girl, whose father keeps her jealously hidden. The lad tries in vain to gain secretly her sexual favors ("Mommy doesn't want, neither does Daddy / How are we going to make love . . . ," as an old Italian stornello goes). In the end, and to gain such favors, he asks her in marriage. Once the girl's father gives his consent to the marriage, he will be the one to impose by law the very consummation he had once sternly prohibited. And the young man becomes himself a husband and a jealous father: a political microcell. Which is to say, he learns "the stupid work of being a husband," as poor Figaro muses melancholically to himself while lurking in the woods trying to catch Susanna in the act with the dirty old Count—that very same Figaro who was once a master in the art of playing the field, and who, in his capacity of trickster, had become the Count's hired ally and confidant. Funny how our lot can change in one's lifetime.

319. Gyges faces his sexual little death in private complicity with the queen; then, a reparatory wedding will allow the positing of the eternal life attained through the sexual act as the political foundation for community law: everyone will become eternal through their symbolic participation in the king's intercourse (to be ritually repeated within their own four walls) and in the following "law of the name"—in the

name of the king you are eternal (as the king is eternal in the name of the gods and their ancestral embraces).

In this sense, it is noteworthy that some scholars doubt whether Gyges is a person's name: it might well be the name of a whole line of sovereigns. In fact, Gyges does not really have a name, it is not even clear who he is. A shepherd? A groom? His status remains obscure, until, having joined himself to the *chasma* of the woman (lover and mother), he becomes a king, that is, an eponymous character, a public name.

320. In other words, in the exchange of looks between Gyges and the queen we see what we should not have seen because it cannot be seen: *the ultrasensible law of speech*. We see what speech forbids, that is, its complementary root. We see the naked truth, stripped naked by the sign, or rather, made so by the sign's cloaking.

Of course, what we must not see becomes at once the object of desire, and thus the fulfillment of the desire for eternal life (a desire implicitly inscribed in the sexual act before speech retroflexes onto it its known desire), which is the foundation of the Political and of the law—starting with the law of speech, which, by signifying, both shows and hides.

For all these reasons Gyges, who dared, will be king. Gyges dared to see, but more precisely, he dared to speak, in the sense that he dared to know what he saw. And yet it is the queen, as you will recall, who does the speaking. It is, in other words, the woman—which cannot fail to lead to further reflections, just as we should not forget (as I empha-sized earlier) that it is Eve who offers the forbidden fruit to Adam, so that she can later become, in the figure of Mary, the instrument of his eternal salvation. Faust's eternal feminine. But this, of course, sounds a bit like a man's tale.

321. By providing the foundation of the sign and the sign's *transferal value*, politics is not there to be the sign for a supposed thing prior to the sign. If I have at least succeeded in putting out of your heads this naïve naturalistic belief (shared by all modern sciences and several empirical semiotics), then my backstage work will not have been in vain.

The sign is there to be a sign for itself, that is, for its value, for its supersensible meaning.

It is this retroflexion of the sign into itself and onto itself (an operation which sums up the essential dynamics of speech and the name) that validates the body, by constituting it as a body and making it desirable—making it into the *object* of desire. It is speech that makes things desirable, by turning them into anthropological objects. Infants do not desire the breast; they simply want it.

And we should remember that the very constitution of things as mere things, devoid of any meaning and indifferent in themselves—a constitution carried out by modern science by virtue of the signs of mathematics—in reality obeys a desire for objectification which is already implicit in speech, and which subjugates things to a specific desire for power and control.

In this sense, science, its will to truth—which Nietzsche found to be ultimately nothing but will to power, and which we like to call a will to control life and death—is only the continuation of the very old "male" project to make woman into the transferal object par excellence: the locus of control over life and death, the tool for obtaining eternal life.

But don't even dream about believing that science and mathematics are only that. In fact, the meaning of their future destiny has yet to be thought out, especially when they contribute to the so-called "woman's liberation," insofar as woman has been more and more escaping her simple subjugation to the generative project, for example by personally taking control of it, with all the problems and paradoxes that this stance inevitably entails.

322. But now, follow me on this: political signs, the insignia of power, fulfill the same function of unveiling-revelation-veiling of power, that is, of the desire that tinges it. Revealing a political project, making it known, without distinction, to all citizens, hides at the same time an *arcanum* that intertwines with the hidden complicities of power itself, that is, of those who are holding it at any given time (I mean the rulers and the social categories which they represent and, on whose behalf, like it or not, they *can* rule).

Power keeps hidden the violence it inevitably promotes. On the one hand, power displays the signs of the universal desire for eternal life, a desire it shares in a complicit way with all its subjects, legitimizing itself before their eyes. On the other hand, however, this ostentation of *salus publica* is only a deceptive mask, because the holders of power pursue eternal life *for themselves*. They create—we could say figuratively—and build their own pyramids.

323. Power, therefore, acts essentially *by taking possession of speech*; or—which is the same, as Adam Smith taught—*taking possession of money*. So, power takes over the supersensible meaning of the object of desire (eternal life, precisely) seizing its transferal signs: words and money. In ancient times: culture and gold. In modern times: information and financial capital.

Precisely because it allows this taking over, political power is highly desirable in and of itself; and even prior to that, the quintessential object of desire is the sociopolitical privileged condition (possession of money and culture, capital and means of information production) which has in the insignia of politics its own vehicle for representation and fulfillment.

324. Everybody, in brief, wants power, that is, domination over eternal life as a sign of their own absolute recognition (in this sense, everybody is personally greedy for love and praise, rather than for money, although money is indeed a powerful means of achieving recognition and the crucial instrument to politically guarantee one's progeny—that is, the preliminary choice of the dead and the unborn. And since power circulates, as Foucault has shown, its desire does not merely concern political and institutional power but runs through the whole of society. Everyone wants power over someone else— essentially, over their complementary—paying a high price for their inconsistency: the man over the woman, the mother and father over their children, the manager over the employee, and so on. "Every porter wants to have an admirer," Nietzsche said ironically.[2]

The powerful in charge promise their subordinates that through their subjugation they will gain the very simulacrum of eternal life (i.e., of supersensible meaning) which the powerful themselves fantasize obtaining by subjugating them. They reassure their subordinates by saying: if you obey, it's for your own good, because one day you'll be like me, you'll be in my place. But what they are really saying is: obey for *my*

---

2. Friedrich Nietzsche, "On Truth and Lie in an Extra-Moral Sense" (1873), in *The Portable Nietzsche*, edited and translated by Walter Kaufmann (Viking Penguin, 1954), 42—Ed.

own good, because, by identifying myself with the power I wield—that is, with its "name" (of the father, etc.)—I attain the eternal universality of the meaning which gives a sense and an infinite future to my life. And this suffices to explain why humans are often ready to risk other people's lives as well as their own in a no-quarter fight to defend power, even the most futile and ephemeral kind.

325. The democratic project—that is, the modern democratic state—prides itself on having publicly revealed, once and for all, the *arcanum* of power, on having unmasked it for everyone to see through information. First through journalism, which, ever since the French Revolution, informs public opinion to deflect it from the *arcana* of political and economic powers.

Unfortunately, this project has gradually turned out to be largely naïve and deceptive. In its undeniable good and equally certain evil, it is but an inner episode and an effect of the modern dynamics of sign or of language. Let me explain what I mean.

326. A naïve project, I said. Naïve insofar as it does not understand that the *veiling* is a consequence and structural necessity of the sign, *that is, of desire*. A power that is *unveiled* in its actual reality is no longer desirable. Venus without her girdle is no longer Venus, but just some girl more than a bit overweight, at least to our modern taste; and a sign reduced to a mere thing is no longer a sign. This is how toupees, wigs, and corsets were banished to the attic once they stopped being the signs of seduction and desire.

Besides being naïve, the project is also deceptive, insofar as information itself (or journalism, which, as Nietzsche had anticipated, has by now replaced culture even in universities and colleges, and brazenly calls itself "culture") has established in turn a new occult power, often in no way different from, or better than, the one it exposes.

The possession of the signs of information—cloaked, just like the signs of power, in hypocritical and conformist prudery—inevitably degenerates, yielding well-known effects: journalism does not inform at all, but rather misinforms systematically and knowingly (that is, scientifically); it keeps quiet about what really matters, while spreading triviality and moral corruption; it produces vulgarity and substantial foolishness, monsters and violence precisely like the power it criticizes and with which, whenever and wherever it can, it enters into a mortal political dispute.

Nowadays, owning the media is the desired goal of every politics, to be pursued at any cost through the most fraudulent means, and indeed, the very first thing the revolutionary forces set out to do is to occupy the television building.

327. It would really be too sad, worthy of justified despondency, if we stopped here. That is why, before I take leave of you with my scene and my backstage, I would like to offer a few words of hope.

Here they are. While it is true that the democratic project cannot really unmask power and, above all, cannot limit effectively or efficiently the damages, the violence, and the superstition it generates for everybody, including those who fortuitously hold it, nevertheless, through the democratic project, *the sign itself—speech, and language and writing—comes to the fore.*

What this means or what this might mean we will discuss briefly, and very softly, in private as soon as the curtain comes down.

(End of Act III)

Epilogue

328. Here I am, like I was at the beginning, on the proscenium, this time acting out the figure of the Epilogue.

We were saying: with the democratic project, the sign itself comes to the fore. What does this mean? It means that the *arcanum* of power and of desire (of the power of desire) becomes visible in its domination.

And this is precisely our auto-bio-graphical scene, the one within which we have been moving from the beginning; the theater of words which I have shown to you. It is the displaying of a will to knowledge—knowledge, for example, of what is *behind* the worldwide figures of democracy, of journalism, of information, of the global market, and so on. A will to knowledge which is certainly stirred in turn by a figure and a backstage of desire—that is, by *our* desire.

329. What desire?

Or rather, and in very simple and direct words: Why do you do what you do? Why are you running around so much, Mr. Prologue, Epilogue, and all the rest of you? What kind of figure do you think you are embodying with this sort of "(pseudo) philosophical theater" of yours?

And yet the reality is that "our" desire cannot but remain largely unknown to us, in its personal and social motives, in its will to dominate and control. Except that we can no longer delude ourselves that it is not there, and thus we can no longer dress up for the usual performance of the martyr / clown / town crier who suffers and perhaps even dies *in the name* of truth. In fact, truth, now that we think we have really encountered it, at least in the figure of *our* truth, demands that we recognize ourselves primarily in the name to which, before any other name, we are entitled—any name for *error*, for our constitutive being-in-error.

330. Of course, we could also say, there is in us the legitimate desire to stage a figure of parting from the sort of truth that has long characterized us in our forms of knowledge, starting with the claims of political science and anthropology. We have undoubtedly become skilled at showing the hidden will to power inhabiting those forms.

For instance, there is the desire to denounce—also a political act (because theater, as we said, is always political)—the violence and folly of modern technological knowledge in its superstitious features, which mortify the profound desire for complementarity that characterizes life, and thereby mortify life itself—although we cannot rule out other unquestionably positive features that certainly accompany them.

331. But now let's focus on the most important point. It concerns the coming to light of the desire behind the sign. Now, this unveiling of the "segnic" dynamics of desire (with its secret removed) *is the unmasking itself of the dynamics of the sign: we can finally see what the sign covers up.*

We are here at the conclusion or at the intersection of a long road that had its initiators in the so-called "masters of suspicion," who had in turn a great forerunner in the pale and solitary Spinoza, equally hated and persecuted by those who in his days feuded with each other, because, as Merleau-Ponty would have it, he did not intend to be a militant member of one side or the other and therefore was, from their point of view, a suspicious man and potential betrayer. Indeed, all feuding villains get along far better with each other than with anyone else who strives to sympathize only with justice. They know very well, and even share, the passions and desires they hypocritically hide, whereas what the desire of a man like Plato might be, who in dissolute and wild Syracuse would rather sleep alone every night, they could never understand in their dreams—which is precisely why they feared it.

We could read the entire philosophical journey of the twentieth century as a progressive unveiling of the deep nature of the sign. An obscure journey, at times, even for those who were undertaking it; the end stages, however, are by now well known to everyone. For example: reduction of everything to sign and of the entire reality to interpretation; centralization of the language issue, in the two complementary and antagonistic versions of formal logic and hermeneutics; semiotization and cyberization of all forms of knowledge, so that the computer model has taken over science, from neurology to cosmology; development of a technical thought understood as applied computer science, from which economic globalization would derive; and so on. Forgive me if I am going over this in very broad terms and quickly, but I think you get the idea.

332. This whole set of consequences could be summed up as the *political project of science*, which is, as we know, largely the legacy of metaphysics mathematically transcribed, and therefore it is not only this, because mathematical transcription itself, introduced by Galileo, calls for a genealogy that is not yet clear to us and that we have not mastered yet (as far as I'm concerned, I haven't; maybe some of you will someday).

An outstanding part of this project is the systematic destruction, in the West, of education and school humanistically intended: a phenomenon that is there for all to see, at least for those who are still not blind. The justifications of official politics for this situation (economic promises to young people: you will find a job, you will be able to settle down, and so on) are the same old vague reassurances serving the promises of eternal life which are constantly broken. Something else is actually at stake, something that is entirely beyond the grasp of the poor nonentities at the ministries of education and culture.

As a matter of fact, nobody can tell where this ongoing great project will lead. Those who are subject to it and blinded by it are only offering ideological tales and convenient fantasies. Those who oppose it are completely in the dark as to the tangles of practices this project will entail, and only talk from their prejudices and fears. Those who merely cross it (or are crossed by it) behave like migratory birds, driven unconsciously by the climate to change their habits and routes: they do not know and cannot know whether in this way they will live or die.

333. And yet we do know one thing here, because, thanks to our theater, we are able to observe it with our very eyes, and it is an important thing: a thing I have carried expressly with me on this proscenium of the epilogue—a final gift from your backstage (I say "your" in the literal sense, because this matter is also "yours," that is, it walks beside you, perhaps without you realizing it).

We can see, then, that the unveiling of the sign—that is, the unveiling of what every sign covers, which is to say, desire—*points inevitably toward the gradual reduction of the sign to mere desire*. This is, then, the hidden truth which, if we only care or dare to look at it, is no longer so hidden from us.

We are placed again on the threshold like Gyges, between a promise of life and the risk of death (a threshold on which humans, perhaps, have always been standing).

It will only be up to us *to abolish the dazzle of the sign*. Which does not mean that we should return to supposedly natural things, to all the naïve ontologies of a genuine reality, to an immediate being-natural of the world as it is without mediation or interpretation.

Clearly, in our time, with the failure of the eminence of the sign, such naturistic nonsense is to be expected; and indeed, there is no shortage of ideological desires for a way out or escape route which, however, tell us of a world that never existed, that cannot exist, either on principle or in practice; a world for which the concept of existence is inapplicable and meaningless.

334. The desecration of the sign, of its authority and of its power implies then, as a sociopolitical consequence, *the reassessment of all desires*, no longer shaded in any way by the sign.

Of course, this, too, is a senseless and impossible thing. A dream of city birds imagining themselves to be forest birds without realizing that the forest is burning.

Dream or no dream, the matter spreads in many ways according to *its* logic, which we could reword like this: if behind the sign there is desire and this is the only thing validating the sign (finally unveiled in its arcane veiling), then desire itself represents value-in-itself. Is this clear?

We witness therefore the universal reassessment of biological individuals, considered in their pure desiring life. To this need proclaimed to the city and to the world, *urbi et orbi*, all powers have by now bowed: churches, states, notoriously conservative political parties, and so on. No one really dares to fight it, because it seems to incarnate everywhere an indispensable feature of contemporary sensitivity and conscience—without exception from New York to Moscow, from Paris to Beijing, from Rome to Buenos Aires: the end of every authority and dignity of political institutions and their representatives. These people must at least *show* that they are serving the fulfillment of everybody's desire: every faux pas in this regard would spell the end of their political careers.

It should be added that the means of information push furiously in this direction, interested as they are in becoming the protectors of public desire, both for economic reasons and because of their ongoing conflict with traditional political powers, with which they are always vying to capture the people's approval (provided they enjoy a certain degree of autonomy—which is mostly not the case in Italy—as opposed to merely serving as the sycophants of power).[1]

To the very same logic, here concisely described, must be ascribed also the reduction of the universal meaning to the massified and artificially induced phenomenon of universal outrage—a global moral reaction (no matter how justified) that the media triggers as soon as individuals are perceived as not being respected in their biological rights and in their real or supposed desires. And yet, we must admit that this phenomenon, too, is inalienably bound up with the exposure of the *arcanum* of politics, which everyone in every corner of the globe by now understands and knows how to value.

335. Yet this whole defense of the individuals' rights to pursue happiness—that is, to fulfill their desires—is ambiguous.

It is ambiguous primarily because, within the universal semiotization—that is, the universal spread of digital information—the individual has ceased to be merely "substance" for a long time now (a journey that, for us philosophers, started as early as Locke, Hume, and Kant). The individual has been totally reduced to being-a-sign and an image of a desire freed from any universal, that is, from any universal meaning and name, and therefore from any *belonging and circumscribed complementarity*.

In a short time, we have moved, in the West, from a society based on sacrifice as the pledge of eternal life to a society which, as has been said, has secularized its goal into immediate and contingent pleasure. A society that invests less and less in the future of eternal life—that is, in the sense of physical and spiritual generation—and thereby lives

---

1. To understand Sini's scathing critique of the knot tying together the information industry (the current incarnation of the "sign," in its primordial sense of *signum* coming from the stars or the gods as supreme authorities) and politics, we must keep in mind that *La virtù politica* was written when Italian politics was dominated by Silvio Berlusconi, who was both prime minister and a media tycoon—Ed.

the death of God in a completely nihilistic and mostly unknowing way.

A strongly disconcerting society, especially for the younger ones, of whom no one dares ask for the least sacrifice or commitment anymore, but for whom the offer of pleasure that replaced the latter does not yield any real happiness or a clear sense of living.

I think I can read in your looks: "What do you suggest, then?" If that's the case, the question is not worthy of you. Why! Are you really exhorting me to repeat Plato's experience, to imagine totalizing and definitive solutions, just and happy states, healthy and satisfied young citizens? Haven't we just realized, thanks to our theater, that this isn't the real issue at all? There is never a general solution or an abstract choice between sacrifice and pleasure. There is only the contingency of life in which we find ourselves, and the *occasion* for complementary love and participation that we can derive from it, with its concrete possibilities for action and thinking. If only you would look at things this way, you would see a virtually endless list of good and beautiful things that you could accomplish, starting as soon as today or tomorrow—things truly worth their while. A list so long there would be no point in trying to compile it now.

336. Therefore: the individual is now at the point of death, because every "concrete universal" is dead and the two things, at least for those who know a little about philosophy, go together. There remains, however, a new kind of universality, congruous with the abstract identification with desire and with the dreamed immediacy of its fulfillment. We could call it the "universality of the *occasions*." The Universal is reduced to the unlimited possibility of occasions "for all." For all, precisely in the sense of the advertising idiocy that has taken over the world: "Come on over, *all* of you, to the most *exclusive* place there is."

It is the cosmopolitan city of Cockaigne, where fulfillment is followed by the media's imposition of ever-new desires: the desire for desires. This creates a habit of conformist like-mindedness which is once again the reverse of "individual." Indeed, those who do not conform, those who fail to abide by the conventional ways, are deemed socially nonexistent: they no longer have a right to any consideration at all, nor the right to have desires—not even the desire to be left in peace—and they are generally stigmatized as culprits.

337. The picture I am painting for you with short impressionist brush-strokes—a picture which has moreover been known for a long time to anyone who thinks carefully enough—does not show at all the failure of the illusionistic domination of the sign! What happens is something else entirely. What happens is that all signs, once they have lost their prestige to be a signifier for some meaning, are reduced to being only one sign: *the sign of money*.

This is by no means obvious. Just try to define money, and you will be in real trouble. Will you seek the advice of economists? Good luck! Your Epilogue already did so and found out that even economists, especially the best and smartest, find themselves today in serious theoretical trouble.

But now, thanks to our journey, we can say something about it. First, we can reflect on the fact that, if it is the *arcanum* itself of the sign that is being manifested and questioned, then it is natural for money to appear in the foreground: because money, just as speech, is the quintessential transferal object (as we have observed). Indeed, money carries within itself the very same unlimited, universal potential to be exchanged for anything else as words, too, have.

Secondly, unlike words—which maintain a relation of complementarity with life's being "in situation"—money shows the extraordinary homogenizing and objectifying power of the quantification that characterizes it. And we can see immediately how science and capital could not but have arisen together to define the birth, as it were, of modernity.

338. Money is the means and sign of absolute translatability: the logic of exchange, the logic of the market and the world stock exchange, which act in real time. In fact, they act in the most imaginary and unreal character of time. Nonetheless, this exchange action translates abstract into concrete (as Marx observed about economic categories, and Whitehead about scientific categories).

Anyone who thinks that, by stating this, I merely intend to criticize the current world, the modern identification of science, capital, and democracy—all three predicated on the reduction of value into measurable quantities and on the reduction of reality into performative objectivity—has not understood a single thing about our theater and our representation.

The rampant power of money (which Plato exorcized in vain at the very moment when, with the establishment of the supersensible conceptual meaning, he was paving the way for its arrival) is one of the most impressive phenomena defining our predicament, and we have no time to waste either with the self-interested fanatics who ideologically extol money, or with the zealots who, on the contrary, thunder against it and curse it.

It is true that money has long been the occult force driving the *arcanum* of politics, and this is by no means what's new about money today. Rather, what is new is that money, following its own implicit logic, universalizes itself to the point that it absorbs and sums up every notion of value. No "thing" can have any "value" anymore, if not to the extent that it can be translated, as William James used to say, into "cash value."[2]

339. No "thing" and no "individual" (and you can talk about a "person" as much as you want). Individuals are only worth anything for the occasions they have, that is, for the opportunities they come across to invest a certain amount of money in the market of endless goods—the object of desire's unlimited drive, a desire created and stirred also for the sake of profit.

Even so-called spiritual or cultural products are more and more assimilated to commodity logic, often veiled under the expression "service offered." The fact is that the massified consumers of these services confuse the enjoyment of the pure occasion (of sharing in the spectacle of an exhibition, a concert, and so on) with the meaning it could have, if consumers were still able to understand it. But meaning, too, has been massified into the small commodities of cultural information, sold at newsstands or translated into a curriculum for some academic discipline, in exchange for tuition fees.

Just as every state reduces its identity to its gross domestic product, every individual is worth exactly as much as their yearly income (with their innocent frankness and ignorance of European good taste, Americans always make sure to inform you about how much money they make).

---

2. William James, "Philosophical Conceptions and Practical Results" (1898), appendix to *Pragmatism: The Works of William James* (Harvard University Press, 1975), 268. James' 1898 address to the Philosophical Union in Berkeley, California, was the first time he introduced the "cash-value" metaphor. See George Cotkin, "William James and the Cash-Value Metaphor," *ETC: A Review of General Semantics* 42, no. 1 (Spring 1985): 37–46—Ed.

For better and worse, this quantitative translatability is the only conceivable functioning criterion that is left, after all the traditional values have shown their ultimate nihilistic consistency—that is, their being constitutionally vitiated by zealotry and error, and invariably molded as masks for the desire for power and control.

In this sense, the boundless devastation that the logic of the market and financial capital is spreading on earth might also spell the beginning of a great occasion for a humanity in the process of freeing itself from superstition and from the illusionistic yoke of the sign.

340. How this might happen is a matter about which your Epilogue doesn't profess to know much. The best thing we can do here, then, is to look at our situation with clear eyes, without hiding to ourselves its dramatic aspects, yet without the absurd notion that we are condemned to them, and thus we find ourselves in a catastrophic end-of-the-world scenario. Of course, many worlds do come to an end, but—as Nietzsche observed—that is because, in some measure, they probably deserved to.

The logic of the market, and of capital, is obliterating the historical figures that have from time immemorial characterized the different practices of life and knowledge on earth. The differences in cultures and traditions are quickly being erased or at best translated into mere touristic occasions for those who can afford them (the exotic paradises of nature and sex). And so, by severing all individuals' ties to their past—a past that is, however, constantly reactivated in the current, independently unfolding practices of life—there remains only the logic of the market, and our abstractly biological identity: human beings are, in a sense, thrown back on that very *animalitas* which they themselves had hallucinatorily constituted by difference.

In practice, everyone remains the keeper of the sense of living and of the rights that the logic of the market, one way or another, may translate into economic advantage. Yet, at the same time, everyone loses that sense and those rights entirely. An emblematic example is the recent brutal revelations made by international authorities about the disposal of damaged and noxious technology, as well as of industrial waste: such disposal, they admit, is routinely exported to developing countries. Of course, it makes total sense. What place could be more economically advantageous?

The same goes for the admission—this, too, official—from a few years ago, that the output produced in developing countries accounts for over sixty percent of the world production, but the earnings amount to less than forty percent of those achieved by entrepreneurs and workers in the highly industrialized West. This exploitation is evident, no longer concealable (although the means of information talk as little as possible about it, and very late at night, busy as they are with pop stars, fashion parades, and Miss World contests), accompanied as it is by the devastation of lands, local economies, traditions, identities, and of any other possible value, all in the service of financial capital, the only remaining true value, supranational and universally exportable.

341. Philosophically, we can see all this as the triumph of the scientific naturalism that Husserl had denounced in his time. A naturalism that has translated itself into the a-historical, circular, eternal logic of the technological society, as Heidegger also foresaw.

Directly affecting the logic of the sign, this naturalistic project involves language itself, turning it into an information bit, which leads to a stripping away of every meaning that is not the supersensible itself, reduced to a visible object producible at will. With the obliteration of meaning, the sign acquires an ambiguity that hints at a sort of a-chronic and a-topic *continuum*: the direct sign and immediate image of eternal life.

This is just further confirmation of what we have already discussed, that is, of the *arcanum* that governs the political project of science: the control and production of life as the gift (or the dream thereof) of eternal life. And in this sense, science—by its nature universal and international (as scientists never tire of boasting)—politically supplants the national states, whose promise of a symbolic eternal life doesn't appeal to anyone anymore. Nobody dreams anymore, at least here in Italy, of resting in the Heroes' Cemetery. But elsewhere, too, a new form of eternal rest has become widespread: the rest of evening television.

342. The political project that is driving us, in the days of the demise of politics in its traditionally metaphysical sense, results then in the anthropological project of the creation of a new man—a project that had already started troubling Plato's mind, upsetting his nights and days. And what we have been representing here, albeit still in somewhat metaphysical fashion, is the fact that politics is nothing more than the

essential anthropological project leading human beings to experience their truth and their fate.

The new technologically projected man is firmly set on the path to realizing that the metaphysical revolution of soul and body must result in the establishment of the soul in the bodies, which, after being reduced to mere extensions (with Descartes), have become, in our time, mere simulations. The supersensible eternity of the meaning has become a kind of digital eternal life, locked in conflict with so-called natural death.

In precisely this sense we should read today's much-argued-about genetic maps: itineraries of possibilities implying that death might be nothing but a DNA trait, *responsible* for the aging of our cells. A Faustian dream of eternal youth. The same goes for the debates on cloning (the eternity of "me," of most fractional difference) and so forth.

This is not to deny that all these scientific issues may contain chances and tremendously serious and important outcomes, although in a dimension of understanding and thinking that leaves us unprepared and from which we are still very distant. The genealogical understanding of *politiké areté* and its connections with our present—what we have here been trying to undertake—has therefore the sense of a contribution to the understanding of our current anthropological destiny, and of a sort of introduction to a possible human ethology.

343. In this sense we have talked of a *political* "writing of the bodies." Its contemporary trait should not make us forget that the writing of bodies, that is, their inscription in the logic of the sign and the double, has always been the task of *politiké areté*: the *mise-en-scène* of the inscribed body, of its theater qua place of initiation and education for social souls, for community subjects. The latter are, indeed, the spectators and users of this *mise-en-scène* and by reflection recognize themselves in it.

The original desire has always been inscribed in this political theater—a desire for complementarity and recognition which, through sex and speech, makes possible the dream of our return in eternal life. It is not surprising that political utopias often come down to this nostalgia or desire for the Garden of Eden, a place where, precisely, death is absent.

All this generates, as we have seen, the complicity of the art of politics with eternal life, a complicity that undergirds the arcane nature of the political project itself, its highly anthropological and pedagogical function.

344. This is the arcane, and above all ambiguous, nature of every *politiké areté*; hence the recurring anarchic temptation to remove politics and the state altogether: a removal which is, in turn, utopian.

We have shown how *politiké areté*, insofar as it is founded on the communal structure of the name (of speech), casts men into the *chasma* of death, which is no other than quid pro quo for the supersensible character of the meaning of speech: now, I think, you can see it clearly.

And so *politiké areté*, by using speech and staging it in its way, offers man salvation and shelter from death. In this sense, political science qua the project of eternal life has been in the making, as we have seen, ever since Plato's political philosophy, that is, since the establishment of philosophy itself and of its logos. But nowadays the project stages a completely different kind of word and language, which is rather derived from the supersensible of modern science, from the signs of mathematics and electronics, to say it bluntly.

345. Our scene, our philosophical theater, our *mise-en-scène* has been nothing but the showing of all this: a writing which still practices philosophy by circum-scribing it.

A writing which, by revealing the backstage of political science in Plato's philosophical theater, cannot pretend not have its own backstage (starting with Plato's): if it did, it would relapse into the very *arcanum* it set out to denounce in the first place, and thus into some form of unconscious violence.

That is why this writing stops short of presuming to indicate a place where, today, the possible figure of *politiké areté* might be in the making. You cannot expect this from your Epilogue if you understood its gesture.

We need to reject the superstition of *saying the place* of the truth of politics beyond its genealogical and never completed understanding, because every word is always already played by its obscure desire, and desire is in turn the effect of the tangles of life practices and knowledges to which we are inevitably and unknowingly beholden.

346. And there is one more thing I would like to tell you in conclusion, which is more than enough to suggest wise caution and a chaste limit for our saying and representing.

Just now, in this Epilogue, I have mentioned the present-day existence of individuals reduced to the biological and economic universal abstract, individuals totally manipulated by the economy of information and money, and as such de-universalized and de-institutionalized, turned into mere financial occasions; individuals in troubled pursuit of a possible future identity, individuals who do not have a *voice*, within the blaring, horrifying, prying, shocking, foolish chitchat that everywhere fills the earth and sky. It is good that here, at least, we keep quiet about things we have no need or basis to speak about and rather remain open to a kind of renewed listening, in hopes that someday these individuals might regain their speech and join us in the dream of a possible complementarity to be achieved together.

347. And there is one more silence, even more important and disquieting, which we have alluded to, although indirectly. What we have represented on the scene is exclusively the voice, deep and articulate, of an assembly of men and Athenians: a scene of foundational speeches marking the origin of our *politiké areté*, which nowadays is on the verge of becoming global and at the same time of fading away.

As the curtain falls and the scene darkens, the emptiness that did not have a voice now manifests itself, provoking us. Of course, I am not talking about any moralistic scruples or abstract justice. I am once more talking about us, about our auto-bio-graphy which has been marked, in a constitutive complementarity, by the public silence of the voice that still gave us a voice, a hearing, and an identity, in the *chasma* that has guarded us even before we were born into the light, and even afterward: a voice that for a long time, perhaps forever, has been repressed and misunderstood.

If our philosophical theater could really raise the curtain again and give voice to that voice, under the sign of a new complicity that leaves to others the action that is proper to each of them, letting them be others and yet allowing, and facilitating, their access to understanding our own destiny and logic (in the absence of which true emancipation would be difficult—which doesn't mean that this logic should replicate itself and idolize itself, which would lead to repeating the same old mistakes); if someday our philosophical theater were able to do *all this*, then it would have attained true political virtue.

Such virtue would certainly still express our current desire for eternal life, yet it would be a desire accepted without further cloaking and superstition for what it is, and therefore reasonably and politically accomplishable, thanks to a new complementarity of desires carried out under the sign of a complicit *recognition*.

(The End)

Author's Annotations

The many references to "Book I," "Book II," and so on, up to "Book VI" refer to the six volumes of the author's *Encyclopedia* first published separately (Jaca Book, 2004–2005) and then collected in one volume, *Transito verità. Figure dell'enciclopedia filosofica* (Jaca Book, 2012). The present book, whose original title is *La virtù politica. Filosofia e antropologia*, is Book IV of the *Encyclopedia*. In the following annotations, the editor and the translators have added the bibliographical information of non-Italian editions of books quoted in Italian by the author—Ed.

1. See Aristotle, *Politics*, here in *The Complete Works of Aristotle: The Revised Oxford Translation*, Vol. 2, translated by Benjamin Jowett, edited by Jonathan Barnes (Princeton University Press, 1991). Italian translation by Renato Laurenti, *Politica* (Laterza, 1973).

5. Plato staged the dialogue: the theater of philosophy and its new "music" (see Book V, *Raccontare il mondo. Filosofia e cosmologia*, Part V, "La favola del racconto," and Book VI, *Le arti dinamiche. Filosofia e pedagogia*, Part I, 8, "La cifra della sapienza arcaica"). Having taken this staging seriously, we have been *dialoguing* for over two thousand years and, as figures in Plato's theater, we have been grounding our political-democratic truth on "debate." We have been repeating his "virile" relationship as well with Socrates, his master and father—yet through this we have already put woman, too, on stage (Aristotle, in his own way, did not fail to do so), perhaps admitting to a profound yearning for a resolution, a desire to go beyond.

8. The mysterious listeners are of course the protagonists of *Timaeus* (see Book V, *Raccontare il mondo*).

9. The expression "prose of the world" conjures up Hegel and Merleau-Ponty (see my *Il silenzio e la parola*, Marietti, 1989).

11. On Mnemosyne, see Book VI, *Le arti dinamiche*, Part 1, 7 and 8.

12. I follow, here and elsewhere, Mario Vegetti's translation. The *Encyclopedia* is greatly indebted to the admirable work on Plato's *Republic* that Vegetti conducted with the collaboration of his students (a project now being published in its entirety by Bibliopolis, 1998–2005). On Vegetti's important undertaking, see my article in *Iride: Filosofia e discussione pubblica* 15, no. 35 (April 2002): 194–198, published by il Mulio.

14. On the "grandiose homage" to Socrates, see Book V, *Raccontare il mondo*, par. 181–183.

19. On the "symballic" distance, see the chapter "L'immagine come evento simbolico" in my *I segni dell'anima* (Laterza, 1989), 165–212. On the inscribed and the circumscribed, see Book I, *L'analogia della parola. Filosofia e metafisica*, First Figure.

22. The expression "putting bodies to work" alludes to Florinda Cambria's research, *Corpi all'opera. Teatro e scrittura in Antonin Artaud* (Jaca Book, 2001).

23. As we can now see, the "marked (*signati*) bodies" of Book III, *L'origine del significato. Filosofia ed etologia* (par. 169–180) come into being as material things-means (*cose-mezzi*) because of the retroflexed action of desire, rather than from the mere retroflexion of meaning.

25. The tale of Ixion was also mentioned in the chapter "Segno e distanza" in my *Semiotica e filosofia. Segno e linguaggio in Peirce, Nietzsche, Heidegger e Foucault* (il Mulino, 1978), 271–272. It is not a casual reference. Back then, and now, the problem of image and sign was under scrutiny. In fact, these paragraphs of the present book are the place where the whole theoretical apparatus of the first three books of the *Encyclopedia* is fully deployed.

28. As I stated in Book II, *La mente e il corpo. Filosofia e psicologia*, the condition of the subject lies in an object that mirrors it. At the bottom of the self, all that can be seen is the relationship.

29. The expression "decorous idealism" is in Maurice Blanchot's *The Infinite Conversation*, translated and foreword by Susan Hanson (University of Minnesota Press, 1993), 81. See my *Teoria e pratica del foglio-mondo. La scrittura filosofica* (Laterza, 1997), 26–35.

44. The beginning of Book VI, *Le arti dinamiche*, refers to Plato's *Laws*. "The love of the nun" is a reference to an aphorism by Carlo Gragnani in his *Per amor di completezza* (Private edition, 2010), 401.

46. As one can see, what I have oftentimes called Plato's "strategy of the soul" (see also note to par. 207), reveals here its original, deeply political roots. Notions like Platonic spiritualism and psychology—without which Western civilization would be inconceivable—arose on the terrain of a gesture which, in fact, instituted the project of a new political anthropology—a gesture whose consequences are manifestly incalculable. The reference to the myth of Dionysus is explained in full in Book VI, *Le arti dinamiche*, Second and Third Figures.

49. On Solon, see Book V, *Raccontare il mondo*, Third Figure.

50. This paragraph, and the next one, refer to the aforementioned theses of Mario Vegetti (see note to par. 12).

60. The example is drawn from C. S. Peirce, "The Doctrine of Chances" (1878), in *The Essential Peirce: Selected Philosophical Writings, vol. 1 (1867–1893)*, edited by Nathan Houser and Christian Kloesel (Indiana University Press, 1992), 147–151 (2.645–2.654 according to the *Collected Papers*). See also my *Il pragmatismo americano* (Laterza, 1972), 205–210.

62. On the pedagogic turn, whereby philosophy replaced ancient poetry, see Book V, *Raccontare il mondo*, 80–81.

74. The figure of Gyges is thoroughly analyzed in Vegetti's comment to Plato's *Republic* (see note to par. 12).

78. On historical legend in G. F. Creuzer, see my *Il simbolo e l'uomo* (Egea, 1991), chap. 4.

82. The origin of speech, as related to the invocation of the name of God and the establishment of sacrifice as a primordial banquet, is the focus of discussion in the first part of Book VI, *Le arti dinamiche*.

85. On Ariadne, see Book VI, *Le arti dinamiche*, par. 81–82.

89. A reference to the Seventh Figure of the present book ("The Encounter with Death"). See in particular Act Three, Scene VII, "Speech and Death." In other words, the vision of the invisible.

93. On the relationship between genealogy and *epoché*, see the Appendix to my *Filosofia e scrittura* (Laterza, 1994), as well as the present book, par. 94.

95. On the relationship between the institution of value and the institution of rituals driven by the desire to secure eternal life, see Book VI, *Le arti dinamiche*, par. 19–23.

100. On primordial incest, see the myth of Pasiphae (already mentioned in Book VI, *Le arti dinamiche*, par. 81–82). As to "the plague of the political," see my *Teoria e pratica del foglio-mondo*, 46–48.

104. See Alfred Kallir, *Sign and Design: The Psychogenetic Source of the Alphabet* (James Clarke, 1961), Italian translation by Francesco Ferrario, *Segno e disegno. Psicogenesi dell'alfabeto* (Spirali, 1994), 318–327.

106. On Plato's *Cratylus*, see my *Idoli della conoscenza* (Cortina, 2000), Part I, 5.

119. The "construction" of the soul, meaning—as I say—the strategy of the soul, see the present book, par. 122.

130. On the shaping of "objectivity," see Book VI, *Le arti dinamiche*, Eighth Figure, "L'occasione dell'oggettività."

148. For the Good in *Timaeus*, see Book V, *Raccontare il mondo*, Fourth Figure, "La differenza cosmologica." The allusion to the "old snake" recalls the present volume, par. 7.

149. The formation of the theory of the image in Plato as the origin of the "psychization" of Western man is the central argument of my *I segni dell'anima* (Laterza, 1989).

152. On the nonexhaustiveness of the scientific response to the nature of the visible, recall the discussion in Book II, *La mente e il corpo*, First Figure, "La visione iscritta e circoscritta."

154. On the difference between primary and secondary qualities, recall the decisive argumentation carried out in Book II, *L'anima e il corpo*, par. 138–144.

155. On Plato's *Letter VII*, see my *Filosofia e scrittura*, 3–19.

159. The identity of the alphabet with the Latin language in the Middle Ages is drawn from Ivan Illich. See my *Gli abiti, le pratiche, i saperi* (Jaca Book, 1996, repr. 2003), 57–68.

169. See "Analisi e sintesi" in Book III, *L'origine del significato*, par. 40–47. On the man/woman complementarity, see Book VI, *Le arti dinamiche*, par. 266–268.

170. On the origin of self-awareness from the vocal gesture, see chap. 7 ("La pragmatica del linguaggio") in my *Il simbolo e l'uomo*, and Part I ("Il gesto e la voce") in *Gli abiti, le pratiche, i saperi*. Taken

together, these two books resolve once and for all the question of the birth of self-awareness.

173. "Adam, where are you?" ("But the Lord God called to the man, 'Where are you?,'" Genesis 3, 9 NIV) is a reference to Blanchot, *The Infinite Conversation*, 14 and 128. See my *Teoria e pratica del foglio-mondo*, 41.

176. Only the written sign is properly a sign; see Book II, *La mente e il corpo*, par. 184–186.

186. On the notion of "enchantment," see my *Images of Truth: From Sign to Symbol*, translated and with an introduction by Massimo Verdicchio (Humanities Press, 1993), 148–154. Originally *Immagini di verità. Dal segno al simbolo* (Spirali, 1985), 187–195.

193. For a definitive critique of contemporary metaphorology—though one which has largely gone unnoticed—see Anna Cazzullo, *La verità della parola. Ricerca sui fondamenti filosofici della metafora in Aristotele e nei contemporanei* (Jaca Book, 1987). By the same author, see also *Il concetto e l'esperienza. Aristotele, Cassirer, Heidegger, Ricoeur* (Jaca Book, 1988).

207. On Plato's dialectic as the scientific overcoming of Sophistic rhetoric (thus contrary to the thesis of Plato's supposed aristocratic archaism), see my *Passare il segno* (Il Saggiatore, 1981), 293–294 (where the thesis of the "strategy of the soul" is also put forward).

212. See Book VI, *Le arti dinamiche*, First Figure, "Il coro iscritto e circoscritto."

216. The gesture's complementarity is analyzed in Book VI, *Le arti dinamiche*, on the basis of its nature being defined as "having-similar-form" ("similforme").

218. The question is taken up again in the present book, par. 254–258.

219. A paragraph that summarizes and recalls many of the complex journeys undertaken thus far.

222–225. The many allusions here refer to the discussion in the first part of Book VI, *Le arti dinamiche*.

223. *The Theatre and Its Double* is Antonin Artaud's well-known masterpiece. See Antonin Artaud, *The Theatre and Its Double*, translated and edited by Mark Taylor-Batty (Methuen, 2024). Italian translation by Gian Renzo Morteo and Guido Neri, *Il Teatro e il suo doppio, con altri scritti teatrali*, preface by Jacques Derrida (Einaudi, 2000). See also 257.

228. For the reference to the original words as sexual signs and writings, see Alfred Kallir (note to par. 104).
230. EVA/AVE: see Book V, *Raccontare il mondo*, par. 216.
231. On the Nietzschean thesis of Socrates' skepticism about sacrifice as well as of his aversion to theater (except for his accomplice Euripides), see my *Teoria e pratica del foglio-mondo*, 23–24.
242. See Jesper Svenbro, *Phrasikleia: An Anthropology of Reading in Ancient Greece*, translated from the French by Janet Loyd (Cornell University Press, 1993). Italian translation by Valeria Laurenzi, *Storia della lettura nella Grecia antica* (Laterza, 1991).
247. The content of this paragraph will be variously developed in Book VI, *Le arti dinamiche*.
252. See my *Il simbolo e l'uomo*, 252–260.
257. On Artaud's body without organs (and on the theater as "double," 223), see Florinda Cambria's seminal works, *Corpi all'opera. Teatro e scrittura in Antonin Artaud*, and *Far danzare l'anatomia. Itinerari del corpo simbolico in Antonin Artaud* (Edizioni ETS, 2007).
267. On the shout in the Dionysian rite (and on the figure of Dionysius *episcopus*), see Book VI, *Le arti dinamiche*, par. 99.
268. On the theme of the dream, see the third part of Book VI, *Le arti dinamiche*. On Chauncey Wright, see my *Il pragmatismo americano*, especially 65–114.
270–271. See note to par. 252.
271. On the posthumous and artificial character of speech, see Book I, *L'analogia della parola*, par. 48–57.
274. On Leo Tolstoy's *The Death of Ivan Ilyich* (1886), see Rocco Ronchi's fine reading in *Luogo comune. Verso un'etica della scrittura* (Egea, 1996).
283. See Desmond Morris, *The Naked Ape: A Zoologist's Study of the Human Animal* (Jonathan Cape, 1967). Italian translation by Marisa Bergami, *La scimmia nuda. Studio zoologico sull'animale uomo* (Bompiani, 1968).
285. See Book II, *La mente e il corpo*, Third Figure, "L'oscillazione dell'origine."
296. See my *La libertà, la finanza, la comunicazione* (Spirali, 2001).
298–299. These themes are developed in Book VI, *Le arti dinamiche*.
301. On mask playing, see Book VI, *Le arti dinamiche*, Second Figure.
346. On the dream of complementarity, see Book VI, *Le arti dinamiche*, Part Three, "Il sogno del risveglio."

Index of Historical, Fictional, and Mythological Names